PRAISE FOR *ADVOCATING FOR WOMEN WITH POSTPARTUM MENTAL ILLNESS*

"*Advocating for Women with Postpartum Mental Illness* is a comprehensive and eloquent review of this subject that I believe we've long needed. Feingold and Lewis have created a compelling book that is instantly a standard of reference. I have enormous respect for both of their writings and for what they are accomplishing legislatively."—Carl S. Burak, MD, JD, coauthor, *The Cradle Will Fall*

"This isn't just a book, it's an outline and a clear path out of our archaic laws and unjust treatment of perinatal women. Dr. Feingold and Attorney Lewis use their expertise, hard work, and compassion in this groundbreaking volume to bring us into a new age of advocacy for mental health. Readers will see that the importance of this work cannot be overstated, and they will also have the road map to move forward. This book is essential."—Katayune Kaeni, PsyD, PMH-C, host, *Mom & Mind* podcast

"Smartly written and insightful, Feingold and Lewis offer a comprehensive and absorbing guide to both the history of postpartum mental illnesses and the law. They provide a clear roadmap to becoming an advocate for women navigating the legal system, and they educate the reader on the complexities of incarceration and maternal mental illness through sensitively told personal stories and case examples."—Linda Klempner, PhD, chair, Postpartum Support International Advisory Council

"Feingold and Lewis's writing strongly illuminates the need for the United States judicial system to change laws to postpartum legal cases. It is high time to bring mercy and justice for those women who suffer from postpartum psychosis. By developing laws that specifically deal with postpartum illness, the U.S. legal system can join the 37 other countries that have criminal law, which reflects judicial fairness—educated, advanced, case sensitive judiciary processes for mothers affected by postpartum illness."—Catherine Hunter, LCSW, CADC, PMH-C, Catherine Hunter & Associates, Ltd.

"Feingold and Lewis are the dynamic duo for incarcerated postpartum women in Illinois. This book outlines their expertise and experience around the tragic intersection of the law with postpartum mental illness and provides a guide for making change wherever it is needed. A compassionate, fascinating, and necessary read!"—Lita Simanis, LCSW, PMH-C, coordinator, Pregnancy and Postpartum Mood & Anxiety Disorder Program, AMITA Health

"I am a PPD survivor and don't really regret my experience because of the opportunity to meet such wonderful maternal mental health advocates as Susan Feingold and Barry Lewis, whose dedication to preventing tragic outcomes is inspirational. Their revolutionary work on laws governing maternal mental health is detailed in *Advocating for Women with Postpartum Mental Illness: A Guide to Changing the Law and the National Climate*. All individuals who care for expectant and new mothers—whether it be OB/GYNs and their staff, general practitioners and their staff, hospital staff, midwives, doulas, lactation consultants, therapists, social workers, or a new mother's family members and friends—should read this book. Public awareness is critical in decreasing stigma of postpartum mood disorders."—Ivy Shih Leung, author, *One Mom's Journey to Motherhood*

"A tremendously important work on a topic that has been grossly misunderstood, stigmatized, and marginalized, creating immeasurable suffering for affected women and families. Feingold and Lewis are a dynamic duo, bringing together mental health and legal expertise on postpartum psychosis and drawing from case studies, first-person advocacy experience, and a thorough review of the scientific literature and applicable legislation, creating a roadmap for those wishing to increase their understanding and join the revolution for change in how postpartum illness is viewed and managed from medical, legal, and societal perspectives."—Jo Kim, PhD, director, Perinatal Depression Program, NorthShore University HealthSystem, and professor, University of Chicago Pritzker School of Medicine

"Susan Feingold and Barry Lewis have written an educational and inspirational account of their path to passing a revolutionary law in Illinois. Read this book and expand your knowledge of perinatal mental health and the history of law in cases of infanticide/filicide. The authors were extremely instrumental in the passing of a new law affecting such cases in Illinois, and this book will do nothing short of expand this ability nationwide."—Kristina Dulaney, RN, PMH-C, cofounder, Appalachian Perinatal Mental Health Alliance, and founder, Cherished Mom

"So well written and easy for anyone to follow and take out the important aspects of advocating legally and emotionally."—Christena Raines RN, MSN, APRN-BC, assistant professor, Women's Mood Disorder Program, Department of Psychiatry, UNC Chapel Hill

“Feingold and Lewis have created a unique and comprehensive book through exhaustive research and insight. By exposing past mistakes in perinatal psychiatry, they provide the foundation for their legal success. A deep and moving triumphant contribution to our movement.”—Jane I. Honikman, MS, founder, Postpartum Support International

“Feingold and Lewis’s book makes a landmark contribution to the literature on postpartum mental illness and the law. Together they harness their mental health and legal expertise to enable the reader to understand the forces driving the tragic line of U.S. cases involving mothers who kill their children while suffering from postpartum mental illness. With stories and interviews, they demonstrate the miscarriage of justice that results when these mothers are not permitted, in their own defense, to introduce evidence regarding postpartum mental illness. After showing why the time is right for responding to postpartum mental illness at many levels, the authors offer a pragmatic guide to making meaningful legal change at the state level. The story of their successful campaign to reform Illinois criminal code to permit women to file post-conviction affidavits regarding postpartum health is a true inspiration. Filled with practical guidance, useful footnotes, and compassion, this book is a must-read.”—Michelle Oberman, JD, MPH, Katharine and George Alexander Professor of Law, Santa Clara University School of Law, and author, *When Mothers Kill: Interviews from Prison*

“Finally a book that sets the record straight about the need to change laws that punish women for psychotic illnesses beyond their control. Dr. Feingold and attorney Barry Lewis have skillfully crafted a text that clearly makes the case for why the criminal justice system needs to reform sentencing guidelines. This work belongs on the bookshelf of every attorney and medical and mental health professional who works in this field.”—Diana Barnes, PsyD, expert in women’s reproductive mental health, and editor and contributing author, *Women’s Reproductive Mental Health across the Lifespan*

“Having treated both peripartum psychiatric illnesses and evaluated women in criminal justice systems for over twenty-five years, I admire the historical context and significant work documented in this book. I know it will provide much needed education to anyone interested in women’s mental health. Hopefully it will provide a model for legislation in many other states. This book is an admirable contribution to every field that intersects with mental health policy and the law.”—Lisa A. Rone, MD, clinical assistant professor of psychiatry, Northwestern School of Medicine

“A profound and essential book leading to transformation in establishing postpartum legislation in the United States every step of the way. Susan Feingold and Barry Lewis’s masterpiece is a call to action and a must-read for maternal mental health professionals, advocates, lawyers, judges, jury members, social workers, police officers, forensic experts, psychologists, and psychiatrists. These trailblazers detail their journey moving the postpartum law in Illinois through legislation. They provide a roadmap in this comprehensive volume, which is filled with descriptions of pivotal cases, personal accounts, facts, interviews, stories, and words from incarcerated mothers amid the heart-warming and gut-wrenching reality of the potential destruction in postpartum mental illness and the lost lives, not only of children, but mothers caught in the quagmire of the United States legal system. This team is awe-inspiring, tireless, courageous, and effective in saving mothers lives. ‘Be the change you wish to see in the world’ is personified.”—Gina Wong, PhD, professor, program director, and chair, Graduate Centre for Applied Psychology, Athabasca University, Canada

Advocating for Women with Postpartum Mental Illness

Advocating for Women with Postpartum Mental Illness

A Guide to Changing the Law and the National Climate

Susan Benjamin Feingold, PsyD

Barry Michael Lewis, JD

ROWMAN & LITTLEFIELD
Lanham • Boulder • New York • London

Published by Rowman & Littlefield
An imprint of The Rowman & Littlefield Publishing Group, Inc.
4501 Forbes Boulevard, Suite 200, Lanham, Maryland 20706
www.rowman.com

6 Tinworth Street, London, SE11 5AL, United Kingdom

British Library Cataloguing in Publication Information Available

Library of Congress Cataloging-in-Publication Data

Names: Feingold, Susan Benjamin, 1951– author. | Lewis, Barry M., 1950– author.
Title: Advocating for women with postpartum mental illness : a guide to changing the law and the national climate / Susan Benjamin Feingold, Barry M. Lewis.
Description: Lanham : Rowman & Littlefield, [2020] | Includes index. | Summary: "Complete with case studies and the authors' experiences in changing the law in their own state of Illinois, this book is a necessary resource for furthering dialogue and action around maternal mental illness."—Provided by publisher.
Identifiers: LCCN 2019040292 (print) | LCCN 2019040293 (ebook) | ISBN 9781538129852 (cloth) | ISBN 9781538129869 (paperback) | ISBN 9781538129876 (epub)
Subjects: LCSH: Postpartum psychiatric disorders. | Women—Mental health. | Mental health services.
Classification: LCC RG850 .F45 2020 (print) | LCC RG850 (ebook) | DDC 618.7/6—dc23
LC record available at https://lccn.loc.gov/2019040292
LC ebook record available at https://lccn.loc.gov/2019040293

To Bill Ryan, Janet Jackson, and Paula Sims.
And to our mothers, although no longer with us,
Diana and Ruth.
Also to our children, Hadar, Rachel,
and twice to our Seths.

Never doubt that a small group of thoughtful, committed people can change the world; indeed, it is the only thing that ever has.

—Margaret Mead

You can't go back and change the beginning, but you can start where you are and change the ending.

—C. S. Lewis

Contents

Preface

In 2017, Bill Ryan, a widower and retiree, teamed up with two people he had never met before: Dr. Susan Feingold, a psychologist, and her partner, Barry Lewis, a lawyer. With a budget for only gas and a few dollars to print a handful of documents, the three navigated the halls of the legislature. They overcame the opposing lobbyist and near fatal parliamentary procedure difficulties.

More than a story of three people, it is a story of hope. Hope for twenty Illinois women unjustly incarcerated for decades. Hope for women in the forty-nine other states who suffered the same. And hope for those who might believe there is nothing that can be done to change the law.

Bill, Susan, and Barry did this the right way. They showed the law should be changed, using only facts and examples. In this way, they attracted the necessary support of influential members of the legislature.

The bill sailed through the House justice committee after Dr. Feingold testified, and then the House. It stumbled at the Senate criminal law committee under the influence of the prosecutor's lobbyist, but passed unanimously. Finally, after overcoming parliamentary difficulties, it passed the Senate with a total of only two opposing votes. Governor Bruce Rauner signed the bill into law in January 2018.

The law is ground-breaking. For the first time in Illinois, there is a judicial procedure for changing a sentence years after it was finalized. For the first time, a particular form of mental illness that is highly curable is recognized in the criminal law as an exceptional matter to be dealt with differently.

Prologue

Weekends, ideally, are never filled with work. Instead, my free time is enjoyed with reading, watching sports, hanging out, and dancing. It was May, and in Chicago free time finally includes the hope of the kind of weather when the outdoors becomes sometimes inviting, although other times not. It was the beginning of the time when walks might replace rushing from the house to the car to some indoor destination. A south wind brings warm air to the city that only recently lost the last of the piles of snow. A wind off the recently thawed lake can remind us of winter. But this particular weekend was not promising for a different reason. I had a head cold. So the prospect of doing a few hours of rushed work was not upsetting. It was a challenge. It was important—perhaps the most important work I'd ever done.

The entire time I had known Susan, not quite five years, her passion was treating postpartum illness, and her free time was for dancing and spiritual expression. A few weeks before, she had made a sudden trip to Springfield. She made herself available to travel to the Illinois House of Representatives and is highly qualified to speak to its criminal justice committee in support of a proposed law on the subject of postpartum illness. She was asked to speak by Lita Simanis, the head of the legal committee of Postpartum Support International. I encouraged her involvement despite the short notice. She returned happy; the bill had unanimously passed in committee following her testimony. And, I thought, that was the end of that. There was no more to do.

Susan noted, quietly and contentedly, when the House passed the bill unanimously. A month passed as the bill went to the Senate. The committee was about to take up the issue of that bill, as well as other routine business. We marked its progress from time to time, a traveler whose journeys we would note when brought to our attention. No more, no less, for neither of us were politicians. Our interest in politics had never before extended beyond voting.

But the law—a ground-breaking first in the nation law—had hit its first pothole. This one was potentially fatal. The prosecutor's lobbyist objected to the law. Consideration of the law had been put on hold. The objection was learned of by our contact late one Friday, and the committee was to address the bill the very next Tuesday. Susan turned to me. My field was criminal law. I had to step up. This law was important.

So what was it and why was it so important? Nearly one million women in the United States each year suffer postpartum illnesses. The most common is postpartum depression, a depression distinct from and far worse than the "baby blues." A surprising number of women become psychotic following childbirth. A woman is twenty-five times more likely to have a psychotic episode in the month following childbirth than at any other time in the rest of her life. Of these unfortunate women, one in twenty commit suicide, and one in twenty-five kill their children. As to the latter group, half commit or attempt suicide. The work was to help pass a law regarding the survivors of all of this, and I had to learn all about this law quickly.

The problem was, as soon as the law was gaining some traction, the state's attorneys objected. Their lobbyist claimed the law was unconstitutional. It took, he claimed, powers of the governor and gave them to the courts. This violated a fundamental concept of our Constitution: separation of powers.

Lobbyists, I have been told, tend to be a personable, likeable lot. If not, they can only function by threats or promises. Matt was no exception; he was both. He shared with me his theory: the law was unconstitutional because it infringed on the governor's power to pardon and commute sentences to a lesser sentence.

After a sentence was finalized by the courts, the power to change it was a power exclusively of the governor.

One of our Constitution's fundamentals is there are three branches of government: (1) the legislature that creates laws, (2) the courts that interpret the laws and determine the rights between citizens under those laws, and (3) the executive, personified by the governor (or president) under whose authority are such agencies as are needed to put the laws into effect, such as law enforcement agencies. It is part of the famous checks and balances, under which no person is above the law. The problem with this law, he said, is for almost two centuries, only the governor could change a valid sentence, once the judges' decision was final. This law took that exclusive power from the governor and gave it to another branch of government. The prosecutor's argument was based upon the court's own interpretation of the interplay between a valid sentence by the judiciary and the governor being the only person who could change a valid sentence once the sentence was finalized.

The attention that has been given to postpartum illness has been plainly inadequate until recently. With a frequency of as much as 10 to 15 percent for each pregnancy, almost one-third of childbearing women have this disease at least once in their lifetime. This is a greater number than any class of illness other than infectious diseases.

Women coming into power in such agencies as the American Psychiatric Association have begun to direct attention to this illness. Organizations have formed specializing or emphasizing this disease, such as Postpartum Support International, the Marcé Society, 2020 Mom, and others. Some of these have created hotlines for women to call for help, and some hospitals such as Illinois's NorthShore University HealthSystem have done so as well. Too often, nonetheless, women don't know what is happening to them. Fortunately, some prominent women, most commonly in the arts, have come forward to tell about their experiences. In the past when women sought treatment, the disease was often unrecognized. This is changing.

What hasn't changed is the law, particularly the criminal law in the US. In this area it is lagging far behind many developed nations. About thirty nations recognize this is a disease and deal with it accordingly.

I set to work to prove the lobbyist wrong. With this modest beginning, I found my calling and my life's work.

Barry M. Lewis, JD

Introduction

In this book, we will help readers understand the various forms of perinatal mood and anxiety disorders from the mildest forms of mood disorders such as maternity or baby blues to postpartum depression and then the severest form, known as postpartum psychosis. Knowledge is the critical first step in treating these perinatal mental disorders, and certainly necessary for our goal and purpose of advocating to change laws and the national climate.

First, we must comprehend the full landscape of perinatal illnesses, the prevalence and symptoms of each type of postpartum disorder. Then we can focus on the most severe and rare form, postpartum psychosis, of which a small but significant percentage of those afflicted women attempt suicide (4 to 5 percent) and a smaller number (1 to 4 percent) commit crimes, most notably neonaticide or infanticide.

Most people currently view these heinous crimes committed by postpartum mothers as a vile act of selfishness, a total disregard of responsibility, or the deficiency of the "normal" maternal love that we associate with new mothers. Many who read or hear about these cases are quick to judge these women perpetrators as "monsters" as it may be one of the most repulsive acts imaginable, and totally in conflict with our myths of motherhood and the Madonna-like images in magazines and the media that we as a society adhere to. However, the real misleading myth associated with new motherhood is that serious mental illness is not a possibility or that it is not a risk factor for a significant number of women with pregnancy.

I myself have found many people are disgusted and appalled when I try to describe the legal advocacy work we are involved with in trying to help these unfortunate women who are incarcerated for decades or a lifetime, due to crimes committed during postpartum psychosis, a temporary psychotic episode. In a few social situations, women have walked away or accused me of being unsympathetic or indifferent to the victims. I have even been accused of being a lover of "baby killers" by a few anonymous online people. Some have been outspoken in public, saying things such as, "Those women should be punished for what they did. What about the child or children they killed? Who is advocating for them?" Others have just walked away after giving me a look of disapproval or, worse, disgust.

Despite the negative evaluation of some, I feel it is not only the children who were lost but also the women themselves with postpartum psychosis. They are victims as well. In most cases, these women had no history of mental illness, but just as any other woman, they had dreams of a family, having a baby, and becoming a mother. They had no idea that pregnancy would take them into the depths of despair or a psychotic episode with hallucinations and delusions that led to the worst tragedy imaginable. Following their horrific postpartum experience and the loss of their dream of a happy family, they most often face the end of a marriage and a lifetime or decades in prison. Unfortunately, the stories of these women and the babies or children they have killed haunt me. These are real-life nightmares that have happened and have resulted in ruined lives and indescribable suffering. While I continue to advocate for these living victims, I am repeatedly grateful that this is not my reality or my life story.

I myself suffered from a postpartum depression with despair and intense anxiety more severe than I could have ever imagined. It was not what I was expecting after the birth of my second child. I struggled to regain my mental health and finally recovered with help from a therapist who specialized in anxiety. At that time twenty-six years ago, I could not find the specialists and resources that exist and are available today. Over months I regained my health and refocused my clinical work on specializing in perinatal mood and anxiety disorders so that others would be able to find a perinatal specialist. This became a mission and my passion over the last twenty-five years of my practice as a clinical psychologist. I was one of the lucky ones. I survived, have a wonderful relationship with both my now-adult children and never became psychotic or committed terrible acts. For this I am truly grateful. I realize that "there but for the grace of God go I." It could have happened to me, and instead of a life as a healer, I could have been one of those incarcerated women I am now trying to advocate for.

We as a society are naïve, judgmental, and lack compassion about severe mental illness. This is particularly true in the US when maternal mental illness results in the death of a baby or children. First we must eliminate the stigma and silence that surround mental health issues. We must open our eyes to the reality of postpartum psychosis, a maternal mental illness that affects one to two out of a thousand childbearing women a year in the United States.

Then we will have a more realistic opportunity to help these women get treatment to prevent infant death and other catastrophic occurrences.

In the UK and approximately thirty other countries, there are far less harsh penalties such as misdemeanors, probation, and mental health treatment as options, rather than incarceration and punishment. Apparently, there is a better understanding by the legal system and by the general public of maternal mental illness. While the UK has had laws to address maternal mental illness related to infanticide since 1922, our society in America cries out for retribution. We associate these crimes with child abuse or even relate these tragedies to attempted abortion. Social media posts are filled with harsh judgments, sometimes even calling out to "kill the woman," an eye for an eye mentality. These women are often referred to provocatively as "baby killers," and there is support for the harshest sentences imaginable for them, even when possible the death penalty.

Although our subject is postpartum mental illness, the principles in this book apply to all advocacy work. This book is primarily about changing and transforming outdated laws and replacing them with more humane mental health treatment. It is also about changing the national landscape to transform the stigma and social climate in this country to be more congruous with other developed countries that are more sympathetic to maternal mental illness. This must start with knowledge, as through education we as a society will gain an understanding and compassion for perinatal mental illness, the most common complication surrounding childbirth.

Susan Benjamin Feingold, PsyD

Disclaimer

This book is based on both authors' research, personal experiences, interviews, and real-life experiences. In order to protect privacy, names have been changed and identifying characteristics have been altered except for contributing experts and those who have already been identified in the popular press.

For purposes of simplifying usage, the pronouns she/he and his/her are sometimes used interchangeably.

The information contained herein is not meant to be a substitute for treatment or professional consultation with mental health professionals or attorneys.

Part I

UNDERSTANDING AND TREATING WOMEN WITH POSTPARTUM PSYCHOSIS

Chapter One

Maternal Mental Illness Is a Serious Risk to Families

You are not alone. You are not to blame. With help, you will be well.

—Postpartum Support International

Maternal mental illness is an unexpected and unwelcome addition to motherhood. Women and couples prepare excitedly for becoming a family, unaware of the risks of perinatal illnesses. Who considers depression, severe anxiety, or a psychosis when they contemplate pregnancy or childbirth?

In the best-case scenario, women with maternal mental illness are identified early and treated by a knowledgeable perinatal mental health professional, and their symptoms remit quickly. They are then able to adjust to the myriad of mothering duties and new roles that come for all new parents with a baby. In this situation, their timely treatment and quick remission leaves their self-esteem intact with no negative aftereffects from their brief illness.

The ideal to which we aspire someday is to provide preventative care and early intervention for all women who are at risk or begin to exhibit symptoms during their pregnancy or shortly after delivery. However, this happily-ever-after tale is not very likely, even in the most affluent and psychologically minded communities with accessible medical services in the US. And the likelihood of this happening in underserved areas, developing countries, and poor or rural communities is liable to be nonexistent.

Presently, effective and timely perinatal treatment is a fairy tale for many women in both the US and around the world. According to the World Health Organization, depression affects 13 percent of women within a year of delivery.[1] Women are at a higher risk of having mental health problems during the perinatal period than at any other time of their life. It has been reported that depression is the fourth leading cause of disability worldwide and affects approximately 121 million people globally.[2] In underdeveloped countries the rate may be as high as 19.8 percent.[3]

In the US, up to eight hundred thousand women a year suffer from perinatal mood and anxiety disorders, a prevalence rate of 10 to 15 percent of all pregnant and postpartum women. This is an illness that needs to be taken seriously. Early intervention and treatment by a perinatal trained specialist reduces the incidence of the depression worsening and the potential for tragedy. Women with severe depression are at higher probability to commit suicide than those with other illnesses. Those with the most serious form of maternal mental illness, postpartum psychosis, have an increased risk of both suicide (4 to 5 percent) and infanticide (1 to 4 percent).[4]

Recently we have become aware that men can suffer with postpartum depression and anxiety disorders as well as women. Estimates for paternal postpartum depression in the first year after delivery vary internationally from 1.2 percent to 11.9 percent.[5] According to a study in 2010, data from 1993 to 2007 found approximately 4 percent of fathers experience depression in the first year following the birth of their child. Younger fathers, those with a history of depression, and those from deprived areas were more likely to experience symptoms.[6] A meta-analysis concluded the rate of fathers' prenatal and postpartum depression was 10 percent.[7] However, this occurrence in men has just begun to be seriously studied in the last few years, while more is known about the prevalence and course of the illness in women.

DISTINGUISHING THE VARIOUS SUBTYPES OF POSTPARTUM MOOD DISORDERS

Although men can suffer too, we will focus on the occurrence in childbearing women and the signs and symptoms of each type of postpartum disorder, from the mildest form known commonly as baby or maternity blues to the severest form, postpartum psychosis. Postpartum emotional disorders vary in their time of onset, severity of symptoms, and duration. The newest publication of the American Psychiatric Association's coding, classification, and diagnosis of mental disorders, the *Diagnostic and Statistical Manual of Mental Disorders*, fifth edition (*DSM-5*), indicates that

> fifty percent of "postpartum" major depression episodes actually begin prior to delivery. Thus, these episodes are referred to collectively as *peripartum* episodes. Women with peripartum major depressive episodes often have severe anxiety and even panic attacks. Prospective studies have demonstrated that

mood and anxiety symptoms during pregnancy, as well as the "baby blues," increase the risk for a postpartum major depressive episode.[8]

The mildest of the biochemically based disorders is the blues (though some doctors prefer to classify this transitory condition as a normal adjustment, because it's so prevalent) affecting 75 to 80 percent of new moms. While less common, the severer postpartum emotional disorders, usually lumped under the term postpartum depression (PPD), still affect a huge number of women—as many as eight hundred thousand Americans and many more worldwide each year. That's roughly 10 to 15 percent of all new mothers. It is considered the most common complication following delivery. This statistic represents only the women who are diagnosed clinically with the illness. These figures are probably lower than its actual occurrence.[9]

Postpartum depression is an umbrella term for a variety of moderate to severe symptoms of depression or anxiety, a psychiatric syndrome following childbirth.[10] Although postpartum disorders are most common in the first three to four months, this maternal mental illness can present anytime in the first postpartum year.

These emotional disorders are identified by their cluster of symptoms, their severity, and the time of onset. A woman's subjective experience of distress and the effect of her symptoms on her current level of functioning also assist in diagnosing the illness. Any one case of postpartum depression can include symptoms from any combination of four subgroups: depression, anxiety, panic disorder, and obsessive-compulsive disorder, each of which has its own different indicators. The clinical symptoms of postpartum mood and anxiety disorders can include insomnia and sleep disturbances; lack of clarity in thinking; extreme fatigue; sad and depressed mood; lack of appetite; worrying and severe anxiety; panic attacks; obsessive thoughts; feelings of hopelessness, worthlessness, and poor self-esteem; loss of pleasure and motivation in usual activities (which can include a lack of interest in the baby); difficulty functioning at one's usual level; feeling overwhelmed, inability to cope with life's demands; suicidal thoughts; and not feeling like oneself.[11]

Depression is not always a component. Don't be confused by other names you may have heard postpartum depression called, such as postpartum illness, postnatal disorder, postnatal depression (used frequently in the UK), and perinatal mood and anxiety disorders.[12] They mean essentially the same thing.

However, postpartum blues and postpartum psychoses are distinct from postpartum depression and postpartum anxiety disorders; these terms are not interchangeable.[13]

POSTPARTUM PSYCHOSIS: THE SEVEREST FORM OF POSTPARTUM MENTAL ILLNESS

The least common and severest postpartum illness that is the subject of this book is known as postpartum psychosis. These women lose touch with reality and can experience alternating depression and mania. Other symptoms can include cognitive confusion and disorientation, disorganized or racing thoughts, bizarre behavior, excessive restlessness, minimal need for sleep, delusional beliefs, and hallucinations. These women are very ill and need immediate hospitalization and medication to stabilize their moods and protect them as well as others, including their infant, from harm. In that they are psychotic, by definition they are not responsible for their actions, lack rational thought, and may be experiencing "command" hallucinations or delusional beliefs that put them and others at risk.

Research supports that the single strongest predictor of postpartum psychosis is a personal history of bipolar disorder, followed by a family history of bipolar disorder.[14] With all the hormonal and biochemical changes that accompany pregnancy, lactation, and the postpartum period, some previously healthy women are psychologically naïve and caught unaware when their first bipolar episode or incidence of severe clinical depression occurs at this time.

Postpartum psychosis or postpartum mood (major depressive or manic) episodes with psychotic features affect only a small minority. These episodes with psychotic features may be more common in primiparous[15] women. The risk is elevated for women with prior postpartum mood episodes or those with a prior history of a depressive or bipolar disorder (especially bipolar I disorder) or a family history of bipolar disorders.[16]

A review of 24,273 publications of the maternal morbidity working group found the global prevalence of postpartum psychosis to range from 0.89 to 2.6 in one thousand women in five of six studies that met their rigorous criteria. One study reported a higher postpartum psychosis prevalence with five in a thousand women.[17] It has been estimated that even of those women with postpartum psychosis, the incidence of women harming their infants is rare, despite the sensationalism associated with this serious illness.[18]

PSYCHOSIS AS A PSYCHIATRIC CRISIS SITUATION THAT DEMANDS URGENCY

Due to the possibility of a tragic outcome and heightened potential for suicide, postpartum psychosis is a psychiatric crisis. Immediate hospitalization is essential. The concern is that families and even health care professionals may observe a waxing and waning of symptoms that can accompany this illness. While sometimes the woman may exhibit unusual behavior and a shift from her previous typical functioning, this can be followed by more "normal" behavior that may be mistaken for a sign of improvement. The best option is to have a woman with psychotic symptoms taken to a hospital to be evaluated by trained mental health professionals to avoid any potential risk.

When we as a society become more educated and tolerant of mental health issues, it will encourage new mothers as well as fathers to admit their symptoms without shame and to pursue the necessary mental health treatment. This is the shift needed in our national consciousness. Research findings support the critical need for early identification and prompt intervention in women with postpartum depression and postpartum psychosis for the sake of the mother's mental stability, her attachment with her baby, and the overall health of the family unit. As a society, we need to replace old notions of shame linked to depression and substitute these outdated ideas with a focus on improved self-care and empowerment.

There is a current trajectory in many areas of the country for people to work on changing laws and the climate of mental health in the US. However, in order to accomplish these lofty goals, it is first necessary to educate the public, legislators, and the health care community about mental illness. Knowledge of perinatal mood and anxiety disorders and their prevalence is the vital initial step. It is unlikely that the public or our legislative representatives will back provocative areas of mental health legislation such as an "infanticide law" without being educated about the range of disorders that are represented by maternal mental illness.

Better prenatal and postpartum education and the dissemination of information is necessary. The general public and health care professionals need to be well informed about the signs and symptoms of the various perinatal illnesses. As we become more open and knowledgeable, patients and their families may feel less stigmatized, leading to prompt treatment. Further research is needed to more fully understand postpartum psychosis, which has gotten much less consideration and study than has postpartum depression. Hopefully with the growing attention to these illnesses, future generations will be better informed and equipped to avoid undue suffering as well as catastrophic circumstances of perinatal depression and psychosis.

THE HISTORY AND DEVELOPMENT OF EVIDENCE-BASED TREATMENT

Awareness of postpartum depression is suddenly experiencing an information explosion. Articles discussing perinatal issues are at an all-time high. New research efforts requesting PPD sufferers' participation are posted on social media sites. Issues correlating postpartum depression and anxiety disorders with C-sections, high-risk and traumatic childbirth, infants admitted to the NICU, the use of Pitocin in delivery, serious maternal complications after early preterm delivery,[19] breastfeeding problems, and so forth are being explored.

Major studies are under way by researchers led by a University of North Carolina team and project leader, Dr. Samantha Meltzer-Brody, to understand with an iPhone App the genetic underpinnings of mood disorders during and after pregnancy.[20] "The goal is to collect about 100,000 DNA samples and compare them with DNA from women who have never experienced depression in hopes of discovering genetic factors that could lead to better prediction, diagnosis and treatment for maternal mental illness."[21] The Center for Psychiatric Genomics is coordinating the project's genetic analysis.

I (Dr. Feingold) have supervised new perinatal therapists and been on half a dozen or more dissertation committees for students researching some aspect of maternal mental illness.

With an increased understanding of the high prevalence rates of maternal mental illness, there has been a growing emphasis among clinicians and researchers in the mental health field on evidence-based treatment for pregnant and postpartum women. Due to the predominance of research studies using cognitive-behavioral psychotherapy[22] or an interpersonal model,[23] there is a preference for clinicians to provide psychotherapy using these approaches with a perinatal population. However, a few new studies have shown the effectiveness of the evidence-based Dialectical Behavior Therapy (DBT)[24] for postpartum mothers and the growing application of Eye Movement Desensitization and Reprocessing (EMDR) for women with traumatic birth experiences.[25] One might expect the inclusion of other novel treatment approaches as a larger group of mental health providers become interested in perinatal issues or identify this niche area as a specialty in the years ahead.

Decades earlier there were so few clinicians providing treatment with this specific population that it was difficult to find a therapist, yet alone a recognized expert. As discussed in the introduction, my motivation to specialize in perinatal mental health was precisely my own struggle to find a knowledgeable mental health provider with experience in treatment of postpartum depression and anxiety. Many of my fellow postpartum sufferers likewise reported seeing numerous therapists until they found one who could help them navigate their healing journey. I recall a colleague and I comparing our desperate searches—who had the most difficult struggle locating a therapist. By comparison with my own search, she "won" with appointments to more than twenty-five doctors and mental health providers whom she deemed incapable or unwilling to help her. I lost the bet, as I was lucky enough to only visit a dozen doctors or therapists until I located a therapist that could help me. He was a social worker who worked with anxiety disorders, yet he was willing to learn about perinatal illnesses and try his best with a trial-and-error approach to help me recover. Despite his lack of expertise, he was well meaning, and we eventually found some useful interventions in a basically "hit or miss" treatment plan.

It was by pure persistence and a refusal to give in to the illness that led my colleague to locate a provider who could help her as well. We both eventually focused our clinical work on helping women with perinatal depression, as both of us were motivated by our own difficult experiences in getting well-informed treatment. Unfortunately, we were not unique.

This has led to developing the perinatal mental health two-day "Components of Care" training within Postpartum Support International (PSI). This course is meant to equip providers with the skills necessary to assess, screen, treat, or refer patients for perinatal mental health complications and to provide additional resources for patients. In 2018, PSI introduced a perinatal mental health certification with the required passage of an exam administered in coordination with Pearson VUE.[26]

Unfortunately, despite all this progress that has centered on perinatal depression and anxiety, there has been little focus on the severest form of maternal mental illness, postpartum psychosis (PPP) until now.[27] Recent initiatives by postpartum psychosis sufferers have led to developing a postpartum psychosis task force within Postpartum Support International.

Lee S. Cohen, MD, is leading the MGHP3 Postpartum Psychosis Project at Massachusetts General Hospital's Center for Women's Mental Health in coordination with Harvard Medical School.[28] He was the keynote speaker at the 2019 Annual Postpartum Support International Conference. His project is establishing a registry of women who have experienced an episode of postpartum psychosis within the past ten years. As new postpartum laws and research attention and interest turn to postpartum psychosis, this may lead to a new body of knowledge about this underserved and underrepresented population.

TREATMENT CONSIDERATIONS WITH POSTPARTUM PSYCHOSIS

Mental health professionals need to be forewarned that there is an inherent challenge in treating cases of women with severe postpartum depression and postpartum psychosis. There is a potential for crisis, as moods can change rapidly and symptoms may alternatively wax and wane. This makes treatment an anxiety-provoking situation for even an experienced clinician. As a mental health provider, one must be aware that the stakes are great. A miscalculation can come with a high cost. With the concern of suicide and infanticide in an unstable severe mental illness, I have learned to err on the side of caution. It has not been a common occurrence in my own clinical practice, but in those cases where there is any doubt about someone's potential for self or other harm, it is advised to have the patient evaluated in a hospital setting. In one case in my own practice, this led to a patient who was expressing suicidal ideation and a plan for self-harm to be promptly sent to the hospital emergency room for an assessment. Later after spending hours at the hospital emergency room followed by hospital admission (as apparently the hospital crisis team agreed), the patient was livid. A few days later upon discharge, she was resentful and quit therapy. I did not feel sorry for my actions. I have no reservations that I acted with goodwill and appropriate therapeutic judgment. I would do the same today if faced with a similar situation. I would prefer a patient be upset or angry with me than take a chance with her life or the lives of others.

Maternal mental disorders are a group of illnesses in which an error in judgment by a clinician comes with so great a cost that it is not worth the risk. The possibility of tragedy is not only for the mother but also for her baby, other children, and the potential for a catastrophic outcome for the whole family. Therefore, be forewarned. This is not a good professional road or specialty niche for a therapist who is a people pleaser and wants to be liked and is unwilling to have patients unhappy or displeased with their provider. Despite this caveat, most of my patients are very grateful, and only very few have been perturbed and quit treatment. Yet this cannot become more important than the need to act in the best interest of patients.

A TRAGEDY AVERTED BY A QUICK CALL BY A CONCERNED SPOUSE

Abby was a new patient for me, referred by her psychiatrist following her hospital discharge in a neighboring state. I had met with her one Friday in the comfort of my home office in a suburb of Chicago. As with all patients,

I take a detailed history as part of my intake procedure and begin the process of developing an outpatient treatment plan.

She was a lovely new mother to multiples, had no prior mental health history, and had worked in a professional capacity. Abby and her spouse were a successful upper-middle-class couple living the good life in their newly purchased suburban home. There were few notable stressors: they had a solid marital relationship, were financially sound, and had wanted children after waiting until they were well established in their mutual careers. They could afford to have outside help, once Abby returned to a job that she enjoyed. They even seemed to have a good network of friends and family to help, as both were aware that multiples would be a real challenge.

Yet within a few weeks of giving birth, Abby's prior characteristically cheerful demeanor had changed to sadness and even despair that was surprising to her, her spouse, and all who knew her. Within a short period of time, she sought out treatment with a psychiatrist for medication at the recommendation of the obstetrician who had delivered her babies. Abby had no prior episodes of depression, so mental health treatment and the idea of psychotherapy was new to her. She decided that she would work with a psychiatrist for medication but was reluctant to begin psychotherapy as she thought that was more appropriate for women with serious issues and mental illness.

During the weeks before I met her, her spouse and family were sufficiently concerned about the depth of her depression. When her psychiatrist recommended hospitalization, they readily agreed as she was already more than four months' postpartum and had been not responding well to the various medications prescribed. Abby was struggling with the demands of caring for her babies and was consumed with anxiety about returning to her job in the near future. It was likely around this same time that Abby decided to abruptly stop nursing as she decided she could not handle the demands of work approaching and pumping for multiples in the coming weeks.[29]

After about a week in the hospital, Abby was feeling a little better, and based on that brief improvement and likely her limited health insurance benefits, she was prepared to be discharged. This was when I received the call and request to provide outpatient psychotherapy within the first week of her discharge home. I was able to schedule Abby for an appointment within days of discharge. Reports from the hospital as well as her attending psychiatrist made it sound as if she was responding well to the new medications. The hospital staff was optimistic about her continued recovery.

As a perinatal psychologist who has seen the best and worst outcomes over my more than two decades of specialization, I was hopeful, yet somewhat skeptical, about so quick an improvement. When I met Abby two days after her discharge, she seemed in good spirits, what a psychologist would call a euthymic mood. She was a lovely, engaging young woman who seemed bright and introspective and a good candidate for a course in psychotherapy to assist in her continued improvement. I was encouraged and expected that I could help her toward a complete recovery over the next few months or possibly even weeks.

The next morning was a Saturday, and although I anticipated a slow morning and a relaxing day off, things changed rapidly when my business and cell phones both had early voicemail messages from Abby's husband with her home number. I am generally careful not to call a patient's family members without a patient's written consent. However, I was concerned and I have learned to trust my instincts. As Abby was a new patient and had just come out of the hospital and the call sounded urgent, I decided I would call immediately. Her spouse answered. He was not frantic but said she was acting weird and he didn't know who else to call. *Thank God he made that call!*

I told him I had just seen Abby the day before and she seemed to be doing fine. Abby's spouse was concerned but vague about what he thought was weird or out of character for her. At that point, I suggested he put her on the phone. Abby quickly launched into some irrational, barely coherent discourse about how her grandmother is evil and that she knows I am good and related to Jesus's mother, Mary. I calmly told her to put her husband back on the phone and then explained to him that she was floridly psychotic and needed to be immediately transported back to the hospital and I would call 9-1-1. As I have explained earlier in this chapter, symptoms can wax and wane or change rapidly at times. Any improvement needs to be measured over the long haul; time is the true test of improved mental stability.

After my brief call to Abby's house, I followed up by contacting the hospital emergency room to tell them I was sending her in and to expect her with the need for a psychiatric assessment and hospitalization. Then I called her treating psychiatrist by pager (it was a weekend emergency). He said he had just had an appointment with her and she was doing great. I listened and agreed that I had the same impression only a day ago. However, currently she was floridly psychotic and needed a rehospitalization. Once I described our conversation, he agreed.

Abby spent another few weeks in the hospital and this time was discharged more slowly and was truly more emotionally stable. I continued to work with her upon her release from the hospital. After several months of treatment, she returned to her work and her normal mothering duties and life.

Following Abby's second hospitalization, she revealed some chilling information during one of our psychotherapy sessions that still haunts me to this day. The Saturday morning that I had called her home, she had been having olfactory and visual hallucinations. Abby disclosed about the time that I telephoned her home, she had smelled smoke and was about to throw her babies out the second-floor window to the fireman waiting below. She believed she was saving her babies from the fire she smelled and assumed was consuming her home. She proceeded to tell me that she now understood there was no fire or any fireman under her window waiting to catch her babies as she had believed in her psychotic state. Both of us breathed a sigh of relief at the catastrophic outcome averted.

The critical part in relation to maternal mental illness and legal issues is that if this tragedy had occurred we may have considered it a disastrous outcome of a psychotic mom or possibly an "altruistic filicide."[30] However, the judicial system would have considered it a double homicide, and she would likely receive life imprisonment with no parole in Illinois. In some states she may have gotten the death penalty.

NOTES

1. World Health Organization, "Mental Health: Maternal Mental Health," accessed July 30, 2019, https://www.who.int.

2. M. S. Reddy, "Depression: The Disorder and the Burden," *Indian Journal of Psychological Medicine* 32, no. 1 (January–June 2010): 1–2, doi:10.4103/0253-7176.70510. National Center for Biotechnology Information, accessed July 30, 2019, https://www.ncbi.nlm.nih.gov.

3. World Health Organization, "Mental Health: Maternal Mental Health," accessed July 30, 2019, https://www.who.int.

4. Statistics vary as to the prevalence of suicide and infanticide in cases of postpartum psychosis. According to one authoritative source, the rate of suicide is 5 percent and the infanticide rate is 4 percent. Dorothy Sit, Anthony J. Rothschild, and Katherine L. Wisner, "A Review of Postpartum Psychosis," *Journal of Women's Health* 15, no. 4 (May 2006): 352–68, doi:10.1089/jwh.2006.15.352; National Center for Biotechnology Information, accessed July 30, 2019, https://www.ncbi.nlm.nih.gov; Criminal Justice, accessed July 30, 2019, http://criminal-justice.iresearchnet.com.

5. John Cox, "National Center for Biotechnology Information," *Lancet* 366 (2005): 982, https://ncbi.nlm.nih.gov.

6. S. Dave et al., "Incidence of Maternal and Paternal Depression in Primary Care: A Cohort Study Using a Primary Care Database," *Archives of Pediatrics and Adolescent Medicine* 164, no. 11 (2010): 1038.

7. J. Paulson and S. Bazemore, "Prenatal and Postpartum Depression in Fathers and Its Association with Maternal Depression: A Meta-Analysis," *JAMA* 303, no. 19 (May 19, 2010): 1961–69, doi:10.1001/jama.2010.605.

8. American Psychiatric Association, *Desk Reference to the Diagnostic Criteria from DSM-5* (Arlington, VA: American Psychiatric Publishing, 2013), 112.

9. Susan B. Feingold, *Happy Endings, New Beginnings: Navigating Postpartum Disorders* (Far Hills, NJ: New Horizon Press, 2013).

10. Ibid.

11. Ibid.

12. Perinatal includes pregnancy as well as the postpartum period.

13. Feingold, *Happy Endings*.

14. I. Jones and N. Craddock, "Familiality of the Puerperal Trigger in Bipolar Disorder: Results of a Family Study," *American Journal of Psychiatry* 158 (2001): 913–17; R. E. Kendell, J. C. Chalmers, and C. Platz, "Epidemiology of Puerperal Psychosis," *British Journal of Psychiatry* 151 (July 1987): 135.

15. Referring to a first pregnancy.

16. American Psychiatric Association, *DSM-5*.

17. R. VanderKruik et al., "The Global Prevalence of Postpartum Psychosis: A Systemic Review," *BMC Psychiatry* (2017), doi:10.1186/s12888-017-1427-7.

18. Margaret G. Spinelli, "Postpartum Psychosis: Detection of Risk and Management," *American Journal of Psychiatry* 166, no. 4 (2009): 405–9.

19. U. M. Reddy, M. M. Rice, W. A. Grobman, J. L. Bailet et al., "Serious Maternal Complications after Early Preterm Delivery (24–33 Weeks' Gestation)." *American Journal of Obstetrics and Gynecology* 213, no. 4 (2015), PubMed.gov, https://www.ncbi.nlm.nih.gov/pubmed.

20. Pam Belluck, "Hunting the Genetic Signs of Postpartum Depression with an iPhone App," *New York Times*, March 21, 2016, https://www.nytimes.com.

21. Reddy et al., "Serious Maternal Complications."

22. H. Wilson and A. Donachie, "Evaluating the Effectiveness of a Dialectical Behaviour Therapy (DBT) Informed Programme in a Community Perinatal Team," *Behavioural and Cognitive Psychotherapy* 46, no. 5 (September 2018): 541–53; G. Apter-Danon and D. Candilis-Huisman, "A Challenge for Perinatal Psychiatry: Therapeutic Management of Maternal Borderline Personality Disorder and Their Very Young Infants," *Clinical Neuropsychiatry* 2, no. 5 (2005): 302–14.

23. S. Stuart, "Interpersonal Psychotherapy for Postpartum Depression," *Clinical Psychology and Psychotherapy* 19, no. 2 (2012): 134–40.

24. S. Stone, "Empowering PPD Recovery with Dialectical Behavior Therapy," *New Jersey Psychologist* 56, no. 3 (2006), accessed October 16, 2019, http://www.perinatalpro.com.

25. Wilson and Donachie, "Evaluating the Effectiveness of a Dialectical Behaviour Therapy (DBT) Informed Programme in a Community Perinatal Team," *Behavioural and Cognitive Psychotherapy* 46, no. 5 (September 2018): 541–53, doi:10.1017/S1352465817000790; M. Van Deursen-Geldrop and E. Bakker, "Is EMDR Effective for Women with Posttraumatic Stress Symptoms after Childbirth?" *European Health Psychologist* 17 (2015): 873; M. A. Baas, C. A. Stramrood, et al., "The OptiMUM-Study: EMDR Therapy in Pregnant Women with Posttraumatic Stress Disorder after Previous Childbirth and Pregnant Women with Fear of Childbirth: Design of a Multicentre Randomized Controlled Trial," *European Journal of Psychotraumatology* 8, no. 1 (2017), https://doi.org/10.1080/20008198.2017.1293315.

26. For more information about the perinatal mental health training and certification, see "Certification in Perinatal Mental Health-PMH-C," Postpartum Support International, 2009, http://www.postpartum.net.

27. C. Burak and M. Remington, *The Cradle Will Fall* (New York: Donald I. Fine, 1994). The was the first book I encountered on the topic of postpartum psychosis and infanticide; it was given to me in 1995 by psychiatrist and fellow Depression After Delivery board member Carl Burak.

28. "The MGH Postpartum Psychosis Project," MGH Center for Women's Mental Health, accessed July 30, 2019, https://www.womensmentalhealth.org/the-mgh-postpartumpsychosis.

29. Abrupt cessation of breastfeeding can trigger hormonal changes and escalating symptoms in some women while the increased estrogen with weaning can be helpful to others. I advise my own patients to wean slowly when they decide to cease nursing. If the baby stops taking the breast quickly, I suggest using a breast pump to "pump and dump" or to donate their milk to a milk bank or friends. I tell them to monitor their moods and, if decreased nursing is associated with worsening symptoms, then the nursing mother needs to slow down the process and to wean slower. I also advise my patients to work with an understanding lactation consultant to help her in the process of weaning, while being careful not to refer her to a consultant who is more concerned with the benefits of lactation than the mother's mental health.

30. "Altruistic filicide" is a term coined by forensic psychiatrist Phillip Resnick, MD (1969), referring to a mentally ill mother who in her psychotic delusional state believes that out of love for her baby or child, she must take the life of that child to end the suffering she imagined.

Chapter Two

Silence and Stigma

A Deadly Combination for Postpartum Psychosis

> We must work to eliminate the stigma that surrounds mental illness. It is the key reason that women fail to seek treatment.
>
> —Susan B. Feingold, PsyD

On a societal level there is a need for recognition of maternal depression as a legitimate illness that affects mortality. It can be as deadly as cancer and other physical diseases, and its victims as with other illnesses often respond best with prompt identification and immediate treatment. However, due to the stigma and shame that has been associated with mental health disorders, too many individuals deny symptoms and resist treatment until their depression has worsened. Research suggests often depression is undiagnosed and untreated, as 65.9 percent of pregnant women with depressive symptomatology do not receive a clinical diagnosis, and up to 50 percent do not receive treatment.[1]

Depression, similar to cancer, can invade other areas of a person's life and ultimately shorten their lifespan, with the known increased risk of suicide. Furthermore, it can certainly alter the joy expected by every new mother. The stigma of a mental health problem often leads individuals to suffer silently, and many families as well as some ethnicities and cultures are more prone to reinforce the tendency to keep this type of illness a secret.

THE STIGMA OF MATERNAL MENTAL ILLNESS ENCOURAGES SILENCE

Our society at the present time does not encourage women to speak up about their less-than-ideal experiences. Instead, we as a culture reinforce silence in survivors and families, leaving them to feel isolated and socially alienated from other new parents. Only recently have postpartum psychosis survivors banded together to discuss and support each other as they form online support groups and begin the process of creating a postpartum psychosis task force within the safety of the mothership, the nonprofit organization Postpartum Support International.

Secrecy and denial are even more likely a problem for women experiencing mental health issues during pregnancy and the postpartum period than at any other time of a woman's life. Women are bombarded by images of blissful mothers on social media that add to unrealistic pressures and societal myths of perfect motherhood. The joy expected and anticipated by every new parent is commonplace. Magazine covers with starlets who have shed all their baby weight in weeks and declare the ecstasy of new motherhood only add to their shame and self-loathing. Those struggling depressed mothers begin to wonder if they are permanently flawed and if they were ever cut out for motherhood. The lack of information about perinatal mood and anxiety disorders leaves new mothers fearful and ashamed of admitting they are suffering, rather than joyful. They often assume that every other new mother is blissful and that they alone are experiencing symptoms of anxiety or depression. This has led perinatal professionals and organizations to the well-known motto "You are not alone. You are not to blame. With help, you will be well."[2]

THE VULNERABILITY OF THE POSTPARTUM PERIOD

Even without a perinatal mood disorder, this is a vulnerable time as women adjust to the major changes in identity and their new roles as a mother. Sometimes a propensity toward perfectionism along with unrealistically high expectations can make it even more difficult. Many new mothers are self-critical; they mercilessly compare themselves to others and feel inadequate in their mothering duties. These women oftentimes fear the wrath of others judging them as a bad mother, as they likely regard themselves with such self-defeating harsh labels.

Combine these normal stressors with the stigma of mental illness, and it becomes more evident why new mothers would resist discussing their symptoms and getting treatment. Some research suggests that only 6 to 10 percent of women with perinatal mood and anxiety disorders actively seek out treatment.[3] This is highly significant. According to a 2014 report in the *Harvard Review of Psychiatry*, while the majority of postpartum depression (PPD) cases improve over a relatively short time with proper treatment, for roughly 38 percent of women diagnosed, postpartum depression becomes a lifelong chronic condition.[4]

WHY ARE WOMEN NOT GETTING TREATMENT?

Often sufferers are not aware of the risks of delaying treatment or avoiding it altogether. Sometimes they are in denial and associate their symptoms with sleep deprivation and the stress of adjusting to motherhood. Many new mothers fear exposure and express concern at being identified with abusive or "bad" mothers. They voice apprehension that their baby might be taken away by a child protective service agency if it became known that they were suffering with a mental illness. The secretiveness about postpartum disorders is self-perpetuated and adds to potential for disaster at times when the illness gets worse because the mother hides her symptoms or does not seek professional help.

Other barriers to women seeking help for perinatal depression include social vulnerability factors such as living in a poor neighborhood with limited local resources (poverty), having public insurance such as Medicaid, being a single parent with limited childcare options, exposure to trauma, and being a member of an ethnic minority. Racial disparities are issues that disproportionately affect African American and Latina women, and they are less likely to seek professional treatment versus low-income Caucasian women.[5]

In the study by Katy Kozhimannil, 9 percent of white women initiated postpartum mental health care, compared with 4 percent of black women and 5 percent of Latinas. "With analyses controlling for clinical factors, the odds of initiating treatment after delivery were significantly lower for blacks and Latinas compared with whites. Among those who initiated treatment, blacks and Latinas were less likely than whites to receive follow-up treatment."[6] There is no doubt that complex interactions exist that create barriers to accessing health care. This is an important area for further attention and study as apparent in a recent publication about the barriers to care for women with postpartum depression in the well-respected *Journal of AWHONN, the Association of Women's Health, Obstetric and Neonatal Nurses*.[7]

EARLY INTERVENTION IS CRITICAL TO PREVENT SERIOUS NEGATIVE OUTCOMES

There is still much to learn about perinatal illnesses. What we know is that the timely detection and treatment of maternal mental illness is essential for the health and well-being of parents and children.[8] The failure to detect these disorders and to provide treatment can lead to personal tragedy and the loss of lives. When we as a society become more educated and tolerant of mental health issues,[9] it will encourage new mothers to admit their symptoms without shame and to pursue the necessary mental health treatment. This is particularly critical with postpartum mood and anxiety disorders.

The American Psychiatric Association dedicated their 2019 annual meeting to collaborative models of care, a multidisciplinary approach that is the optimum method for prevention and treatment of mothers with postpartum mood disorders. An editorial in *Lancet*, the well-respected psychiatric journal, stated,

> Although several mental health conditions would benefit from a collaborative care approach, arguably postpartum depression should be high up on any physician's list. Physical and mental health care for mothers and babies in the USA is disjointed to say the least, despite the overwhelming evidence that a baby's health is directly linked to the mother's health after delivery: a period that is sometimes referred to as the fourth trimester.

The editorial goes on to point out that "a fourth-trimester collaborative care model that involves access to a night nurse after delivery, case management, temporary safe housing, family education, and a team-based approach to regular physical and behavioural health checks for both mother and baby could all go a long way to improving outcomes" of this large population of historically underserved patients.[10]

Likely with more attention to these illnesses, future generations will be better informed and better equipped to avoid undue suffering as well as catastrophic circumstances of perinatal depression and postpartum psychosis that lead to mothers being involved with the criminal justice system. Society and the legal system must work to prevent these tragedies and to understand that when a woman is not treated and tragedy ensues, excessive punishment is inappropriate. "It makes no sense for a brief mental illness to cause a lifetime of incarceration."[11]

As I have discussed in the last chapter, education and early intervention are critical to prevent catastrophic outcomes. Conversely the caveat in order to have this happen is for the woman and family to disclose signs and symptoms to family and friends, as well as health care and mental health professionals. It is evident that the more people are aware of a woman's symptoms of maternal mental illness, the more likely it will be that someone will reach out and encourage her or her family to seek professional help. This could not be clearer than in the catastrophic case in 2013 of Cynthia Wachenheim of New York.

All too often many of us visualize women with psychotic mental illness with the too-familiar image of a tattered, incoherent homeless person. Yet, Cynthia was far from that. She was a beautiful, articulate, well-educated, successful attorney. She serves as an excellent example to destigmatize women who have suffered with postpartum psychosis. It is a poignant example to bring home the point that this illness is nondiscriminatory. There is no specific socioeconomic class or race of woman who acquires postpartum psychosis, although a genetic predisposition for bipolar disorder is a well-accepted and known risk factor.[12] It is a shock for pregnant women with no prior history of mental health problems when they experience their first episode of depression or psychosis as a consequence of pregnancy and childbirth, rather than the joyful motherhood they anticipated.

THE POIGNANT STORY OF CYNTHIA WACHENHEIM

> "I love him so much, but it's obviously a terrible kind of love," she agonized in a 13-page handwritten note. "It's a love where I can't bear knowing he is going to suffer physically and mentally/emotionally for much of his life."[13]
>
> —Cindy Wachenheim

Enter Cynthia (Cindy) Wachenheim, a talented and well-respected attorney who wrote position papers for judges in the State Supreme Court in Manhattan. Cindy was living the "good life" that comes with education and privilege. She was her high school's valedictorian and attended a well-respected college followed by Columbia University Law School. Cindy would be one of the last people that others would associate with maternal mental illness. Yet in 2013, the forty-four-year-old first-time mother strapped her ten-month-old son to her chest in a baby carrier and leapt to her death from the eighth-floor window of her Harlem apartment. She had become obsessed with the idea that she was a failure as a mother and had caused him irrevocable brain damage when he was a few months old. (She believed in her delusional mind that the cause of the brain damage was the small falls and scrapes that her son experienced, something that is normal to all children learning to walk.) Nothing could shake her from that certainty, not even repeated assurances from doctors that he was normal.[14]

Cindy, a proficient writer and loving mother, left a rambling, mostly incoherent thirteen-page suicide note, stating her need to protect her child from a lifetime of suffering from what she believed were his disabilities. These disabilities existed only in her own delusional mind. Her jump from her high-rise only took her life; she landed on her back; the child was protected by his mother's dead body and suffered only mild injuries. It was the ultimate irony, in that Cindy judged herself as a failure as a mom in that she couldn't protect her son from minor falls. In the end, it was her own body that protected her son from the intentional fall that was meant to kill them both.

If Cindy's family or doctors had only understood what was happening to her, that she was having psychotic delusional thoughts about her son, they might have been able to save her by having her hospitalized. Her own psychiatrist may have prescribed an antipsychotic or mood-stabilizing medication had he understood that the depression she was experiencing was based on her own psychotic delusions.

Cindy did see many physicians during those ten months following childbirth. She repeatedly sought treatment for her son from numerous pediatricians and pediatric neurologists who reassured her that her son was perfectly normal and not hurt from the minor falls that are so common to babies exploring their environment and learning to walk. What the medical physicians failed to understand was that no reassurance could comfort Cindy. Her frequent troubling thoughts were not the common normal fears or concerns of an overprotective mom. Her thoughts were the unrelenting and delusional beliefs of a woman with a psychotic disorder. Likely because Cindy was well educated, or due to the waxing and waning that can be a part of postpartum psychosis, she was unfortunately able to pass as just another worried new mom.

It is also an example of a case that might be understood as an "altruistic filicide,"[15] had Cindy survived and the baby died instead. With the present laws in the US it is likely she would have been charged with murder and spent years or a lifetime in prison. It is unlikely she would have been found *not guilty by reason of insanity* as no physician, family, or friend detected her mental illness.

Excerpts from an Interview with Karen Wachenheim, Board Member of Postpartum Support International and the Sister-in-Law of Cindy Wachenheim

Karen was gracious enough to agree to an interview to shed light and to explain from a family member's prospective what happened that led to the tragic death of Cindy. Karen was no stranger to maternal mental illness, as she herself had suffered from postpartum depression that ironically was identified first by Cindy who helped her find treatment to assist in her recovery.

Did you personally or did your family know what was going on with Cindy? Did any of you realize this was not just obsessive thinking or your typical new mom adjustment behavior?

When things first started happening with Cindy, we did realize that something was going on. We figured she had some form of postpartum depression. We didn't realize how severe, and we didn't know there was such a thing as postpartum psychosis at the time. We tried to get her to get some help. She was going to see someone, possibly a psychiatrist in that she was on some medication, but it wasn't the right one. She believed she was depressed because she had brain-damaged her baby son.

Was she seeing someone who specialized in postpartum mental illness?

No. We couldn't convince her to see someone who specialized in postpartum. She saw a generalist, and we really didn't know if she was taking her medication, or if the medication was making her worse. Cindy's sister was trying to help connect her with someone else, but Cindy insisted on staying with who she was working with. We also couldn't convince her to believe something different than that he was brain-damaged and it was her fault. Unfortunately, Cindy couldn't forgive herself.

It sounds like the family recognized that it was crazy thinking, but you couldn't dissuade her from these irrational beliefs?

Correct. Cindy didn't start showing any symptoms until the baby was about four months old. It was at that time that she started sending us videos where she thought she saw the baby's arm doing something strange. She believed he was having seizures. She started seeing one doctor for something, and although he said the baby was fine, she went on Dr. Google. You know how dangerous that is.

Then she decided it was something else, so she took the baby to another specialist. The family became concerned, and we started talking to the pediatrician and got her to agree to see someone to get help for herself.

Did the doctors who were assessing her baby, who found nothing wrong with the child, understand that there was something wrong with the mother?

Who knows what Cindy was telling the doctors? We never got a chance to talk to her therapist to say this is what we are seeing as her family. That is one of our regrets. We didn't say this is what we see and what we think should be done.

How would you have known what was about to occur and that things were about to go off the rails? Now we know more and the importance of seeing someone who specializes in postpartum mental illness.

At that time, I'm not sure we even knew that there were therapists who specialized in this. In fact, I suffered postpartum depression with both my boys, and it was Cindy who saw it in me. I just went to my regular doctor and she gave me some medication. The doctor never suggested going to see someone; she only said, "Here, take this." Luckily for me, I was fine, but I wish I had seen someone to help me through my postpartum anxiety. Since that time, I have learned so much from being involved with Postpartum Support International.

With postpartum psychosis, symptoms can wax and wane, and sometimes someone seems fine and other times not, acting or talking in a peculiar or bizarre way. Was this the case with Cindy?

There was a time we saw her go downhill. We didn't live nearby, but she stayed with us for about a week at Thanksgiving, a few months before she took her own life. We had never seen her this low. We tried to get her to stay with us longer, as she said she felt safe and happier being with us. But her husband was working in New York City, and she missed him and wanted to go back to be with him.

Then, she came back for my son's birthday a few months later and she seemed a little bit better. She was aware that people were starting to think she was crazy. I think she was starting to fake it, to make people think she wasn't crazy. We told her we didn't see anything wrong with him, but either way we would love him. We didn't want her to feel alone and we really tried.

When I look back, I wonder if she was starting to get a "plan." She was starting to appear calm and seemed better about things. That was the last time we saw her. It was January or February, and then in March is when it happened. She took her life.

One of Cindy's biggest fears was that the baby would never walk, because he was a little bit slower with developmental milestones. Right after she died, we were visiting my brother-in-law and the baby was right on the verge of walking. It was bittersweet as, had Cindy seen that, maybe she would have been convinced that the baby was normal. Although perhaps the delusions were too powerful and strong to even override that reality.

Cindy was so brilliant and kind, but once the delusions took over her brain, we had lost her. She couldn't be away from the baby for a second, yet when she was with him she seemed so detached and disconnected. She became a person we didn't know.

NOTES

1. J. Y. Ko et al., "Depression and Treatment among U.S. Pregnant and Nonpregnant Women of Reproductive Age, 2005–2009," *Journal of Women's Health* 21 (2012): 830–36.

2. The well-recognized motto has served as a slogan of Postpartum Support International.

3. Katherine Stone, "BabyCenter Finds PPD Moms Don't Seek Help Due to Guilt and Shame," *Postpartum Progress* (blog), November 2014, https://postpartum progress.com.

4. Erin Heger, "When Postpartum Depression Doesn't Go Away," *Atlantic*, September 4, 2018.

5. S. M. Simpson, L. L. Krishnan, M. E. Kunik, et al. "Racial Disparities in Diagnosis and Treatment of Depression: A Literature Review," *Psychiatric Quarterly* 78 (2007): 3–14.

6. Katy Kozhimannil et al., "Racial and Ethnic Disparities in Postpartum Depression Care among Low-Income Women," *Psychiatric Services* (journal of the American Psychiatric Association) 62, no. 6 (2011): 619–25, doi:10.1176/appi.ps.62.6.619.

7. B. Grissette et al., "Barriers to Help-Seeking Behavior among Women with Postpartum Depression," *Journal of Obstetric, Gynecologic, and Neonatal Nursing* 47, no. 6 (November 2018): 812–81.

8. E. O'Connor et al., "Primary Care Screening for and Treatment of Depression in Pregnant and Postpartum Women: Evidence Report and Systematic Review for the US Preventive Services Task Force," *JAMA* 315, no. 4 (2016): 388–406; Simpson, Krishnan, and Kunik et al., "Racial Disparities."

9. A study in *Stigma and Health* reports that an hour-long slide and video presentation from the National Alliance on Mental Illness called "Ending the Silence" can help end mental health stigma. "Ending the Silence," *Monitor on Psychology*, May 2018.

10. "Editorial: Seeing the Whole Picture of Postpartum Depression," *Lancet* 6, no. 7 (July 2019): 547, http://www.thelancet.com/psychiatry.

11. Barry Lewis, "Postpartum Disorders: A New Law Offers Hope," *Champion* (National Association of Criminal Defense Lawyers) (March 2018): 20–25.

12. I. Jones and N. Craddock, "Familiality of the Puerperal Trigger in Bipolar Disorder: Results of a Family Study," *American Journal of Psychiatry* 158 (2001): 913–17; R. E. Kendell, J. C. Chalmers, and C. Platz, "Epidemiology of Puerperal Psychosis," *British Journal of Psychiatry* 151 (July 1987): 135.

13. P. Belluck, "A Case Study in Maternal Mental Illness," *New York Times*, June 16, 2014.

14. Ibid.

15. Coined by Phillip Resnick in 1969, "altruistic filicide" is one of the five theories of classification identified as to why mothers kill.

Chapter Three

Legal Implications of Postpartum Illness in the Criminal Justice System

Abandon hope all ye who enter here.

The reader may believe the system of checks and balances within the justice system will protect the mentally ill from severe punishment. When trying to protect its own, outside pressure results in the legal system scapegoating the extremely guilty only as a last resort, still protecting the less notorious. Unfortunately, the system seems incapable of withstanding outside pressure and ends up punishing the powerless. This is especially true regarding the mentally ill.

Andrea Yates wanted children, as many as she could have. Her ambition was to be a great mother. She gave up her nursing career to raise her children. Her children's deaths took her on the notorious side of the criminal justice system.

Paula Sims's notoriety made her the subject of a television call-in poll: a popular vote whether she should be executed.

Both Sims and Yates were spared because the jury failed to unanimously vote in favor of their execution. Both had suffered postpartum psychosis at the time of the crime but were convicted nonetheless. Both, like many other sufferers of postpartum psychosis, face a lifetime in an institution.

WHY DOES A BRIEF MENTAL ILLNESS CAUSE A LIFETIME OF INSTITUTIONALIZATION?

Long-standing ingrained culture and firmly set laws have failed to stay abreast of medical knowledge. The criminal justice system faces many challenges. It deals with the innocent, the falsely accused, the onetime criminal, the lifetime criminal, the white-collar criminal, the armed offender, the drunk, the vagrant, and the murderer. The criminal justice system is charged with sorting the innocent from the guilty, the rehabilitatable from the few who would be a danger to society if released before aging makes them incapable of causing harm. It also includes the concept that fairness means persons with severe mental illness or infirmities are to be excused in part or in entirety for their wrongs. The latter concept has lately become more lacking in mercy. It is particularly flawed with respect to postpartum illnesses.

Most of the time, this system operates outside of the general public's awareness. Perfection cannot be expected. Short of the rare cases of outright fixes, it actually performs its job fairly well. This is because it does have its own checks and balances. The greatest problem it has, actually caused by its own form of checks and balances, is in sentencing. Imagine a system wherein sentences are set within a limited range by legislators who may be entirely unfamiliar with mental health issues, and who have never learned a thing about the defendant. Add to that, those imposing sentences are actually discouraged from leniency by a voting public that encourages them to give harsh sentences.

This, then, is the firestorm into which a sufferer from postpartum illnesses walks, or perhaps is dragged. "Abandon hope all ye who enter here."

The issue of "knowing" right from wrong is critical in the law. No one could rationally claim Yates was not seriously mentally ill. While the witness for the prosecution testified that Yates was responsible for the deaths of her children because she knew right from wrong at the time of the act,[1] the expert for the defense testified, "Even though she knew it was against the law, she did what she thought was right in the world she perceived through her psychotic eyes at the time."[2] Yates's motivation was to kill the children before they would reach the age where they could, and would, be sent to hell for eternity. This is another example of "altruistic filicide" where a mentally ill mother kills her children ultimately to save them. In her first trial, Yates narrowly escaped execution.

WHAT ABOUT OTHER MENTALLY ILL ACCUSED?

While the very nature of postpartum illnesses screams out for special treatment in the law, what about all other sufferers of mental illness? Can all mentally ill persons who commit crimes be treated with mercy equal to those whose crimes were caused by a temporary mental illness and were committed against one's own infant?

The first issue is one of definition, or extent. What degree and kind of mental illness is to be given grace? All would agree that no particular mercy is to be given the sociopath, one whose mental illness is exhibited primarily by a willingness to commit crimes or other antisocial behavior. But how will we determine what group of persons who, by reason of a mental illness, are granted a categorical ban protecting them from the severest punishments?

The US Supreme Court provides only a limited answer. It has intervened prohibiting the death penalty only in extreme circumstances. Most recently, Vernon Madison was finally spared execution. Madison's attorneys claimed he was constitutionally unfit to be executed. Strokes had slurred his speech and left him incontinent, unable to walk, and suffering profound disorientation and confusion and without memory of his crime or understanding of why he was to be executed. The prosecution hired an expert contradicting this claim; the execution was allowed to proceed. Months later, the defense filed a supplemental petition to stop the execution that established the doctor, whose testimony had contradicted Madison's doctors, was addicted to drugs, was forging prescriptions, and had since been arrested. Also, Madison's condition had further deteriorated. The Supreme Court ruled five to three the execution should be barred.

Significant rulings by the US Supreme Court pertaining to mental capacity and punishment also include (1) *Miller v. Alabama* that held a life sentence for a minor is unconstitutional because of their not fully formed brains and (2) the pair of *Ford v. Wainwright* (1986) and *Panetti v. Quarterman* (2007). *Ford* held that the execution of the insane is barred; in the early common law in both England and the US, execution of the insane was considered "savage and inhumane." Panetti was to be executed despite believing he was to be executed because of the spiritual warfare between angels and devils. The court held that delusion was sufficient to show he lacked a rational understanding of why he was to be executed; after a substantial showing of unfitness to be executed, the prisoner must be granted a judicial hearing to determine if he knew he had committed the crime, knew he was to be executed, and knew he was to be executed for the crime.

Hall v. Florida (2014) and *Atkins v. Virginia* (2002) are mental competency cases, partially but not wholly distinguishable from mental illness cases. Atkins was intellectually disabled, so his execution was barred. Hall was on the borderline of that definition. The court ruled further hearings were necessary to determine whether Hall's intellectual capacity was sufficient to treat him as competent.

Despite these rulings, the severely mentally ill can still be executed. Nothing stopped the 2015 execution of Andrew Brannan, a Vietnam War veteran. An "outstanding" and "exemplary" officer, he was awarded the Bronze Star and, twice, the Army Commendation Medal. His posttraumatic stress disorder (PTSD) was linked to his service, notably having observed an officer stepping on a land mine and twice taking command of his unit after his superior officer was killed. His bizarre behavior at the crime scene, caught on a dash-cam, was noted. He had never before committed a crime. Back in 1994 the Department of Veterans Affairs declared him "100 percent disabled" due to depression and bipolar disorder.[3] The otherwise senseless murder he committed is explained entirely by his PTSD.

The American Bar Association, the American Psychological Association, the American Psychiatric Association, and the National Alliance on Mental Illness have adopted resolutions opposing the execution of the mentally ill.

The National Association of Drug Court Professionals in association with Justice for Vets, among others, is seeking justice for the mentally ill.[4] Veterans' Courts have been formed in numerous states. This useful, but categorically limited, approach avoids the harshness of criminal justice for those servicepersons who have had difficulty adjusting to civilian life.

Hardworking attorneys have had some limited success expanding those US Supreme Court rulings in scope and jurisdiction. Recently, on June 17, 2019, Pakistan's Supreme Court in Islamabad stopped the execution of a mentally ill prisoner.[5]

Legislatures have nearly universally enacted laws that call for mitigating punishments for crimes committed by the mentally ill. These laws provide only limited benefits. They do not reduce minimum penalties. They are not mandatory; their application can be rejected almost arbitrarily.

Presently, relief from harsh sentences is on an ad hoc basis. Changes of a global nature depend on the establishment of general rules that are difficult to create. Relief depends on the mercy of the courts, not universally present, to balance the sometimes-harsh requirements imposed by legislators.

We believe the current approach is wrong. It is too strongly in favor of convictions and harsh sentences, including at times execution, of the mentally ill. It is the duty of each state to correct this.

WHERE DO THINGS ACTUALLY BEGIN TO GO WRONG IN THE CRIMINAL JUSTICE SYSTEM?

The criminal justice system begins with various law enforcement officials. This is actually the location of the greatest chance of corruption, because the infamous blue code of silence limits the willingness of officers to disclose wrongdoing by other officers. The police officers would refer to this as "ratting out" their fellow officers. The police enforce this internal prohibition with absolute universality and greater zeal than they enforce the law out in the streets. There is a hierarchy that restricts corruption in the other portions of the criminal justice system, but the supervisors of the police rarely successfully encourage violations of the blue code of silence. The police code of silence is difficult to overcome. It is ingrained into the very structure of many police departments.

The Chicago Police Department has received a great deal of attention. Likely it is no better or worse than other large city departments. While it has been made a scapegoat, events such as the Rodney King beating in Los Angeles show it is similar, unfortunately, to other departments. The police code of silence has been exposed on multiple occasions, but never cured.

In my career, notable code of silence incidents include the street files case, the systematic torturing of young African American men by Detective Jon Burge, and the murder of Laquan McDonald.

Enforcement of the police code of silence reached its zenith in the largely forgotten "street files" case in the early 1980s in Chicago. This incident exposed the impunity with which officers conduct their business and demonstrated the blatant enforcement of the code of silence.

In that incident, Chicago police detective Frank Laverty investigated a crime and concluded, based on evidence he uncovered, a particular suspect was innocent. That detective went to the state's attorneys involved in the prosecution and informed them the defendant was innocent, explaining carefully and in detail just why that was precisely so. The prosecutors told him they would dismiss the charges. The detective believed them. He returned to performing his police business. The prosecutors, however, lied to the detective, the court, and the public, and proceeded to prosecute that innocent man in a jury trial. During that trial, a scene dramatic enough to make a large story in the local press took place. A relative of the victim was surprised by the prosecutor showing a photograph of the victim lying dead at the scene. The anguished scream in front of the jury was described in the *Chicago Tribune*. This drama was planned by the prosecutors: in addition to prosecuting an innocent man, the prosecution wanted to inflame the jury's passions, itself a highly improper objective.

The article in the *Chicago Tribune* was read by many, including the police detective who told the prosecutors the defendant was innocent. He went to the courthouse again. This time he spoke with the defense attorneys who were far more receptive to the information that their client was innocent than had been the prosecutors. The defense demanded a hearing, because the law is clear on this point: if there is evidence of innocence in the hands of the police or prosecutors, the defense must be informed. The evidence presented by the defense disclosed the existence of an entire system of "street files," a set of reports that contained the real evidence. These street files existed throughout the police department. Their function was to hide evidence that contradicted the official, disclosed reports. This is completely illegal, and absolutely morally wrong.

The disclosures set several firestorms in the department. The biggest firestorm was the burning (or disposal) of countless reports—the burning also, figuratively, of the police detective who disclosed the systematic fabrication of and withholding of evidence.[6] Of the many police involved in the murder prosecution of an innocent man, of the hundreds who engaged in the systematic suppression of evidence, and of the prosecutors who prosecuted a man knowing he was innocent and hid that evidence, only one man was punished. That was Detective Frank Laverty, the honest police detective who disclosed what his moral compass told him he must.[7]

Meanwhile, Chicago police detective Jon Burge for years was torturing young African American men. He was seeking confessions. Nothing else mattered to him. Guilt or innocence did not matter. The law did not matter. The unreliability of forced confessions did not matter. The number and form of tortures did not matter. The burns, the electrical shocks, and the physical scars were all, ultimately, well documented.[8] The interview and detention rooms in detective area headquarters are not soundproofed. There were plenty of staff there hearing the screams of the tortured. None spoke up. It took investigations by two Chicago newspapers, a report by Amnesty International, and a lawsuit by victims before an internal police report was uncovered documenting twelve years of torture.[9]

None who were aware of the torture were prosecuted or even disciplined. Burge himself was promoted to watch commander and retired in Florida with his police pension before decades of pressure, settlements, and legal expenses of more than one hundred million dollars of taxpayer money and before special prosecutor investigations finally forced him to answer to justice. That is the same Detective Burge who ordered the punishment of Detective Laverty.[10] Those who followed the code of silence were unpunished, and even promoted.

A few decades later, Laquan McDonald was executed by an armed offender, Chicago police officer Jason Van Dyke. Van Dyke pumped sixteen bullets into McDonald. There were several videotapes of the execution, unfortunately for Van Dyke and the many police officers who observed this. This cover-up went all the way to the mayor, who was concerned this damning video might hurt his election chances. The video was suppressed for a year and a half. Then the mayor blamed the chief of police for the cover-up. The chief, scapegoated, was fired by the mayor. In a very real sense, this cover-up went all the way to just short of the president of the United States.

As a consequence of this shooting, various civic interests opened negotiations and lawsuits attempting to make the police department more transparent and more in touch with the needs of the community, which according to every marked squad car, was there to "serve and protect." An agreement was reached creating greater transparency and making the department more sensitive to the needs of the community.

Jeff Sessions, the attorney general handpicked by our forty-fifth president, found this agreement between the community and the police department so intolerable he did his best to interfere with this local agreement. At least this time, there were actual prosecutions, both for the shooter and for those who wrote false reports attempting to exonerate Van Dyke. Somehow, although the reports were directly and clearly contradicted by the videotape, those who wrote the false reports were, of course, acquitted.

How were the three officers who were prosecuted for their false reports and cover up found not guilty?

The felony trial was assigned to an "associate" judge. An associate judge is one protected from the ballot by being appointed to the position by the Illinois Supreme Court justices. Thus, insulated from public opinion, she was able to find the three officers not guilty. The lawyers for the three then expressed righteous indignation for being forced to go to trial despite what they called flimsy evidence, such as an actual videotape of the event.

The sad point is not only that police reports and testimony cannot be trusted; additionally, the executive office of the United States could not tolerate a local police department's efforts to improve itself. Nor can we rely on the prosecutors to exercise lenity in prosecution and sentencing. The prosecutors must justify lenience, not lengthy sentences, to their superiors. And their superiors must justify lenience to their superiors, who ultimately are the voters.

Members of police departments understand the lesson. Do not disclose torture, murder, or corruption. The "code of silence" became enforced for all to see. Could any lesson be clearer? Police may be rewarded for heroic risks to save a life or rescue a victim. They will be unpunished for obeying the code of silence. Punishment comes only to those who violate that code and to the extremely rare officer whose conduct becomes too visible despite the code of silence.

At least judges hopefully think of the shame and loss of income from a corruption conviction. They should think of Judge Al Rosen, who chose to end his life rather than face justice; such is the irony of what is known as higher justice.

Returning now to public pressure on judges who are vulnerable to that, it always acts to increase and never decrease sentences imposed. A sad fact of our system under the Citizen's United law is that judges never become vulnerable by giving excessive sentences but are more vulnerable than ever to special interests such as corporations spending fortunes to remove a judge who acts leniently or against their interests. We have seen too much of this. As an example, Justice Louis Butler was the first sitting Supreme Court justice in Wisconsin to be voted out of office in forty years; in that election only about 20 percent of registered voters cast ballots. His opponent attacked him for actually defending criminals earlier in his career as a public defender, with ads funded by conservative groups such as right to life supporters and corporations that would benefit from less restrictive pollution laws.[11] Butler was guilty of no wrong.

In another infamous situation, a supreme court candidate in West Virginia, Brent Benjamin, was supported by ads totaling three million dollars from a corporation that had a case in front of that supreme court. Three million dollars swayed the election in his favor. Of course, in return Judge Benjamin refused to recuse himself and tried, until the US Supreme Court ordered him off the case, to rule in that corporation's interests. Even in the face of outright corruption affecting the integrity of both the election and the judicial system, the decision to prohibit that judge from participation in that case was five to four.

The tendency toward harsh sentences is worsened by punitive laws enacted in the interest of showing voters that their representative is "tough on crime." Prior to "Truth in Sentencing" statutes, a set of laws popular with the tough-on-crime crowd, the typical sentencing laws accommodated an actual truth in sentencing: as it is in life, people change. It is well known in the legal and sociological communities that even young adults with a criminal mindset almost universally give up a life of crime somewhere in their thirties at the latest.[12] Accordingly, parole laws were universal up to the mid- to late twentieth century. Parole was a rational system of releasing prisoners who demonstrated rehabilitation. "Truth in Sentencing" laws largely took away parole and a great deal of a judge's authority to choose a sentence based on the totality of the circumstances. Instead these laws compelled the court to impose a particular, harsher sentence. The limited range of sentences was chosen by the legislature without consideration of the relative involvement or lack thereof of a convicted person. His or her past, potential, entire nature, rehabilitative potential, and remorse, normally significant to any rational sentencing decision and normally significant to any early release, became immaterial.

In many states a lookout for a burglar who had no inkling the burglar had a gun is required to be sentenced to life imprisonment without parole if two or more die in the burglary. Clearly such a situation merits punishment. But life with no possibility of parole seems to be extreme.

If these laws were enacted for the purpose of ensuring criminals all face certain punishment, they do no such thing. Rather, they create a compulsion for innocents accused to bargain for a plea to a lesser charge and a sentence they could live with. This causes innocent persons to have felony records. The opposite also occurs. These laws tie up courts with trials for people who are guilty, and know they are almost certain to be found guilty, but have nothing to lose because, if convicted, they have no hope to see daylight again. It encourages perjury, because they have nothing to lose. Since conduct in jail becomes immaterial for the timing of one's release, the jail authorities lose the control they had from that source of authority. About half of prisoners are in a penitentiary for lengthy terms that were mandatory upon conviction. They have no hope of early release after rehabilitation. Many are innocent. Many others suffered from mental illness. Some of those have been cured, some not. Some are curable, some not, but are all punished rather than treated for their illness because they failed to be found not guilty by reason of insanity. It has been said that Cook County Jail is America's largest mental institution.[13]

Certainly, the lookout in a burglary in which a murder occurs does deserve punishment. The severity of that punishment can be debated. It is unfortunate when that debate is resolved by application of a mandatory sentence imposed by legislators seeking a reelection platform rather than consideration of the defendant's history of good and bad acts, the circumstances of his birth, his mental status, his contribution to both the crime and to society, his childhood, or his development into adulthood. In that class of cases, like many others, the law is not in touch with the actual situation. But in no class of cases is the law as out of touch with reality as it is with respect to mothers suffering from postpartum illnesses. The sentences are out of line. The determination of whether the sufferer is not guilty by reason of insanity is structurally flawed. The crime of infanticide by a suffering mother is much different from the same crime by an opportunistic criminal.

A BRIEF HISTORY OF THE LAW: HOW DID WE GET OUR SYSTEM OF JUSTICE?

With the exception of Louisiana, and its French heritage, our laws derive from William the Conqueror, whose 1066 invasion of England changed history. He took over a country whose laws varied from baron to baron, from county to county. That was a confusing patchwork of laws, with a Northumberland law, a Nottinghamshire law, a Derbyshire law, and so on. King William replaced all that with law consistent in all jurisdictions within his realm, a "common law." The term is still used today. A hallmark of it is its consistency, not just throughout the realm but over time.

The law would change but at a glacial pace. Once a change was successful, or popular, it might spread over a period of years through our nation and perhaps among the many common law nations. As an example, we take for granted today women can control their property. The common law did not permit this. We broke from England more than six decades before one state allowed married women to control their property *provided their husbands were incapacitated.* Nine years later, three states enacted laws giving women full control over their property. The lesson from this is, a small change to the law can be made and later expanded. It is not a choice of half a loaf versus none at all or a full one. The wheat can continue to grow. More and better loaves will result.

Under the common law, a judge's decision was final. Appeals were limited to issues of whether the law was applied correctly. Only in the 1500s could issues of fact first become the basis of an appeal.

Our states diverged from the other common law countries with respect to appellate court review of sentences. Sentences by most courts in the US were final, and could be reviewed only if the sentence was illegal. In virtually all common law jurisdictions outside the US, appellate review of sentences has been the principal method used to develop consistency in sentencing.[14]

Our laws diverged from the English common law roughly the time each state joined the union. From that point, state legislatures began to change laws that had worked for hundreds of years. Often this was due to advances in technology. Laws that applied to horses were not suitable for aircraft. Nevertheless, after the US diverged from Britain, the British realized that the appeals courts were the place to make punishment for crimes equal and fair, under equal circumstances. While the British and those jurisdictions following them have sought to rationalize sentencing and make sentences consistent throughout the country based upon appellate review with consideration of the crime and the nature and background of the offender, the states made no such effort. Whatever sentence the judge imposed could not be touched as long as the sentence was within the very broad requirements of the law.

DID THE COMMON LAW TREAT THESE MOTHERS AS BADLY AS WE DO NOW?

It is an interesting question whether the early common law would call for a murder conviction and harsh punishment of such women. The early common law, drawing from even earlier sources, did not make all homicides murder. Murder was an intentional act, a "premeditated act" with "malice aforethought." But what do those phrases mean? They are vague, and of a broad brush. What acts would be other than premeditated acts? What acts would and would not be with "malice aforethought"? The phrases limit the application of a murder conviction. Would it permit or limit a murder conviction to a mother for whom the judge or jury had sympathy? The available records do not permit a conclusive opinion but would allow a sympathetic outcome under the very general and nonspecific laws' requirements. Shakespeare could have that in mind when he wrote, "The quality of mercy is not strained."

Now the quality of mercy is strained. The accused must jump through specific "hoops," those that the law imposes on a defendant. Over many years, the concepts of premeditation and malice aforethought became legislated into specific categories. Within those categories, common enough fact patterns were specifically defined as less than murder. All other homicides, with the intent to kill or cause "great bodily harm," were murder in the first degree. Sadly, for whatever reason, infanticide did not make the "cut." Whether "premeditated" or not, whether by "malice aforethought" or not, or just by stress or mental illness not amounting to "insanity" under the statutes, these are now murder.

CRIMES RESULTING FROM MATERNAL MENTAL ILLNESS ARE TREATED AS ANY OTHER CRIME IN THE US

This brings us to the crimes resulting from a most treatable form of mental illness and problems with applying the insanity defense to crimes committed under the strong influence of postpartum illness. Postpartum illness is not the result of a depraved mind. It is literally the result of motherhood. There is no reason a side effect of motherhood, however severe, should exclude one from society, especially once it is cured. With treatment, even severe postpartum psychosis is cured rapidly. Without treatment, about one-quarter of perinatal sufferers will not be cured. However, the majority of those who commit a crime while floridly psychotic in a postpartum condition are condemned to severe penitentiary sentences or a lifetime in an inpatient "treatment facility." In fact, in the cases drawing significant attention in the media, it is the universal result. Only in those cases slipping under the radar is there a chance for a fair result.

A delusional psychotic mother who kills her children, like Andrea Yates of Texas, often does so for altruistic motives. This strange and unfortunate circumstance has a mother protecting her children from a worse outcome than death, such as an eternity in hell or a lifetime of disability. As with Yates, it can be the compulsion of voices in her head. The most likely outcome for a woman who kills her children with an altruistic motive while suffering from acute psychosis is not a "not guilty by reason of insanity." It is not a period of mental health treatment, which, once successful, would allow her to return to society. It is a guilty finding followed by decades or a lifetime in prison.

This is because of the nature of the laws governing insanity and consequences of "Truth in Sentencing." Yet it makes more sense that following treatment and the mother's recovery, the postpartum survivors should be welcomed into society as though they never had an illness.

It is logical as an individual to be skeptical of a claim of insanity raised by a defendant who is caught red-handed and has no prior history of insanity. The law as an institution is skeptical of such claims. This notion is generally accurate, except with respect to postpartum psychosis, which comes on without warning and oftentimes without a prior history of insanity. Temporary insanity is very real in postpartum psychosis. Even those a century ago who erroneously denied postpartum psychosis was a distinct illness noted the absence of prior psychosis in the majority of postpartum psychosis cases they analyzed.[15]

HOW DID INSANITY COME TO BE A CRIMINAL DEFENSE?

Insanity as a defense in modern times reflects the M'Naghten case in England. M'Naghten's not guilty by reason of insanity became a polarizing event. Parliament took up the issue. Stripped to its essentials, Parliament's M'Naghten makes insanity a defense only if the person does not realize what he or she is doing or, if the person does know what is being done, the person does not know it is wrong. Under either prong of the defense it requires that the person behaves with a belief that his actions are not what they really are.

The M'Naghten rule was criticized as too narrow. The M'Naghten rule is so narrow, so restricting in its application, that Daniel M'Naghten would not have been found not guilty by reason of insanity under that rule. We see this conflict between popular opinion and the use of insanity as a defense again and again.

The Model Penal Code (MPC) rules proposed in the US responded to the criticism of the M'Naghten rule and left it up to individual states to decide whether to adopt their proposals. That code, a set of recommended laws for the states, adds to the grounds for findings of insanity that the person lacks substantial capacity either to understand the criminality (or "wrongfulness" in some versions) of the conduct or to conform his or her conduct to the requirements of the law.

The MPC code on that subject was derived from the "irresistible impulse test" and the "Durham Rule." The irresistible impulse test allows for a finding of insanity despite the defendant being aware of the nature of his acts; if he cannot control it because of his mental illness, the crime is considered the result of insanity rather than the result of criminal impulses. The Durham Rule never had broad acceptance. The Model Penal Code tests, which had once been broadly accepted, lost popular support after John Hinckley was found not guilty of the attempted murder of Ronald Reagan based on that code. This was the M'Naghten history repeating itself. After a single unanimous jury's decision became unpopular, the US tightened rational rules and returned to the M'Naghten standard. Burdens of proof were switched. The accused had to prove insanity to a higher standard than previous law called for. Another widespread consequence of the Hinckley case is the abomination of "guilty but mentally ill." That is literally an invitation to send psychotic people to jail as soon as they have recovered, to suffer a sentence that cannot be modified.

One constant in all laws regarding the insanity defense is particularly harmful and inappropriate for the treatment within the justice system of the sufferer of postpartum illness. It is ingrained in the system. It is the belief, institutionalized and universal in the law, that a claim of insanity not supported by prior evidence of insanity is to be rejected. This is generally a rational and proper application of the concepts of insanity in the law. It is generally a proper filter to separate the real from the false claims of insanity. Most people who are insane have had their chemical or mental imbalances for much of their lifetime. This is not the case with postpartum psychosis. It is a sudden-onset condition, without prior insanity. The law therefore is structurally incapable of dealing with it. So the woman who has a first episode of mental illness due to pregnancy, delivery, or lactation is less likely to receive an insanity defense than others, due to the lack of severe prior mental illness and treatment. Selling insanity as a defense becomes a problem for the defendant that is specific to women with postpartum psychosis, because often it is the first time a woman experiences a severe mental illness.

Lawmakers who pretend to know more about what punishment is to be imposed upon any individual than those who have knowledge of the actual offender and have continuing daily experience in the criminal justice system are demonstrating their own hubris at best, their self-interest, ignorance, and malice at worst. Punishing a multitude of mentally ill persons to show the legislature is tough on crime is unjustifiable. These laws are written and passed by individuals in the legislature to draw attention at election time to their popular work and divert attention from matters the voting public would scorn. These tough on crime laws are particularly unfair to those who are unlucky enough to be mentally ill. It was never necessary to reduce the very infrequent not guilty by reason of insanity verdicts. For example, the main criminal courthouse in Chicago has existed for nearly a century. Yet there has never been a jury verdict of not guilty by reason of insanity in its history in a case involving serious injury to the victim. It has been estimated resolutions of not guilty by reason of insanity occur in one case in one thousand.[16]

A single study of verdicts in cases involving postpartum psychosis surprisingly claimed the particular formulation of the insanity defense in local laws had no effect on the rate of success of the insanity defense.[17] We can only speculate why. It is possible there is jury nullification, where the juries decide someone is so mentally ill they should be treated as such regardless of details within the judge's charge to them (the judge's written instructions to the jury). It is possible these surprising results arose from issues with the methodology of the study. There was no possible way to evaluate all such postpartum cases; it is impossible to locate them in a statistically accurate manner. The study admitted that problem.

In postpartum cases, the crime was the result of a temporary mental illness. The criminal justice system's outcome was horribly inconsistent. Only changes in the law can restore consistency and fairness.

THE INFAMOUS CASE OF ANDREA YATES OF TEXAS

Andrea Yates was valedictorian of her high school, captain of her swim team, and an officer in the National Honor Society. She became a nurse, got married, and started giving birth to and raising as many children "as nature would allow."

Nature had its own ideas. After the birth of her fourth child, Luke, Yates's mental health deteriorated. One day, unexpectedly, she was visibly upset. The next day she attempted suicide by overdosing on pills. Subsequent treatment appeared successful, and she was released from the hospital only to return days later following another suicide attempt. The next month, she suffered a nervous breakdown leading to two suicide attempts and the hospitalizations that followed. She was diagnosed with postpartum psychosis. Her doctor advised her not to have any more children, because her doctor was certain Yates would have a repeat of her psychosis. Sadly, that is exactly what happened. Initially she was mentally stable following the birth of her fifth child, a daughter. But four months later, Yates's father died. Yates stopped taking her medication, stopped feeding her youngest, began mutilating herself, and was "feverishly reading the bible." Incapacitated, she was hospitalized, treated, and released.

The next month was May 2001. In a near catatonic state, she took what may have been the first step toward ending her children's suffering. She filled the tub with water. Fortunately, she attended a scheduled doctor visit. Her doctor logically concluded the tub incident was done with the intent of drowning herself. Yates was again hospitalized. However, Yates later told police she planned that day to drown her children. She could not bear the thought of the children she desired and adored to spend eternity in hell. She was the only one who would *save* them from that fate. Videos of Yates in police custody showed how mentally ill she was. The contrast between her appearance that day and later following treatment was obvious.

Before harming her children, Yates had so many psychotic incidents, so many hospitalizations, and so many suicide attempts one could have lost track of them all. Her postpartum diagnosis was made more than a year before the crime. Her doctor's diagnosis was that she would have the psychosis return if she had another child. That is precisely what happened. Doubtless one would assume that rather than being sentenced to death, she would be found not guilty by reason of insanity and, following extensive treatment, would be sent home. The reader would be wrong on all counts.

Yates was obviously deserving of at least a not guilty by reason of insanity verdict. Nonetheless, under the M'Naghten standard, Yates was guilty. She knew she was drowning her children. Under the Model Penal Code standard of lacking substantial capacity to conform her conduct to the requirements of the law, again she knew what she was doing was contrary to law. She elected to do it to protect her children from an eternity of suffering. Yet she was certainly clearly, floridly psychotic.

What Is It About Her that Drove Her to Murder?

She loved her children. She was deeply religious, so she gave up her nursing career to homeschool her five children. Because she loved her children, she could not bear the thought of them suffering and burning for eternity in hell. So she killed them all before, according to her religious beliefs, they would reach an age at which they would be held accountable for their sins.

For Yates's altruistic desire to protect her children the prosecution sought the death penalty. Hers was a terrible confluence of psychosis, religious beliefs, and societal pressures that came close to resulting in her execution. The jury did not unanimously vote to execute her. She was sentenced instead to life without parole.

The discovery of the prosecution's perjury awarded her only a retrial. As is always the case, this perjury by the prosecution's witness who upheld the prosecution's theory went entirely unpunished. Yates's second trial, absent the perjury, resulted in her being found not guilty by reason of insanity.[18] Two decades later, though never a danger to society, she remains in a mental institution. Recurrence of her psychosis is not likely. A repeat of the occurrence is impossible without another pregnancy, which can be easily prevented.

POSTPARTUM LAWS IN COUNTRIES OUTSIDE THE US

In great contrast to the United States, some thirty countries have laws to deal with this specific disease, postpartum illness. These laws, like so many others, arose in England. The recognition of the poor fit of the criminal laws to mothers who commit acts of infanticide resulted in the ill-named British Infanticide Act of 1922. This law eliminated the death penalty for those mothers. This was a huge benefit. Sixteen years later, in 1938, the law was again changed. Recognition of the illness, and the law-abiding general character of the victims of postpartum illness sufferers, was expanded again. The mother was recognized less as a criminal and more as the victim of the disease herself. Treatment was emphasized, and penalties generally reduced.

Many countries have adopted this model. A survey of thirty-four countries showed twenty-eight of them had a specific law pertaining to mothers who kill their infants.[19] All the countries surveyed indicated it was always a crime, typically a homicide of a lesser degree. The average maximum penalty was six to ten years. In five, including the US, the maximum penalty was life. Only in the US and no other country surveyed was the death penalty an option. Giving the death penalty for an illness is God's job, not governments'. We believe justice should be tempered with mercy. That is often not possible in the US. Other countries are generally more advanced.

Following the rather polarizing commentary on the Yates case, in 2009 a law was presented to the Texas state legislature modeled after the British Infanticide Act. It failed to gain any traction and was never enacted into law. Nine years later, Illinois had the first, albeit limited, criminal law recognizing the pernicious effects of postpartum illness on the mother. It gives those mothers a new sentencing hearing. The new law carries the same maximum sentence, including sometimes life imprisonment, but the law, PA 100-0574, is nonetheless ground-breaking. In no other situation will the Illinois courts change a lawful sentence after appeals are completed. PA 100-0574 was passed by the Illinois House in early 2017. It passed the senate on November 9, 2017, was signed by the governor on January 8, 2018, and became law on June 1, 2018.

The British acts were a part of the upward arrow of refinements to the checks and balances of the judicial system, generally, but with exceptions, seeking greater fairness to all. After the first half millennium of the common law, it was recognized there needed to be a process for appellate review of finding facts. It took another half of a millennium for the next attempt to enhance judicial fairness to gradually come into existence. The process of reviewing facts had required a very specific compilation of the testimony presented to the trial judge. This developed into having at the trial trained shorthand court reporters who would type out word for word as exactly as humanly possible what evidence was presented to the judge or jury. This allowed for the accurate review of facts necessary. But what was to happen if important facts were somehow overlooked? What if the attorney somehow failed to present a motion, or some evidence, crucial to the case? What if the witness later recants the trial testimony? What if a critical missing witness is located after the trial?

The problem is, none of that would be clearly demonstrated by the original trial record. Therefore, none of it could be addressed by traditional judicial methods that required reference and adherence exclusively to the trial court's written records. What developed was an expanded use of habeas corpus, a federal constitutional procedure, or a brand-new procedure called typically a Post-Conviction Act. These called for the petitioner to submit one or more affidavits, statements under oath subject to penalty of perjury, showing the petitioner had a valid claim. A specific requirement in the Illinois Post-Conviction Act is that the claim had to be on the issues of guilt or innocence. New evidence pertaining to issues of whether the sentence was proper, excessive, or unfair was just not allowed. It was the Illinois courts' viewpoint, taken to an extreme, that a sentence imposed by a judge could not be touched even if the appellate court or supreme court would never have issued that sentence.

PA 100-0574 STOOD THIS AND ALL OF UNITED STATES' LAW ON ITS EAR

It was the first law in Illinois to specifically grant a new sentencing hearing for someone convicted in accordance with the law and sentenced within its requirements. This law was the first criminal statute in the entire nation that recognized postpartum illnesses for what they are, a unique, involuntary, and pernicious effect on a mother's ability to care for and protect her child. The doorway opened in Britain a century ago was finally cracked open for the first time in the United States.

To take advantage of the law, every woman in Logan Women's Correctional Center has the opportunity to and needs only file a petition, supported by her affidavit, which states at the time of her offense, she was suffering from a postpartum illness that was undiagnosed or untreated at the time and that no evidence of such illness was presented at trial or sentencing. If the judge finds the evidence of postpartum illness compelling, a new and lesser sentence can result. Most of the women in Logan who would be eligible to win such a petition have spent decades in jail and would be eligible for immediate release if sentenced mercifully. What PA 100-0574 does not do is allow for any greater mercy than the minimum sentences for any conviction of the same crime. Still, it permits the judges to be merciful and to consider postsentencing rehabilitation or good deeds of a person who was unsuccessful at motherhood. The legislature had previously taken away everyone's right to consideration of these things.

Few would dispute there are degrees of homicide, and few would dispute there are murders that deserve greater punishment than others. Factors such as motivation, the relationship of the offender to the victim, and the manner of the homicide are recognized in murder as reasons for a judge to show more or less mercy, or none at all.

Yet laws such as the ill-named "Truth in Sentencing" acts not only tie the judge's hands but also prevent any rehabilitation or postoccurrence good deeds from changing a sentence once imposed. In the case of sentences of decades or longer, the "Truth in Sentencing" acts bizarrely ask a judge to accurately determine years in advance to the day when a given individual will be rehabilitated and fit to enter society, or bars that judge from any exercise of judgment.

The legislatures have erred in their judgment. They are not in a better position to determine sentences than the judges who actually encounter such persons. Judges have the opportunity to hear professional and lay opinions regarding the character of the individual as extensively as the prosecutor and defense may choose. Taking the power away from professionals to exercise any judgment when an offender should be released is fallacious. It is for reasons such as this that the United States has the largest prison population of all the "free states."

Of all the homicide causes, none is more deserving of universal sympathy than that of postpartum mental illness. It is a disease literally caused by motherhood. It, like most illnesses, is beyond the control of the patient to avoid. It is entirely unlike the situation of the career criminal who must be removed from society for the protection of the general public. And the law simply does not fit the victim of the disease.

NOTES

1. D. Denno, "Who Is Andrea Yates? A Short Story about Insanity," *Duke Journal of Gender Law and Policy* 10, no. 1 (2003): 1–60. Note that Texas law did not clarify whether wrong was to be considered from a moral standpoint or a legal standpoint. This was a key issue in the Yates case.

2. F. Charatan, F. Eaton, and L. Eaton, "Woman May Face Death Penalty in Postnatal Depression Case," *British Medical Journal* 324, no. 7338 (March 16, 2002): 634. doi:10.1136/bmj.324.7338.634.

3. "Murder of Kyle Dinkheller," Wikipedia, accessed August 2, 2019, https://en.wikipedia.org.

4. "About Us," Justice for Vets, accessed August 2, 2019, https://justiceforvets.org/about.

5. "Pakistan's Top Court Halts Execution of Mentally Ill Inmate," Associated Press, June 17, 2019, https://www.apnews.com.

6. The exposure of "street files" did not exonerate all defendants whose official files were contradicted by the "street files." Many remained under wraps for decades. Jason Meisner, "Old Police 'Street Files' Raise Question: Did Chicago Cops Hide Evidence?" *Chicago Tribune*, February 13, 2016.

7. Detective Frank Laverty was the only person investigated and punished for all that wrongdoing. He was transferred from the detective division to central headquarters where his job became monitoring urine tests of police recruits. Nat Hentoff, "The Wrong Man," *Washington Post*, April 24, 1987. By contrast, the lead prosecutor was made a judge. Steve Bogira, *Courtroom 302* (New York: Random House, 2005).

8. There are literally hundreds of reports regarding "the code of silence" by official investigations completed by multiple organizations, including notably Amnesty International. An example of a report analyzing the code of silence is Elliot Reibman, "How and Why a Code of Silence between State's Attorneys and Police Officers Resulted in Unprosecuted Torture," *DePaul Journal of Social Justice* 9, no. 2 (2016): 3.

9. R. Blau and D. Jackson, "Police Study Turns Up Heat on Brutality," *Chicago Tribune*, February 9, 1992 (Newsbank; archived from the original on January 21, 2016); "Summary of Amnesty International's Concerns on Police Abuse in Chicago," *Amnesty International*, October 1999, AI Index: AMR 51/168/99.

10. M. Smith and M. Davey, "Chicago to Pay $5 Million to Victims of Police Abuse," *New York Times*, May 6, 2015, https://www.nytimes.com.

11. Thomas J. Basting, "President's Message: Gutter Politics and the Wisconsin Supreme Court," Wisconsin Lawyer, May 2008, https://www.wisbar.org.

12. See, for example, the summary of such statistics at J. Ulmer and D. Steffensmeir, "The Age and Crime Relationship: Social Variation, Social Explanations," Sage Publications, accessed July 30, 2019, https://www.sagepub.com/sites/default/files/upm-binaries/60294_Chapter_23.pdf. This report noted the drop-off in crime rates begins at age twenty and is very notable by age twenty-five. "Most street crimes have peak age involvement . . . and begin sharply declining well before age 25."

13. M. Ford, "America's Largest Mental Hospital Is a Jail," *Atlantic*, June 8, 2015.

14. Barry Lewis, "Postpartum Disorders: A New Law Offers Hope," *Champion* (National Association of Criminal Defense Lawyers) (March 2018): 20–25.

15. Edward A. Strecker and Franklin G. Ebaugh, "Psychoses Occurring during the Puerperium," *Archives of Neurology and Psychiatry* 15 (February 1926): 239.

16. See, for example, C. Cirincione, H. J. Stedman, and M. A. McGreevy, "Rates of Insanity Acquittals and the Factors Associated with Successful Insanity Pleas" (bull), *Journal of the American Academy of Psychiatry and the Law* 23, no. 3 (1995): 399–409. This study concluded in large counties in seven states that the rate of not guilty by reason of insanity (NGRI) was 0.26 percent. The study's authors admit it is likely despite their best efforts that unsuccessful insanity defenses could have

been overlooked. This study, as in all we have found, did not evaluate the matters of particular concern resulting in the British Infanticide Act—that the absence of prior insanity, coupled with a contest between experts with contrary opinions, resulted in aberrant and unfortunate variations in individuals' success with that defense.

17. M. Nau, D. McNeil, and R. Binder, "Postpartum Psychosis and the Courts," *Journal of the American Academy of Psychiatry and the Law* 40 (September 2012): 318–25.

18. Deborah Denno, "Andrea Yates: A Continuing Story about Insanity," Fordham University, January 2017.

19. Paul Smit et al., "Homicide Data in Europe: Definitions, Sources and Statistics," in *Handbook of European Homicide Research, Patterns, Explanations and Research Studies*, ed. M. C. A. Liem and W. A. Pridemore (New York: Springer, 2012), https://hoplofobia.info.

Chapter Four

Laws of Neonaticide and Infanticide in Countries outside the US

Cut the living child in half.

The earliest well-known expression of the expectation of maternal devotion is found in the Bible. Wise King Solomon had to decide between two women each of whom insisted a baby was her own. As written in the Bible, the ability to discern the nature of motherly instincts and convert it to justice was a gift directly from God. The wisdom of Solomon's decision is accepted by virtually all, believers and nonbelievers alike.

Even lower animals will often risk their lives to protect their young. Bears will attack someone who steps between mother and cubs. Birds undertake great risks and overcome huge difficulties to protect their nests and feed their young. Even some insects engage in astonishing behavior to protect and nurture their offspring. The opposite behavior, by humans, causes shock and dismay.

The law adopts that moral imperative and punishes the violators. The reader might reasonably, but erroneously believe the prosecution always attempts to make the punishment fit the crime. In the majority of cases this is true, albeit with the prosecutor's personal beliefs informing the prosecution's decisions. Still, there is competition within prosecution offices to obtain more convictions and impose severer sentences than other assistant district attorneys. Nowhere is this better illustrated to my knowledge than what was known as the "Weight and Wait Competition." In the early 1980s prosecutors at the Cook County Criminal Court engaged in a competition to get the highest score. Scoring was simple, but not as simple as a penny a point. In fact, there was no monetary benefit. The scoring was a multiple of the defendant's weight as shown on the arrest report times the number of years (the "wait") he or she was sentenced to. A three-hundred-pound defendant sentenced to ten years was worth three thousand points. I represented a severely obese defendant during that competition. A lot of pressure was put on the overweight accused and on myself because the prosecutor sought the maximum sentence. My leverage was in my implied threat to delay the disposition until after the contest. The judge, James Bailey, was amused by the propositions presented but not so amused to allow that competition to influence his sentence. In part, this was due to Judge Bailey being an honest judge and a decent person. In part too was the influence of his own competition. Judge Bailey also wanted to win. His competition was to resolve more cases than his nearest competitor, Judge Riley. This competition used the yardstick of the number of cases resolved. As a result, the author was sent from Bailey's court to Riley's court with a motion to substitute another judge for Judge Riley after Bailey learned that particular defendant had fifteen cases. A defendant in Illinois is allowed one such motion as a matter of right. The motion had to be granted, although Judge Riley put two and two together. I never dared enter Riley's courtroom again.

The point of this is while technically the law was scrupulously followed by generally honorable (in these cases) civil servants, improper influences pervade the justice system. People are competitive. This includes prosecutors, defense counsel, and judges. Competitions are not only on the ball field. Only the restrictions of the law constrain the outcome. Personal influences abound and require restraints. Other times, the restraints on the law are a result of the law's attempt to treat all equally, regardless of circumstances of birth, provided their crimes are equal. In the case of "Truth in Sentencing" it is a miserable failure. It treats people equally regardless of their degree of involvement in an offense, by requiring a certain minimum sentence. It treats the unrehabilitated and the completely rehabilitated equally, no matter how incorrigible and no matter how overwhelming the proof is of rehabilitation. Inmates can perform good deeds in the prison system. Under "Truth in Sentencing" Mother Teresa would serve the same sentence as would Osama bin Laden.

The restrictions of the law applicable generally to postpartum psychosis cases are onerous in the extreme. It makes no sense to lock up a mentally ill woman who desperately needed help when she succumbed to the desperation of her situation in a fashion that would otherwise deserve a severe punishment. We submit this extends to the loss of a mother's own infant.

When the law is applied as written, as is often the case, the result is terrible. The laws pertaining to crimes of violence are themselves about what one might expect regarding violent offenders who commit unmitigated acts of violence. Issues of infants and motherhood are far more complex.

Michelle Oberman and Cheryl Meyer attempted to interview at length every woman in Ohio who was in the penitentiary convicted of a murder of a child. There were more than sixty such women; the majority of them were interviewed. There is no reason to believe the Ohio women sentenced under such circumstances are a significantly different population, location aside, from those in other states. Oberman and Meyer's conclusion: The various pressures brought to bear on these women, accompanied usually by poverty, single motherhood, abusive upbringings, and lack of assistance from relatives or the father, made the crimes virtually inevitable. Many suffered from various forms of mental illness. In fact, Oberman and Meyer concluded all the women who had intentionally killed their children were suffering from a severe form of postpartum illness.[1]

When courtroom personnel become involved in a murder case, the prosecution often holds all the cards. Before such a case gets to the courtroom, the police have obtained evidence of guilt. This evidence is passed on to a supervising police officer who approves charges. The case is then passed on to the prosecutor's office. At that time, the prosecutor will, if the office desires, contact the national offices of the FBI or the attorney general to gain additional evidence. The prosecutors can send the police officers or other investigators to interview additional witnesses. They can "lock in" the testimony of reluctant witnesses by forcing them to testify under oath at the grand jury. Refusal to testify is punishable as contempt of court. False testimony is a felony. Often that false testimony is admitted under various theories, even though there is no opportunity to *effectively* question the witness further. The prosecutors can use their own forensic tools, those scientific tools made available by the federal government, or those of cooperating sister states. The percentage of guilty verdicts under these circumstances is doubtless very high.

There is very little to incentivize a prosecutor to grant leniency if the proof of guilt is evident. Mitigating circumstances rarely result in a plea to a charge reduced from murder unless those mitigating circumstances would likely result in a verdict of a lesser charge. Usually the prosecutor is little concerned about the risk of a not guilty by reason of insanity verdict. This is particularly true with respect to infanticide by a mother, unless, as is rare, the press takes an attitude against convicting her. A not guilty by reason of insanity verdict is a rarity. More often, strong evidence of a serious mental illness results in a finding of guilty but mentally ill. This verdict sends the defendant to a short stay in a mental hospital, followed by a penitentiary stay for the entire remaining sentence. *This is not leniency.*

The death of a child is a painful subject to approach. It is always a tragedy, regardless of the cause. Even if somehow the child does not suffer, the adult relatives suffer. The closer the relative, the greater is the suffering. This is true especially of the mother. This remains true even if the mother is to whatever degree or for whatever reason responsible for the death of the child. It is surprising then how popular press and internet reports can result in a virtual lynch mob attitude being shared and commonplace in these instances. It is less surprising that a conservative legal establishment, perhaps ignorant of the differences, would treat these crimes the same as any other murder a century after the British recognized the difference.

Infanticide and its cousin, filicide, are both difficult subjects to address in polite company. It is not the stuff of casual dinner conversations, or between innings of a game. The British managed nonetheless to learn to approach the subject with compassion and understanding. Objectively, and subjectively, these cases tend to be different from the kind of cases legislatures had in mind when they required sentences ranging from decades in the penitentiary all the way to a lifetime without parole or even the death penalty. They had in mind the armed robber, the thrill killer, and the fleeing felon. For those, a lack of compassion is the just result of their intentional felonious behavior against members of society whom they may select arbitrarily based on opportunity. For those who act out of not a malicious heart but a deranged mind, the possibility of an alternative exists. The likelihood of a judgment of not guilty by reason of insanity is greatest for those whose psychosis is well documented in years prior to the crime. All this is what the average citizen would expect of the criminal justice system. All this generally fits.

None of this fits the overwhelming majority of the cases of infanticide. Infanticide is so contrary to our concepts of devotion of motherhood as to be unfathomable, unthinkable. Tragically, it can only be contemplated by those whose situation itself is unfathomable—being stressed by circumstances to the point no alternative presents itself. One such stressor is a condition, known to medicine and science, caused by pregnancy, lactation, or childbirth. It is called perinatal mental illness, which in reality is not just one condition but a cluster of illnesses caused by motherhood itself.

EVOLUTION OF THE UK'S BRITISH INFANTICIDE LAW

Enter the British Infanticide Act of 1922. A century ago, the British were the first "Western" nation to recognize almost universally that infanticide was an act of desperation by an ill mother, alone at the time her suffering reached the critical stage. The British Infanticide Act of 1922 barred the death penalty from being imposed as a result of conviction of infanticide by the mother of the child. This was the first law that recognized the penalties for such women were too harsh. These mothers were in a situation that but for the grace of God, Parliament's own daughters and wives would face. The recognition of this by Parliament was and continues to be commendable.

The year 1938 tragically would be the last year of peace until General MacArthur said, "I declare these proceedings closed" when peace was restored after the murder of more than fifty million persons. In Britain, 1938 also marked the expansion of its Infanticide Act. The Infanticide Act of 1938 emphasized treatment and prevention over punishment. The culture of Britain had come to further recognize the difficulties motherhood caused. They acknowledged how different the costs to society were as a result of a suffering mother killing her own child compared to the costs to society resulting from the lifelong criminal type executing those he had no right to encounter. Society needs protection from the latter. Society needs no protection from the former. The former needs help.

It is ironic that in the interwar years this law would be promulgated. The events beginning the following year—the naked aggressions of the Axis powers that resulted in so many millions suffering death, the survivors with losses of loved ones, and so many surviving with horrible injuries both physical and emotional—would result in the conviction in Nuremberg of only eighteen for war crimes, not all of whom were sentenced to execution. This is a pattern seen time and time again. Such is worldwide criminal justice.

Returning to common law justice, from its beginnings the ultimate crime was murder. But it developed that homicide was not always murder. In biblical times, less evil, less responsible homicides resulted in banishment to sanctuary cities. The common law took note of a distinction and gradually codified it.

THE CONCEPT OF PREMEDITATION AS A DISTINGUISHING FACTOR IN HOMICIDE

"Malice aforethought" became by the fifteenth century the fundamental concept distinguishing murder from all other forms of homicide. Over centuries the conviction for murder of certain homicides was recognized as too harsh, and sometimes even entirely wrong. The distinction of murder from such exceptions as self-defense developed in the law. Often the term "premeditation" has been used virtually synonymously with "malice aforethought." The very general and ambiguous terms of "malice aforethought" and "premeditation" were problematical to apply.

What exactly were they? The general concept was clear enough. It was to distinguish the true evildoer, those dangerous to the general public, from people who were in the wrong place at the wrong time. The terms were replaced with more specific terms denominating very specific fact patterns; the general concept was replaced, over the years, with specific exceptions.

Exceptions were for reasonable fear requiring self-defense—even an unreasonable fear resulting in a degree of self-defense—a lack of *intention* to cause serious bodily harm, and serious provocation. A greater certainty was imposed regarding what was murder and what was not. The mercy the law intended through its requirement of malice aforethought was now processed and codified. Mercy obtained specific restrictions. Mercy now existed only for those whose homicides were of a type frequent enough to make it into the law books and considered excusable to some degree. No longer would the prosecution have to prove premeditation or malice aforethought. No longer would a lack of premeditation or lack of malice aforethought exonerate or mitigate the homicide. In the late sixteenth century, William Shakespeare wrote, "The quality of mercy is not strained. It droppeth as the gentle rain from the heaven upon the place beneath." That may have been true then. Thereafter, per the codifications, mercy had to be strained through a tight mesh. It left no room for mothers suffering from postpartum illness to escape the net of justice.

The British Infanticide Act of 1938 recognized that many women who committed that terrible act were either not criminal or a totally different kind of unfortunate "criminal" whose suffering rather than malice aforethought or premeditation caused that act. If any malice or premeditation did exist in these cases, the overwhelming cause was the illness and suffering, not malice or premeditation. While stealing a loaf of bread to feed a starving child was accommodated by the mercy the law allows in some cases, the punishment for crimes against infants did not allow for mercy. Those punishments are mandatory and extreme, which makes perfect sense in most situations. It is terrible regarding those mothers that we are discussing.

The British Infanticide Act of 1938 took some additional steps beyond its antecedent of 1922. Sixteen years after that first act, the recognition that these mothers universally, or at least nearly universally, needed help far more than society needed to punish them took greater hold. So, the act of 1938 emphasized treatment, not punishment. The lessons learned over the next eighty years showed this law to be ameliorative, and not at all pernicious. It was learned that no harmful effects were caused by this law.[2]

OTHER COUNTRIES JOINED THE UK IN ENACTING POSTPARTUM LAWS

About thirty other nations joined in and enacted similar laws. These nations ranged from the Pacific to the Atlantic and touched North American shores. But no inroad was made into any of the United States. Before the Illinois law was enacted, only one other attempt to follow the British act existed. This was in response to the rather polarizing Andrea Yates case, infamous as it was for the attempt to use perjury to bring about the execution of a mentally ill mother. Despite the travesty of the existing law, the 2009 efforts to modernize it in even a single state, Texas, failed to gain any traction.

The reader may innocently believe the laws of insanity enable a mentally ill mother to escape a lifetime in the penitentiary. Unfortunately, not only is that not always the case, but also it is relatively rare that a mentally ill woman suffering from her disease will escape decades or a lifetime in the penitentiary as a consequence of the laws of insanity.

Findings of not guilty by reason of insanity, even in cases in which the most modest of oppositional facts exist, are so rare as to be unicorns. There is no national database covering this, so methodologies are always questionable. Some estimates say one in a thousand trials successfully use that defense. In cases suggesting insanity, such as maternal infanticide, success might be one chance in five. It may even be much less than one in five. At the main criminal courthouse in Chicago, there has never been a jury that found a defendant not guilty by reason of insanity in a case involving serious injuries to a victim. That courthouse has been hearing jury trials for eighty years.

A woman is twenty-five times more likely to have a psychotic episode in the single month following childbirth than at any other time in her life. The law does not account for that. Quite the contrary: A brief psychotic episode is far less likely to result in a finding of insanity. Lawyers and judges are trained to be skeptical of a claim of insanity without an extensive history of psychotic behavior. The absence of a lengthy history of insanity is considered evidence of faking insanity at the time of the crime. Even a lifelong mental illness may not suffice to obtain leniency. American jurisprudence is far more concerned with the possibility that a person will avoid conviction by faking illness than with the ill serving decades in the penitentiary.

A HARSH SENTENCE FOR CAROL CORONADO OF CALIFORNIA

Carol Coronado had been molested as a child and gang-raped as an adolescent. Some believed she overcame that. She graduated high school and entered the army. Injured, she was discharged from duty. She did have problems, hearing voices since she was five. Leading up to May 20, 2014, Carol Coronado experienced no sleep for days, an increasing level of depression, and some erratic behavior, such as turning off the electricity to her home. Dr. Torang Sepah, a former psychiatrist at the Twin Towers county jail where Coronado was housed, stated in court, "Depression . . . has a kindling effect. . . . Neurons start to maladaptively fire together in depression. . . .There's a spreading of that [making it more likely to spark psychosis]."[3] Sepah stated she met with Coronado forty-five to fifty times over the course of a year and diagnosed her with a mood disorder. During cross-examination, Sepah reported that Coronado and her husband Rudy told her she was sexually abused from the time she was five years old until she was a teenager. She was "treated" for a molestation incident when she was five but never again reported the crimes.

On May 20, Rudy Coronado, Carol's husband and the father of two-and-a-half-year-old Sophie, sixteen-month-old Yazmine, and two-month-old Xenia, returned home to a scene of unimaginable horror.

Rudy did not see his wife at the scene. He saw the demon inside her. "It was like a demon possessed. She was a girl with a good career ahead of her." Her blood-spattered body lay next to their three murdered children, all neatly arranged on the bed. Carol had slashed her wrists and stabbed herself in her chest—but was still alive. She was naked. Carol's mother had called Rudy to the scene after seeing the devastation. Carol had called her mother repeatedly, saying she needed her. Yet Carol had no recollection of the calls. When her mother arrived to see her naked, blood-spattered daughter, Carol looked surprised. "Mom, what are you doing here?" she asked. Rudy made the obvious conclusion. "She's crazy." A neighbor Eddie Larsen said, "I can't believe this kind of evil exists. I feel terrible for what happened to the children, and equally as bad for the woman." The children's godfather said he had never seen her angry and continued, "He [Rudy] loved her. He is concerned for her. He understands what happened, but he is adamant whatever happened wasn't her. She needs help." Neighbor Ashley Madrid saw Carol led from the scene by police. She was wrapped in a blanket. Her blood was visible. "She had a zoned-out look and was just looking down."

When the police arrived, they found Carol on the bed next to the children. She was naked and covered in blood. She was looking at the ceiling with a blank stare and had no emotion on her face. She had put her fingers in the stab wound on her left chest and was using them to open up the wound. The police told her to step away from the bed. She looked at the police but did not understand or otherwise respond. The police early on in their questioning tried to develop their revenge theory. Police Sergeant Robert Martindale asked Carol if she killed the children to get back at her husband. Carol asked if she would get a better deal if that were true. Obviously, her thinking was impaired. How could that get her a better deal? Martindale stepped up the pressure. He falsely told Carol that her husband had said Carol killed the children to get even with him. Carol said Rudy was right. Martindale asked what Carol would need to tell him everything that happened. "Bedpan," she replied.

"It was a bad day, Mom," said Carol. Worse was to come. The judicial system had a plan as evil as anything the demon had created. The prosecution invented evidence of a motive—the killings were to punish her husband. This type of evidence is child's play to create. No relationship is perfect. It was the same strategy invented for the Yates case but without that case's perjury by the prosecution witness. Though all the defense witnesses showed Carol was out of her mind, and the first psychiatrist hired by the state prosecutor concluded Carol was insane, that did not deter them. They simply hired another, who concluded she was not insane but "may have been mildly depressed at times." Judge Ocampo, who ruled in place of a jury, of course rejected that ludicrous testimony. "She needs mental health treatment," he determined, a conclusion at odds with the prosecution's psychiatrist because no one "mildly depressed at times" *needs* mental health treatment.

On the day of her scheduled sentencing, Carol was brought to court in the prison jumpsuit assigned to the mentally ill. Judge Ocampo said she could get the mental health treatment she needs in the penitentiary. There will be plenty of time for that, because he sentenced her to three life sentences without the possibility of parole.

Of course, you would expect with that fundamental inconsistency between the testimony and the judge's ruling, the courts of appeal would take care of it. They did not. In an unpublished opinion, the appellate court affirmed the case and left Carol to rot away for life. The California Supreme Court refused the case. And that is that.[4]

So what was the evidence of sanity, other than a single outlandish expert opinion? The evidence consisted of just the invented claims of Carol seeking revenge against her husband, coupled with the expert interrogation of Carol by trained police, and the fact that six days prior she was her usual jovial self. It is impossible to reconcile the claim Carol planned to get even with her husband with the fact that she instead attempted to kill herself. In the doctor's office, Carol was in the same emotional state as Cynthia Wachenheim days before her incoherent suicide note and death. The warning signs of an upcoming psychotic break are limited. They are difficult even for the medical professionals to detect. The psychosis, even once detectible, waxes and wanes. The only fair and responsible conclusion: The law and medicine failed Yates, Wachenheim, and Coronado. What should be done?

From a Prison Cell

You say I can't change
But you don't know my pain.
You don't know where I've been,
Nor how much I've gained.

My tears have long since dried.
My broken bones have healed,
My bruises are long gone.
Yet my fate remains sealed.

Here I sit, life without parole,
For the murder of him.
Who used me, beat me, burnt my soul,
The one I once called my kin.

I grew old in a prison cell,
From young to old as time went on.
My body tired, aching more and more.
I prayed my spirit to be strong.

From night to day, day to night,
Freedom just another dream,
Years passing, decades gone,
Time but an endless stream.

My prayer is for a second chance,
Before I breathe my last,
For one to take and look at me
And not judge me by my past,

Poem by Janet Jackson
Age sixty-three, incarcerated thirty-one years

NOTES

1. Michelle Oberman and Cheryl Meyer, *When Mothers Kill: Interviews from Prison* (New York: New York University Press, 2008).
2. England, Wales, and Scotland are all similar demographically. All have similar rates of infanticide. Yet England and Wales have an infanticide act, and Scotland does not. M. M. Marks and R. Kumar, "Infanticide in Scotland," *Medicine, Science, and the Law* 36, no. 4 (October 1996): 299–305, PubMed.gov, US National Library of Medicine National Institutes of Health, doi:10.1177/002580249603600405.

3. M. Pandika, "A Psychiatrist Told Us Why Her Patient Killed Her Children," *Vice*, May 1, 2018, https://www.vice.com.

4. E. Harrington, J. Watkin, and V. Brady, *Not Carol* (film) (Planet Grande Films, 2019); T. Bigelo (presiding judge), People v. Coronado, No. B269983 California Court of Appeal, 2018; also various news sources.

Part II

ADVOCATING FOR WOMEN WITH POSTPARTUM PSYCHOSIS

Chapter Five

The Road to Public Act 100-0574

Illinois's New Ground-Breaking Postpartum Law

> You mean to tell me that we can't right a known wrong?
>
> —Illinois senator Don Harmon (D 39th district), in criminal law committee before unanimous vote on HB 1764

A thousand or more women are imprisoned in the United States on criminal charges related to psychosis with the onset during the postpartum period—a staggering number. And imagine the countless numbers that will be charged and incarcerated in the future if we do nothing to remedy this multifaceted problem. Although according to experts it is rare even for women with postpartum psychosis to harm their baby or other children,[1] due to the delusional thinking that can accompany this disorder, it is a risk best avoided at all costs.

STEPS NEEDED TO PROTECT WOMEN WITH POSTPARTUM ILLNESSES AND THEIR FAMILIES

What can be done to ameliorate this problem? Prompt screening and treatment of maternal mental illness would be a first step to avoid the risk of mothers harming themselves or their infants. A second step is for passage of state criminal laws to incorporate treatment, such as a conditional-release program. Mothers with postpartum psychosis, who due to lack of early identification and mental health treatment commit crimes such as infanticide or neonaticide within a year of delivery or at the end of a pregnancy, should not be subject to state homicide laws and harsh sentences.

In California, the Department of State Hospitals runs a conditional-release program that provides treatment for the following commitment groups: not guilty by reason of insanity, incompetent to stand trial, mentally disordered offenders, and some parolees who have been released to outpatient status.[2] Having every state create criminal laws offering this type of treatment and conditional-release outpatient follow-up would be a major advance to our existing state laws.[3] In the US we currently focus on punishment rather than mental health treatment and rehabilitation for afflicted women.[4]

The US lags far behind thirty or more developed countries, such as the UK, that have had special laws such as the British Infanticide Acts of 1922 and 1938 that acknowledge the uniqueness of maternal mental illness. These laws provide recognition and some exception to mothers who commit crimes, due to a temporary psychosis outside their control.

With this in mind, new comprehensive legislation has been filed in the Commonwealth of Massachusetts with the name "An Act Relative to the Well-Being of New Mothers and Infants" (see appendix D). Massachusetts is already unique in that it is the only state in the US to have a maternal mental health commission.[5] If the act passes, it will be the second state to change criminal laws that affect maternal mental illness.

ILLINOIS PA 100-0574 IS THE FIRST CRIMINAL POSTPARTUM LAW IN THE NATION

Illinois was the first state in the nation to open the door with the groundbreaking new law PA 100-0574, which amended the Code of Corrections to consider postpartum depression and postpartum psychosis as "mitigating factors" in sentencing when women commit crimes while suffering from these illnesses. It is retroactive. Following the passage of PA 100-0574, approximately twenty incarcerated women at Logan Correctional Center serving long or lifetime sentences have hope for a reduced sentence and the possibility of the long-lost dream of freedom.

In Illinois, as of June 1, 2018, the new law allowed those incarcerated women who had suffered with postpartum depression or psychosis at the time of their crime to file for resentencing under the stipulation that their postpartum illness was not previously identified, treated, or presented at the time of their trial or initial sentencing. The "postpartum infanticide law," as it is sometimes known, is a start and the first time that an exception was considered, allowing for a new sentencing hearing when a valid sentence had been previously imposed in Illinois.

This is a major change as prior to Illinois PA 100-0574, the only chance for these women serving decades or a lifetime in prison to be released was an order by the governor of executive clemency or a pardon. The only other option was for a retrial, due to finding new evidence not presented at their initial trial or by establishing a valid claim that the attorney who represented them had been incompetent. Both are unlikely occurrences and improbable for these women charged with crimes of infanticide.

Another disadvantage that is unique to this group of incarcerated women is that many of them have no history of mental health problems and have never experienced an episode of depression or psychosis in the past prior to their postpartum occurrence. This makes it particularly challenging for criminal defense attorneys to make a case for an insanity defense, such as not guilty by reason of insanity or guilty but mentally ill. Most often the lack of mental health records or history is a real hindrance for this unfortunate population of women. It makes prosecutors, judges, and juries believe that the insanity defense is being used as an excuse or a fallacious rationale for a violent and possibly premeditated offense. The outcome is that the insanity defense is a harder "sell" for these women in the criminal justice system than for other mental health sufferers charged with crimes.

WHY IS IT THAT PRISON JUSTICE ADVOCATES AND OTHERS INTERESTED IN LEGAL REFORM AND CORRECTING WRONGFUL CONVICTIONS HAVEN'T ADDRESSED THIS SUBJECT IN THE PAST?

The initiative for legal change has largely been from the perinatal community of professionals and survivors as well as some lone legal justice advocates such as in Illinois.[6] Likely, this issue has been less popular due to the very heinous nature of the crime. Overall the public has limited understanding and even less compassion for women that kill their own progeny. As stated previously, the act itself is likely one of the most repugnant and least understood of crimes. Conceivably due to that fact, there is limited motivation to help these unfortunate women as well as a dearth of research to comprehend their behavior or the women who commit such atrocities.

WHAT DO WE KNOW ABOUT MOTHERS WHO KILL THEIR CHILDREN?

Are there other reasons than psychosis to explain why a woman would plan a pregnancy, carry a baby to term and then, within hours to days, weeks, or months, suddenly murder their own offspring? A first attempt at typology and an early system of classification was identified by Phillip Resnick in 1969.

He pinpointed five theories of why mothers kill their babies or other children. These include the following: altruistic filicide; acute psychosis; unwanted child; accidental filicide, as a result of neglect or abuse; and spousal revenge. Meyer and Oberman criticized Resnick's classification system as being outdated, as not being specific to women, and for having weak methodology.[7] All the same, it is still often cited when cases of infanticide occur and are brought to the courts, as noted at the 2018 Postpartum Support International conference.[8]

In applying Resnick's typology to cases of postpartum psychosis, the delusional beliefs that led to the infanticide or neonaticide are most congruent with his categories of altruistic filicide or just due to the acute temporary psychotic nature of the illness itself. However, prosecutors in postpartum infanticide cases often attempt to make a convincing case for spousal revenge as the rationale cited for why a mother would kill her infant or children. This of course inflames and incites most judges as well as jurors. We expect a parent to defend their offspring, as a mother lion would guard her cubs. We cannot wrap our heads around or rationalize murdering one's own child for spousal revenge. This is the reason these mentally ill moms generally receive such severe sentences for their crimes.

Other classification systems exist. Meyer and Oberman assert that the typology constructed by Ania Wilczynski in 1997 was "perhaps the most comprehensive of all the previous classifications," identifying ten categories and specifically three groupings that exclusively reflected female motives: unwanted child, psychotic parent, and Munchausen syndrome by proxy.[9]

Another typology exclusively using a US sample and one that incorporates the interaction of mental illness and social factors within each category was one developed in 1996 by Oberman. She reviewed nearly one hundred cases in which there were forty-nine filicide and forty-seven neonaticide cases, resulting in the classification of those two categories. Infanticide was then subcategorized into these groupings: infanticide and postpartum psychosis, infanticide by mothers with chronic mental disabilities, infanticide as a manifestation of an affective disorder with postpartum onset, and addiction-related infanticide. Following this, Meyer and Oberman collaborated to develop a US-based typology in reviewing 219 cases from 1990 to 1999.[10] They identified five categories that are not based on motive or intent but describe patterns from an interactional perspective incorporating social, cultural, environmental, and individual variables. These five classifications include filicide related to an ignored pregnancy, abuse-related filicide, filicide due to neglect, assisted/coerced filicide, and purposeful filicide and the mother acted alone, with and without mental illness. This last category is one that encompasses women with maternal mental illness, specifically postpartum psychosis. All the abovementioned women were in tragic and difficult circumstances.

LACK OF UNDERSTANDING OF POSTPARTUM ILLNESS IN THE LEGAL SYSTEM

No matter what classification system you use, the general public largely has limited understanding of maternal mental illness. Thus, an eloquent prosecutor does not have a very difficult task convincing a judge or jurors that a mother who kills her baby or children is despicable. Consequently, it is no wonder that these women are perceived in the very worst way and accordingly get such harsh sentences. Consider, for example, the earlier referenced case of Carol Coronado of California, who received three consecutive life sentences, and the case of Andrea Yates of Texas, in which many publicly called for life imprisonment or, even worse, the death sentence.

Mental health professionals and those in the perinatal mental health community understand that these women were mentally ill and exhibited classic symptoms of postpartum psychosis. I recall a few years back attending a breakout session at the Postpartum Support International conference in which I, along with a group of my perinatal mental health colleagues, watched a video clip of the eerie catatonic-like stare of Andrea Yates after her arrest. The speaker was none other than Yates's esteemed Texas defense attorney George Parnham. Many in that seminar remarked it is difficult to comprehend how others did not understand what was so obvious to all of us. This was a very disturbed mentally ill woman. We viewed overhead slides with earlier photos of Yates from before her postpartum episode, and photos of her following the act of her taking the lives of her children. She was barely recognizable subsequent to her arrest. It was like looking at two completely different women. How was it that even the general public and nonprofessionals were unable to see the obvious differences in her appearance? The flat, detached affect and zombie-like facial appearance were apparent in the video, a familiar look common to those with severe mental illness.

What was obvious to some was overshadowed by the revolting nature of the crime. Apparently the same can be said in the case of Carol Coronado where the harshest penalty was given, ignoring the woman's long history of mental illness and the fact that her mother called the police after having discovered Carol naked, stabbing herself while huddled above the lifeless bodies of her three children.

THE DILEMMA OF UNDERSTANDING MATERNAL MENTAL ILLNESS IN THE JUDICIAL SYSTEM

This is where the legal world and mental health world collide. The criminal justice system does not understand mental health issues and vice versa. This is particularly evident in perinatal incidents when women with severe depression or psychosis come into contact with the judicial system, particularly when crimes like infanticide are committed. Suddenly a woman and her family are faced with police officers, attorneys, judges, and a complicated judicial system. This is a perplexing system to navigate when you are mentally healthy but lack experience with the legal system. The situation is much worse with the majority of women who are not hardened criminals but mothers with mental illness. Imagine how confusing and scary this is when you are suffering from depression and lack mental clarity. In addition, this becomes even more bewildering when you have an absence of family support, lack financial resources, and/or have inadequate legal representation. Suddenly the tension and confusion become multiplied exponentially when a woman is floridly psychotic and possibly paranoid. This is the overwhelming situation that a woman with severe postpartum depression or postpartum psychosis has to face and negotiate when faced with a criminal charge.

Understanding more about the experience of women with postpartum illnesses in the legal system may be a way to start to comprehend the broader topic of why it is necessary to update laws to reflect the plight of these postpartum sufferers. Author, frequent blogger, and survivor of postpartum depression Ivy Shih Leung wrote in one of her past posts,

> During trial, these women are not allowed to talk about their conditions or have them considered as mitigating factors in sentencing. Although the idea of infanticide is truly tragic and unfathomable, try donning your empathy hat and imagine what it would be like if it were you that was being controlled by neurochemistry gone completely out of whack until tragedy strikes with an act you commit—one that you could not prevent or control due to your illness—that you will pay for dearly for the rest of your life enduring painful, unrelenting regret, many years of life in jail (or even face the death sentence), and with your illness never addressed or treated.[11]

As repeatedly stated by experts, cases of postpartum psychosis are unusual, and tragic ones leading to infanticide are even more rare. Yet all situations of postpartum psychosis are biologically based and neurochemically caused, set off during pregnancy, postpartum or lactation, and related to the hormones, psychosocial stressors, and biochemistry for a small atypical group of women sufferers. It is a temporary mental illness that responds well when mood-stabilizing medications are administered and a woman is hospitalized for her safety and the safety of her baby and others. With quick identification and treatment, psychotic episodes and symptoms can remit in weeks, and not lead to the tragedies discussed previously and those sensationalized by the media.

These criminal-judicial issues have recently become a national initiative in the United States and particularly in our home state of Illinois. Illinois has proudly led the nation and has become the first state leading the cause to amend the criminal Code of Corrections with PA 100-0574. This legislation made postpartum depression and postpartum psychosis "mitigating factors" in prosecution and sentencing of women who commit crimes while suffering from these illnesses. Since adopted, an effort commenced to address the current legal system to consider extenuating factors during the perinatal period with women who are mentally ill and ultimately need mental health treatment rather than incarceration and punishment.

How is it that in the US, we have continued to prosecute mothers as criminals who suffer from postpartum illness? In the UK, a law was enacted by Parliament in 1922 and then expanded in 1938: the British Infanticide Act. This law stated that when a woman causes the death of her child under the age of twelve months, it is assumed that "the balance of her mind was disturbed" related to childbirth or lactation. In lieu of being tried for murder, a jury may return a verdict of infanticide, manslaughter, or guilty but insane. This law was put into place to ensure these women receive psychiatric treatment and rehabilitation rather than an extensive prison term or death sentence. It has been adopted by thirty countries, including Canada and many European countries, while in the US we have continued to prosecute and sentence these mentally ill women as criminals. We treat these cases the same as any other homicide.

PERINATAL LEGAL CHANGE IN THE US COMMENCES WITH ILLINOIS PA 100-0574

> Never doubt that a small group of thoughtful, committed people can change the world, indeed it is the only thing that ever has.
>
> —Margaret Mead

Following is the narrative of how this law came to be in Illinois and how the authors became involved with this important matter and helped to usher this legislation into law. We will discuss the key team players whose contribution made this all possible and ended with the passage of the first criminal law in the US to address this critically important issue.

It all originated with the creation of a bill written by Janet Jackson and Paula Sims, two friends and women inmates at Logan Correctional Center (their story and interview follow). The bill they wrote, known as Illinois HB 1764, proceeded with the efforts of Bill Ryan, a retired assistant deputy director at the Illinois Department of Children and Family Services. Ryan used his retirement to advocate for prison reform and justice. He regularly visited prisons including the Logan Correctional Center in Lincoln, Illinois. He began hearing and listening to the stories of numerous women serving long or lifetime prison sentences for crimes committed while mentally ill with a postpartum disorder.

Ryan was struck by the injustice of it all and began talking to state representative Linda Chapa LaVia (D 83rd district) who ultimately took up the cause and sponsored Illinois HB 1764 in February 2017. The bill was referred to the Rules Committee and thereafter assigned to the Judiciary-Criminal Committee in the Illinois House. It was amended and debated until the end of March 2017.

At that point, I (Feingold) chanced to see an email request from fellow Postpartum Support International member and the coordinator of the Pregnancy and Postpartum Mood and Anxiety Disorder Program at Amita Health, Lita Simanis. The email requested someone with perinatal expertise come to Springfield, Illinois, the next day to testify before the House Judiciary-Criminal Committee on HB 1764, the postpartum depression and psychosis bill. I prepared my expert testimony and accompanied Simanis where we would meet with Bill Ryan and Representative Chapa LaVia the next day in the state capital. After being sworn in, Simanis and I provided oral testimony as experts to the Judiciary-Criminal Committee. The bill was immediately voted on and passed in committee unanimously on March 28, 2017.

Following parliamentary procedure, the bill moved to the full house for a short debate and vote on April 5, 2017. The bill again passed unanimously by a vote of 113–0. As the bill began to pick up steam, it then followed a similar path, arriving in the senate later the same day and gained a senate sponsor, Senator Toi Hutchinson (D 40th senate district) and several cosponsors. It was then referred to the Senate Criminal Law Subcommittee. In May it was put on hold, with the May 31 senate's summer adjournment looming ahead.

Problems arose in the senate. Matt Jones, the lobbyist for the state attorney's offices, became a strong opponent to its passage. Jones stated that the modification to the Post-Conviction Act was an unconstitutional violation of separation of powers. He was openly antagonistic to the passage of the current HB 1764. At this point the only option with time ticking by was to find a knowledgeable attorney who would understand the legislative challenges and quickly respond to the separation of powers concern.[12]

Enter Chicago criminal defense attorney Barry M. Lewis, who talked to the lobbyist, Matt Jones. Lewis researched the stated concerns. Yet when his phone conversation did not change the lobbyist's intent to terminate the bill, Lewis prepared a written brief and joined forces with me in the cause to move this bill along.[13]

With the additional support of Lewis's legal expertise and a written brief sent to the state's attorney's office and to all the committee members, Senator Hutchinson took the postpartum bill off hold. Lewis and I were notified twenty-four hours prior that HB 1764 was moving again and would be presented to the Senate Criminal Law Committee on May 23 for a vote. We were also informed that it was more than likely that Matt Jones would be present and oppose passage. So, Bill Ryan, Lewis, and I rearranged our schedules and again headed to the state capital. The intent was for Lewis and me to provide expert testimony to the Senate Criminal Law Subcommittee, as well as to address concerns of the opponent and lobbyist Matt Jones.

The full senate was working on budget issues most of the day. The committee did not meet until 5:00 p.m., with HB 1764 the second contested legislative matter to be addressed. First Senator Hutchinson presented the bill. I followed with oral testimony to the committee members. My intent was to educate the legislature on the range of postpartum disorders, to explain the importance of considering "mitigating factors" in prosecution and sentencing, and to indicate how this law is a first critical step toward providing postpartum women who are mentally ill with mental health treatment rather than incarceration and punishment.

Next the prosecutor and Lewis took their seats in front of the Senate Criminal Law Committee. Prosecutor Jones provided a lengthy discourse of the unconstitutionality of the bill and was questioned several times by a few skeptical committee members. At this point, Senator Don Harmon spoke up: "You mean to tell me that we can't right a known wrong?" The committee announced they were ready to vote. The final result was a unanimous vote in favor of HB 1764.

Although a victory, Lewis and I learned repeatedly throughout the process of advocating for the passage of the new law that it was necessary to usher the bill along each step of the way to ensure its passage. Various impediments came up. These might have put an end to the postpartum legislation had it not been for the perseverance and the couple's watchful eye in attending to the progress and advancement of the bill.

Although HB 1764 triumphed in the senate subcommittee, it had to be read three times and voted on in the full senate before it could be sent to the governor and become law. Unfortunately, in the remaining days prior to the senate's summer adjournment, the focus and priority of the Illinois Senate was on the passage of the state's budget. The road to make Illinois HB 1764 law had again taken a brief hiatus. With unanimous passage in both the House Criminal-Judiciary Committee and the Illinois Senate Criminal Law Committee as well as the Full House, it seemed certain that when the senate reconvened in the fall of 2017, HB 1764 would finally have the full support of the senate needed for the required three readings and an uncontested vote.[14] After that it would proceed to the governor for his signature, to become law. Or so we thought.

We soon found that there were other snags along the way, and the bill got stalled again and again. The fall came and went, and HB 1764 was placed on hold in the Assignments Committee, unable to move without the agreement by senate president John J. Cullerton and the senate sponsor, Toi Hutchinson. As the end of the year approached, Lewis and I became concerned as the culmination of the Illinois General Assembly in 2017 would mean starting all over in 2018. There was concern that with delay that all may be lost.

At this point, I with help from Lewis prepared a prospectus, and both of us hand-delivered it to Cullerton's Chicago office. Shortly after, the bill was taken off hold and finally moved out of the Assignments Committee to be heard in the veto session.[15] Later we were told that Cullerton was seen carrying that prospectus in the legislature in Springfield.

In early November 2017 at the Third Biennial Perinatal Mental Health Conference in Chicago, within minutes of concluding a presentation on Legal Advocacy and Perinatal Issues, Lewis and I received a call from Senator Hutchinson's office. HB 1764 had the third reading in the senate. A vote followed. The bill passed in the full senate with near unanimity.

Now the final and last step. The bill had to be presented to the governor for his signature.

Again things went amiss. Lewis noticed the final date was approaching and the governor had not signed the bill. So again, we began to make calls, only to find out the house was to send the bill to the governor. However, due to lack of communication between the houses, that had not been done. Within days prior to the deadline, numerous calls were made to house and senate sponsors by this particularly determined couple. At long last the bill was sent to Governor Bruce Rauner's office. The postpartum bill was finally signed by him and became law.

My purpose in this detailed account is twofold: both to inspire the reader about how change takes place and to encourage other individuals to demonstrate the successful path that perseverance and determination can have to produce change. The arduous journey that HB 1764 took to become Illinois PA 100-0574 brings home the point that being an advocate means ushering legislation along each step of the way.

TWO INCARCERATED WOMEN FRIENDS CREATE A LAW

Paula Sims and Janet Jackson, both incarcerated with natural life sentences for different crimes, met at Logan Correctional Center. They were roommates over the years and became best friends. We met them at Logan in early June 2019 to interview them and learned how they came to write the legislation that would become PA 100-0574, the ground-breaking new law in Illinois and the first postpartum criminal law in the nation.

In that it was my first time at a prison, I was expectedly nervous and uncertain what to anticipate. Lewis has a long history as a criminal defense attorney and was used to meeting clients in prison. With years of experience with prison visits, he was expectedly calm.

Within minutes of meeting Paula and Janet, I was put at ease by their warmth, openness, and directness in answering our questions about how this law came to be. It was incredulous to both of us that two incarcerated women would know how to write up new legislation, at the recommendation of Bill Ryan, that was good enough to be taken seriously by the Illinois General Assembly.

Each woman was interviewed individually. Then we spent the last fifteen minutes of our two-hour session with both together. By the end of our allotted time, as set by the prison warden, we hugged as old friends. We promised to stay in touch and hoped to meet again, outside the barbed wire and secure walls of Logan Correctional Center in Lincoln, Illinois.

Janet told us, "Paula is my inspiration, and she's been my best friend for thirty years." She was hoping that the new law would give Paula another chance at freedom, in that it allowed for a second postconviction petition and was retroactive. Incredulously Janet would not benefit and could lose the company of her roommate if Paula's natural life sentence was commuted, following her resentencing hearing. Janet was a domestic abuse victim but never suffered from postpartum psychosis as Paula and others at Logan had.

Janet related how she was moved by the number of new mothers at Logan crying uncontrollably. "Women who suffer from postpartum are so down on themselves. They don't understand; they don't know they were mentally ill but just [that] something is wrong." "Mental illness is a stigma, and a lot of women won't tell you what they were incarcerated for. They don't share." She explained that others in the prison population and their families are against them.[16]

Paula credited Janet who had finished her degree as a paralegal within prison for largely writing the legislation. Paula had also taken classes toward a paralegal degree. Janet insisted that they wrote the legislation together, each contributing. She noted they had access when they were working as law clerks but later spent their one hour of weekly allotted time in the prison law library as well as writing when they had free time in their prison cell. They had talked about doing something for years. They finally decided to stop talking about it and just do it.

Janet had worked on a domestic violence bill, and they mimicked that bill, using it as a model. She had been writing for the *Stateville Speaks* newspaper[17] when Bill Ryan suggested that if she would write something up, he would try to get something passed. Bill too had heard the stories of numerous women at Logan who had committed crimes "often the unthinkable" when they had a temporary psychosis or depression after the birth of their baby. Bill found a sponsor in the Illinois House, Representative Linda Chapa LaVia. They made the bill retroactive. The rest is history.

Janet and Paula give recognition to many. They express gratitude. They credit Lewis and me, Bill Ryan, Representative Linda Chapa LaVia, Senator Toi Hutchinson, and Carol Blocker with getting "the train" moving down the track. They described it as a miracle bill that could not have happened without each of us contributing. It was powerful that two women inmates who came into the prison with only a high school diploma could get a law passed. This is inspirational and empowers everyday citizens and advocates, and means that you too can make a change in the law.

Here are some highlights from our interviews with Sims and Jackson.

How did this all start? How did you know how to write the legislation that became Illinois PA 100-0574?

Paula: We talked about it for years. I've done thirty years and Janet's done thirty-three years, and we've been friends for a long time.

Are you roommates?

Paula: Yes. We are now. We have been over the years. We've been blessed in that area too. We kept talking about doing a bill. And we had worked on a domestic violence bill.

Did you work on that before? Together?

Paula: Yes. Mostly her though.

How did you learn how to write a law? How did a couple of people sitting behind bars create a law that actually got passed?

Paula: Well, we were law clerks at Logan. Janet is a paralegal. I'm a part paralegal because they quit the class [the prison eliminated that program] when I was in the middle of it. Janet came in four years before I did.

We didn't want to waste our time, and we didn't want our lives to have been nothing. And we were trying to make a difference. So, we kept saying we should do a bill on postpartum like we had done on domestic violence.

We just talked and talked about it. And one day I just said, let's quit talking about it and do it. So, we did.

We started really getting into the research. "We used the domestic violence law as a guideline. We got the books out and made sure it's retroactive. Cause the domestic violence bill, they still have problems with that.

We mimicked it off of the domestic violence bill. We made sure, because they had so much trouble with the retroactivity of it and the constitutionality of it. We made sure that it was retroactive the best we could. 'Cause we couldn't use the word "retroactive."

Janet: We talked about the retro . . . but we knew it wouldn't fly. But if you use the postconviction, it's obvious retroactive. The domestic violence was a relief of judgment. The way the domestic violence was written was only allowed to be used in sentencing, not in trial.

In trial, it makes an enormous amount of difference because you might be found not guilty because you are so severely mentally ill that you may be found not guilty. Or it may be a different charge; instead of a murder, it may be a manslaughter. Which is a whole different ball of wax. It became what we were going to do for this relief from judgment.

Paula and I talked about it and talked about it. We stayed up nights talking about it. We didn't want it to be a relief from judgment because it didn't work well. All we had left was a postconviction petition. We knew it had to be something that was already in place. And you can have a successive one if you had already done a postconviction, if you have a new law. We knew that you could insert things in the law. We heard changing things and inserting things is so much easier that writing a whole new law.

Paula: And Bill Ryan said, you present a rough draft bill, I will get someone to introduce it. And he found Representative Linda Chapa LaVia. She came here and met us. It was beautiful. The warden printed it off and gave Janet a copy and me a copy.

It's not over; it's just beginning. There's maybe twenty women here. Maybe five or so that we don't know about, because a lot of women don't talk about this.

It's a mental illness, but a temporary mental illness as you all know. Cause lots of times when people start talking about mental illness, they think you are a danger to society.

Paula, have you been well a long time?

Paula: Yes. And I didn't even know what postpartum depression was.

So, you didn't know anything about postpartum mental illness before the incident?

Paula: No. I heard of the mother blues, maybe you might cry a little bit after you have your baby, but your hormones are getting in line and everything's going to be OK.

I didn't know there was a mental illness, and I didn't know that if it goes into psychosis it could be very, very serious. Where your life could be lost. Your baby's life could be lost. Many lives could be lost and destroyed. Never thought about that. Because this is something I dreamed about being, a mother.

Since I was a little girl playing with dolls, like most little girls. The great American dream. Being a mother, a wife, a nice home.

Did your mom or other relatives have depression around childbirth?

Paula: My mom wouldn't talk about it. I asked her, and she got defensive and thought I was accusing her of thinking about killing us. She got very offended and said never to bring it up again. I'm just trying to figure all this out. Now my aunts told me that they were depressed with their children.

I wish someone would have told me. Why didn't anyone say something? We were afraid we'd upset you. Upset me! It could have saved me from tragedy. I'm not blaming them, I'm not blaming them. But they could have maybe saved this tragedy from happening.

Who knew this would be where you would end up.

Paula: It's devastating. It's the most terrible thing that a woman could do. To take the life of her child. A child is a gift from God. You love that child, it's part of it. And I had psychosis. I didn't know it at the time.

As I said, we aren't gonna waste our time, like a lot of people that may have a long time to do. They sit around playing cards, watching soap operas, getting fat, not being active. And they start losing their mind and they get bitter.

One of my prayers was, when I first arrived in prison and I saw what I saw, Lord make me a better person not a bitter person.

No matter how long I have to be in prison, no matter if I never get out. I want to be a better person. I want to be a beautiful person. It's our choice.

One of the things that surprised me when I came to prison is that women judge each other. When you're in for a child case, and they know that, they call you a baby killer.

We are working on something right now, mainly Janet. It's a compassionate release bill.

Janet: It doesn't take one person; it takes a village.

NOTES

1. C. Klier et al., "Filicide Research in the 21st Century," *Archives of Women's Mental Health* 22, no. 1 (February 2019): 135–37.

2. See Richard J. Loftus, "The Mentally Ill and California Criminal Justice: The Issues and Challenges of Collaboration," Superior Court of Santa Clara County, March 13, 2014, https://www.cibhs.org.

3. Some other states have conditional-release programs similar to California.

4. It is not just a societal cost to incarcerate the already-cured formerly mentally ill. A life sentence in a penitentiary for a woman of childbearing age will cost in excess of a million dollars, with a present expense of about $25,000 per year. Logan's women's jail has an average per inmate cost of $26,440 (FY 2016). With a thousand such, the total taxpayer burden is a waste of more than a billion dollars. "Logan Correctional Facility Data," Illinois Department of Corrections, accessed July 30, 2019, https://www2.illinois.gov.

5. "Ellen Story Commission on Postpartum Depression," Office of Rep O'Day of Joint Committee on Municipalities and Regional Government, 2018.

6. Bill Ryan was a sole prison reform advocate who was instrumental in getting HB 1764 started in Illinois that eventually led to the new law PA 100-0574.

7. Cheryl Meyer and Michelle Oberman, *Mothers Who Kill Their Children: Understanding the Acts of Moms from Susan Smith to the "Prom Mom."* (New York: New York University Press, 2001).

8. Gina Wong and George Parnham, Postpartum Support International meeting, Houston, Texas, June 2018.

9. Meyer and Oberman, *Mothers Who Kill.*

10. Ibid.

11. Ivy Shih Leung, "Maternal Mental Health Awareness Month—2017," *Ivy's PPD Blog*, May 1, 2017, https://ivysppdblog.wordpress.com/tag/hb-1764.

12. Barry Lewis, "Postpartum Disorders: A New Law Offers Hope," *Champion* (National Association of Criminal Defense Lawyers) (March 2018): 20–25.

13. We were later nicknamed in the perinatal professional community the dream team or "the power couple."

14. Each bill introduced must be read by title on three different days in each house before it is passed. The first reading introduces the bill. The second reading allows for floor amendments. A bill is voted on when called for the third reading. "Illinois Legislative Glossary," Illinois General Assembly, http://ilga.gov.

15. Advocate Bill Ryan later informed us that "the veto session is after the two regular sessions. . . . And oftentimes the most important legislation is heard during the veto session. The death penalty was abolished during the veto session. Gay marriage was enacted in the veto session."

16. Women are understandably at risk in the prison for crimes like infanticide and neonaticide. Carol Coronado, serving her sentence in California, had been beaten up

badly within the prison once other prisoners found out she had taken the lives of her three children.

17. A prison newsletter whose primary purpose is to provide a creative outlet—a voice for the voiceless—for those incarcerated in Illinois prisons, as well as to disseminate legislative and legal information.

Chapter Six

A Tale of Two Women

It was the best of times, it was the worst of times . . . , it was the spring of hope, it was the winter of despair.

—Charles Dickens, *A Tale of Two Cities*

THE STORY OF LOGAN CORRECTIONAL CENTER INMATE PAULA SIMS

We first met Paula Sims in a video by Scrappers, an independent film company. Paula had been raised in La Plata, Missouri, a city with half the population of our high schools. It owed its existence to the junction of two main line railroads, making it an ideal place in the nineteenth century for goods, delivered there by horse and buggy, to be shipped on to Chicago. The city has grown little since then. Trip Advisor lists four things to do in La Plata: a golf course and three references to railfanning. It boasts four restaurants: a Mexican establishment, a restaurant with a railfan theme, a carryout pizza place, and a sidewalk cafe.[1] It has a library open sixteen hours each week. Its elementary and high schools have a total of 347 students.[2] There are seven churches and an American Legion Hall.[3] No reference to a daily newspaper is in the internet record.

In her late teens, Paula moved to Brighton, Illinois, a town with two restaurants and one traffic signal. Despite these bucolic, quiet surroundings, trouble has had no difficulty locating the Sims family. Homicide trouble. Presently two women are in penitentiaries for the homicides of the three Sims children.

Randall Sims was the last surviving child of Paula Sims when, on June 20, 2015,[4] the Jeep his father was driving was forced off the interstate by an uninsured, drunk driver. Randall and his father both died on impact. Yolanda McNeely is now serving a twenty-year sentence in Mississippi for the two homicides. Randall was named after Paula's brother Randy who died in an auto accident when he was nineteen.[5] Paula, then seventeen, survived that with physical and emotional scarring.

The news of the deaths of Paula's son and her ex-husband reached her at Logan penitentiary in Lincoln, Illinois. Paula was barely thirty years old when she was sentenced to life imprisonment without the possibility of parole for the death of her six-week-old daughter Heather. She was also sentenced to several years in the penitentiary for obstruction of justice regarding the previous homicide of thirteen-day-old Loralei. She has now spent half of her life in the penitentiary.

Nothing in La Plata prepared her for the trial Paula faced. Unlike what she saw in television, there was no Perry Mason proving what really happened. There was no Della Street investigating. There was a local attorney who handled marital law, family law, criminal defense, DUI, and traffic offenses. That attorney was informed by Kathleen Hamill, a lawyer at Illinois's Office of the State Appellate Defender, of the potential issue of postpartum illnesses. Hamill sent Paula's attorney documents detailing the illness and its relationship to Sims's case. She followed up with a phone call to Sims's attorney, emphasizing the need for quickly conducting certain medical tests.[6] That was not done. The attorney claimed he discussed the insanity defense with Sims. Sims disputes this. What is confirmed is Sims's attorney asked for expert witnesses on five subjects: a trace evidence examiner, a pollster to ascertain the extent and effect of adverse pretrial publicity in Peoria County, a medical consultant, a jury consultant, and a forensic pathologist. Her counsel also sought payment of the experts from the state.[7] That was denied. The record does not show why no experts were paid from the forty-thousand-dollar-bond Sims put up. The money put up for her bond remained available for defense purposes. Note that the list of proposed experts proves there was no attempt to have any expert review the possibility of an insanity defense. The reason given by counsel for ignoring the defense of insanity: he believed the defendant. Defense counsel also failed to object when important, undisclosed evidence was presented to the jury. This was costly to Paula's chance for freedom.[8]

Paula entered prison as a thirty-year-old. Now sixty, her appearance is grandmotherly and broad at the hips. She sits and faces Scrappers cameraman. Her straight greying hair extends past her shoulders. Entirely accustomed to the painted cinderblock walls she has lived with half her life, she speaks with a calm precision. She could only be a murderer in a documentary using actual prisoners. Were this film fictional, the casting director who sent her for an audition would be fired with the words "This is no murderer." She does not appear to belong in a film of murder, except perhaps as a central character soon to be made a victim, which in a very real sense she is. Her voice is clear, soft-spoken, without a hint of anger, and with a tinge of regret over what may have been. She is the victim of laws that do not fit postpartum sufferers.

Paula first heard of postpartum illness during her trial in the briefest of passing mention by the prosecutor, who asked Paula if she suffered from it. Back then she did not know what postpartum illness was. Years later, she was unsuccessful in her attempt to gain a new trial, citing her post-trial diagnosis by a medical expert who concluded that she killed because she had postpartum psychosis.[9]

CONTRASTING PAULA SIMS WITH THE HOMICIDE CASE OF INMATE PATTY COLUMBO

Paula said she finally learned about postpartum psychosis at the women's penitentiary then in Dwight, Illinois, where she shared facilities with several postpartum sufferers. Their behavior is in stark contrast with such offenders as Patty Columbo. Columbo spent months plotting the murder of her entire family: Frank, Mary, and her thirteen-year-old brother, Michael. Columbo had begun an affair with Frank DeLuca who was married with five children. It is unclear if her disinheritance was prompted by her affair. It is unclear to what extent her family knew of her sexual proclivity: swinging, and even photos showing her having sex with DeLuca's German Shepherd dog.

Columbo did not know she had been disowned by her parents and hoped to get her inheritance early. What we do know is the exceptional violence of the murders and the sheer anger Patricia displayed on that night. She cruelly tortured, beat, and stabbed her entire family. The extended description of the murder scene in quiet Elk Grove Village, Illinois, is too violent and disgusting to be laid out in this text. The readers can find the details on their own, such as in Murderpedia, should the crimes of Sims and Columbo seem at all equivalent.[10] There is no comparison. Suffice it to say I have never encountered a report of a single night with more horrific abuse either in fiction or in reality.

Columbo made the best of her stay at Dwight. In 1979 it was reported she was involved in organizing sex orgies involving guards and wardens. High-ranking officials there were forced to resign. Despite all, Columbo is eligible for a parole hearing every three years. In contrast, Sims's sentence bars her from any and every form of release. Only a governor or death's mercy can release Sims from Logan Correctional Center. Columbo murdered for money; there are plenty of potential victims around. Sims is a model prisoner. Sims, like the other postpartum illness sufferers in Logan, has no meaningful chance to make another victim. The reason for the difference in parole eligibility: Columbo murdered before determinate sentencing, a predecessor to "Truth in Sentencing," was passed in Illinois; Sims, a short time after.

The Illinois courts have shown little inclination to give Sims mercy. It is commonplace, even routine, for defendants to claim their conviction was caused by the incompetence of defense counsel. There are plenty of "jailhouse lawyers" whose commissary money is earned by preparing petitions on behalf of their fellow inmates. Second guessing the defense attorneys is commonplace. Everyone's hindsight is twenty-twenty. The courts' reluctance to overturn a verdict based on a hindsight argument is completely understandable. It wasn't until the twentieth century that many states permitted a new trial under exceptional circumstances in a criminal case based on new evidence. The basic concept of trial law is you take your best shot, because you will be stuck with it. It is certainly true that an insanity defense would conflict with and hurt Sims's "I didn't do it" defense. Her attorney claimed he did not use the insanity defense because of that conflict. However, Sims's attorney should never have passed on the opportunity to analyze objectively this issue that Attorney Hamill handed him on a silver platter. He took a pass on getting the then-recommended medical exam. If Sims had a sanity and fitness examination, there is no telling where that might have led. Conceivably, the prosecution would have been unable to effectively rebut the defense expert on insanity. In that case, the judge would have no choice; a not guilty by reason of insanity would be a certainty. Sims was facing the death penalty and horrific popular animus. Establishing a mental illness, albeit with the conclusion she was sane, would still do much to deflect the animus of the popular press pretrial. At the sentencing phase it would do much to make a jury reject the death penalty. As it was, she was spared execution only because the jury could not unanimously agree to it. There was at least forty thousand dollars in her bond money and willing experts available.

With that in mind, the representation of Sims was objectively incompetent. Her attorney was notified of a potential defense and knew Sims was facing the death penalty. Certainly, the local television station's poll whether she should be executed would suggest to even the least aware attorney that Sims's life was seriously endangered. Every attorney knows mental illness is a mitigating factor that must be considered at the time of sentencing. The failure to explore that is clear incompetence. The exploration of the mitigating factor of postpartum illness could be accomplished privately and without publicity. It could be used as an insanity defense. If the insanity defense was deemed weaker than the claim of not having committed the crime, all references to mental illness could be hidden from the jury until the later, entirely separate, sentencing phase.

The obvious attorney error, however, was not grounds for a new trial, or a new sentence. Why not? Illinois law is absolutely monolithic that sentences other than death sentences cannot be challenged in postconviction proceedings. The failure to present strong mitigating evidence, or even seek it, if not raised at the time of trial is not a legal factor at all in postconviction proceedings. The court regarded the insanity defense as an ordinary hindsight claim. Her trial attorney claimed he believed Sims, and an insanity defense would show a jury just why she killed. In other words, it would detract from his chosen defense. Since both defenses could not be used together, it was her attorney's duty to make a choice—not necessarily the right choice. Only a rational, defensible choice is required by law.

SIMS AND OTHER POSTPARTUM SUFFERERS HOPE FOR FREEDOM WITH THE NEW LAW

PA 100-0574, the unique Illinois law, will give Sims a chance for freedom. She should get a new sentencing hearing, unencumbered by the lawyer's past errors. We believe there are nationwide about one thousand like Paula Sims. The law is a start, but it does not go far enough. It is not as all-encompassing as the British Infanticide Act. It is not as comprehensive as we would like.

The life sentence with a possibility of parole does not fit Columbo because she should never be paroled.[11] But that is harmless. No rational parole board will parole her until age enfeebles her. The life sentence without any possibility of parole the judge handed down to Sims or any other lengthy sentence given a victim of this maternal illness does not fit because it is preposterous for someone suffering from a temporary illness to be imprisoned until death.

The solution to the wrongful incarceration of women whose crime is motherhood itself is found by reference to the British laws we have discussed in this and other chapters.

NOTES

1. "Things to Do in La Plata," Trip Advisor, accessed July 30, 2019, https://www.tripadvisor.com.

2. "La Plata, Missouri," City-Data.com, accessed July 30, 2019, http://www.city-data.com.

3. "Missouri Church Directory," Church Finder, accessed July 30, 2019, https://www.churchfinder.com; "Post 282 La Plata, Missouri," American Legion, accessed July 30, 2019, https://centennial.legion.org.

4. Beth Hundsdorfer, "The Estate of Paula Sims Son Could Get Nearly $1M. Here's What She's Done About It," *Belleville News-Democrat*, May 24, 2017, https://www.bnd.com.

5. Ann Knef, "Sims' Petition Describes How Son's Life Was Spared," *Madison-St. Clair Record*, August 10, 2006, https://madisonrecord.com.

6. Fifth Dist. Appellate Court, *People v. Sims*, No. 5-99-0250 (2011).

7. Fifth Dist. Appellate Court, *People v. Sims*, No. 5-90-0287 (1993).

8. Ibid.

9. Patrick E. Gauen, "Twisting Path Continues for Paula Sims Who Killed Two Daughters," *St. Louis Post-Dispatch*, December 14, 2015, https://www.stltoday.com; Fifth Dist. Appellate Court, *People v. Sims*, No. 5-99-0250 (2011).

10. Juan I. Blanco, "Columbo, Patricia," Murderpedia, accessed July 31, 2019, https://murderpedia.org.

11. Technically speaking Columbo was sentenced to a two- to three-hundred-year term for the murders, and another two hundred for the conspiracy and solicitation counts.

Chapter Seven

Recognition of Postpartum Mental Illness within the Medical and Legal Community

> Once I had my baby I experienced postpartum depression. Because I had suffered from depression before, I thought I would know what depression would feel like, but it was totally unlike anything I had experienced before to the point I didn't realize what was happening. It felt like I was living in a post-apocalyptic world.
>
> —Anonymous patient describes the uniqueness of postpartum depression

Medicine is science based. A bacteria-based, virus-based, and organ-based pathology of disease is as fully and universally accepted as the foibles of humankind permit. Of the fields of medicine, psychiatry lags behind. It has failed to find a genetic, microbial, or environmental cure for what ails us. It cannot even agree whether many outlying behaviors constitute a disease. For much of its existence as a recognized field in science, it, sometimes aligned with other medical fields, has debated whether such aspects of human behavior as obesity, sexual proclivity (especially among women), homosexuality, alcoholism, kleptomania, and drug addiction are diseases.[1] The specifics within the massive volume of the latest version of the *Diagnostic and Statistical Manual* stand in stark contrast to the disputes arising regarding its attempt, not altogether successful, to render black and white the shades of grey within.[2] There is no dispute what constitutes cancer. Usually a cancer diagnosis, backed by a pathological examination, does not become a matter of dispute. Rare too is a dispute about the general nature of cancer treatment.[3] The utility of the triad of surgery, radiation, and chemotherapy is accepted by proof of the success rates of these treatments. Only the doses and members of the triad might be debated as pertaining to a specific individual.

By contrast in psychiatry, both the diagnosis and treatment are frequently the subject of ongoing debate. A study showed that in England, the diagnosis of schizophrenia varied from that in one of its former colonies, the US.[4]

Paradoxically, the mysteries of the brain have proven difficult to penetrate by our own brains. A degree of unanimity has developed that a given severe set of symptoms constitutes a psychiatric disease. However, the causes and cures of psychiatric illness are poorly known in contrast to our understanding of the causes and cures of microbiological illnesses.

THE DEBATE: WHERE DOES MATERNAL MENTAL ILLNESS FIT AND IS IT UNIQUE?

Postpartum illness is accepted as both a maternal mental illness and a psychiatric disease. It is unfortunate it is not universally seen as the unique illness it is. The DSM's failure to recognize postpartum illnesses over its many years and many iterations as a unique disease is pernicious. The investigation and treatment of illnesses is dependent upon researchers and treating doctors' proper classification of the illness in question.

To illustrate, let us consider a couple of examples. Legionnaires' disease has its own ICD code (ICD-10-CM-48.1). This coding is distinct from its very similar illness, pneumonia due to a particular bacterium (ICD-10-CM-J15.1). The cause and cure for Legionnaires' disease was discovered by recognition of the unique nature and timing of the population it struck, a group of attendees at the American Legion convention in Philadelphia in 1976. The disease was not spread by casual contact. The timing of the onset together with the distinctive population it struck led to uncovering its cause and cure, a fortunate thing because it is now understood the bacterium causing it sickens annually about twenty thousand individuals who were previously thought to have an intractable pathology. The cause and control of AIDS was discovered also because of the unique nature and timing of the illness. It was recognized its victims were males, often from the San Francisco area, who acquired the disease that was not spread by casual contact, within months after having unprotected sex with other males. There are other examples of defining a disease uniquely that often by a lucky circumstance led relatively quickly to greater understanding of the condition and its cure. It is also a matter of record that the treatment of one disease is different from that of another. No one would prescribe the AIDS drug regimen for Legionnaires' or vice versa.

THE HISTORY AND CLASSIFICATION OF MENTAL ILLNESS

Now consider the history and proper classification of mental illness in modern times that can be traced to the work of Emil Kraepelin (1856–1926) and Eugen Bleuler (1857–1939) building on the work of Karl Kulbaum (1828–1899) that developed into the recognized authoritative classification system, the *Diagnostic and Statistical Manual of Mental Disorders*, or *DSM-5*.

Mental illnesses have been noted throughout most of written history. Homer, Euripides, and Sophocles wrote about it in their original Greek. Madness was attributed to circumstances, "imbalanced humors," or the influences of the gods. Socrates admitted to his "daemon," which today we would call command hallucinations.[5] Sufferers were shunned, cast out, jailed, or even put to death.[6] The Old Testament references a king losing his mind.[7] The explanation for mental illness in the Old Testament pertained to the person's relationship with God.[8] According to Wikipedia, the first written record of mental illness was from China in 1100 BC; treatment was with herbs, acupuncture, or a form of therapy.[9]

Modern treatment of mental illness is not informed by the treatments prior to the eighteenth century. This is a good thing; witch-hunts, trepanning, exorcism, stoning, straitjackets, binding, chaining, and poorhouses have little to commend themselves as loving care or treatment. Shakespeare's works referenced mental illness; no modern treatment is referenced therein and likely did not exist. "Madness" existed as did "madhouses." Rational treatments did not.

Before the dawn of the moral treatment era at the end of the eighteenth century, the antithesis persisted: "mad doctors" claimed a scientifically based expertise in dealing with "lunacy." Unfortunately, their theories had little basis in actual science and treatment often entailed crude procedures. For example, Dr. T. Munro, a physician at London's Bethlem facility in 1800, recalled, "Patients are ordered to be bled about the latter end of May, according to the weather; after they have been bled they take vomits once a week for a certain number of weeks; after that we purge the patients. That has been the practice invariably for years, long before my time; it was handed down to me by my father, and I do not know any better practice."[10] That was not the worst of the treatments. Emotional torments, spinning the patient in a chair to induce vomiting, freezing baths, trepanning, bloodletting, leeches, social isolation, and infliction of pain are among the "treatments" in the house of horrors of the day. Many were in chains, poked at, and left to lie in their own excrement, and that of others. Plato advocated fair and responsible treatment of the mentally ill.[11] It is an understatement to say Munro's institution over two millennia later lacked that Platonic ideal. The "moral treatment" initiative, as reborn, arose in the Western nations in the eighteenth century under a combination of influences, notably Reverend Dr. Francis Willis, as well as many others. This informed the developing early modern psychiatry and was prompted as well by religious and moral concerns. Around that time, King George III developed a series of severe mental illnesses. These necessitated the appointment of regents at various intervals. A king could not be sent to a poorhouse, chained, trepanned, or tied to a bed or chair. His recovery, albeit at intervals, indicated treatment and recovery were possible. The doctor, Francis Willis, thus gave some respectability and professionalism to the mental health physician.[12]

MORAL AND ETHICAL ADVANCES IN PSYCHIATRIC TREATMENT

Another breakthrough also occurred in the eighteenth century across the channel, in Paris. Jean-Baptiste Pussin, a physician at La Bicetre mental hospital, successfully treated a number of its institutionalized. Chaining was barred, the dungeons were replaced over time with well-lit and well-ventilated rooms, and the patients could walk freely in the institution. A part of the treatment was simply getting to know the patients, an obvious predecessor to what is called engagement in modern therapy.

With this success, what is sometimes derogatorily referred to as the "asylum era" took hold in the nineteenth century.[13] The successful La Bicetre model was copied but soon found to be overwhelmed by the sheer volume of patients.

Nevertheless, successful treatment and the elevation of physicians in the specialty to respectability, together with moral concerns, led to scientific examination of the illnesses and treatment modalities. Proper and effective treatment requires an analysis of the nature of various disease modalities so that related illnesses are reliably and consistently recognized and treatment specialized accordingly. Otherwise, the only legitimate function of the DSM and ICD coding is to comply with insurance company demands and expedite insurance payments.

THE *DIAGNOSTIC AND STATISTICAL MANUAL OF MENTAL DISORDERS (DSM)* ESTABLISHES CRITERIA FOR DIAGNOSING AND DESCRIBING MENTAL DISORDERS

The American Psychiatric Association states the function of the *DSM* is not to expedite insurance payments:

The *Diagnostic and Statistical Manual of Mental Disorders* (*DSM*) is the handbook used by health care professionals in the United States and much of the world as the authoritative guide to the diagnosis of mental disorders. *DSM* contains descriptions, symptoms, and other criteria for diagnosing mental disorders. It provides a common language for clinicians to communicate about their patients and establishes consistent and reliable diagnoses that can be used in the research of mental disorders. It also provides a common vernacular for researchers to study the criteria for potential future revisions and to aid in the development of medications and other interventions.[14]

THE DSM DOES NOT ACKNOWLEDGE PERINATAL MENTAL ILLNESS AS A DISTINCT DISORDER

That being the case, lumping a particular illness with specific timing of onset, and encountered by a specific population with all other illnesses with the same symptomatology, is to overlook the exceptional hormonal connections and uniqueness of biological and environmental factors that accompany this illness. Ultimately this is a disservice to this group and impedes "aid[ing] the development of medications and other interventions" in this important population. This group is not just important because of its size. This population is critical to the development of healthy infants, maintenance of family units, and the growth and development of future generations. This is all the more important since US divorce rates have been at 50 percent and single mother households are, per the census reports, at 23 percent.[15]

The existence of the classification system of the *DSM*, to its credit, encourages developing generalized treatments for "mainstream" forms of depression. As an example, we can look at fluoxetine hydrochloride (trade name Prozac). In the 1970s the importance of serotonin was recognized. This led to the discovery of Prozac and the approval of this breakthrough drug for treatment of depression through its effects of inhibiting the uptake of serotonin.[16] Prior to Prozac, the drug regimen for treatment of depression focused on monoamine oxidase, such as tricyclic antidepressants. In March 2019, Zulresso was approved by the FDA, a new drug administered by continuous IV infusion over sixty hours with a cost of $34,000, specifically to treat postpartum depression.[17]

The development of monoamine oxidase and serotonin-related drugs took place prior to *DSM-IV*, a time in which the *DSM* totally ignored postpartum illnesses. Even now, its limitation to a "specifier" as opposed to a distinctive classification continues, because the committee did not find "persuasive evidence" of the distinctive character of postpartum depression from other forms of depression.[18] That decision is worrisome. The development of treatment for Legionnaires' disease was directly related to intense investigation into the unique population affected, rather than simply attributing symptoms to ordinary severe pneumonia. AIDS's cause and cure too was uncovered only after first recognizing its unique origin and circumstances. Perinatal mental illnesses likewise have unique origins and circumstances. Any investigation of causes and cures is not furthered by ignoring the etiology in either its broad or its narrow sense of *any* illness. As an example of the need for unique treatments, two decades after their first development, SSRIs were still only questionably effective in the treatment of postpartum depression.[19]

While *DSM-5* limits the classification of postpartum depression to the perinatal period and up to thirty days postnatal, the majority of experts in the field,[20] the only law in the entirety of the US criminal justice system defining it,[21] and the law of at least thirty nations[22] define the onset of postpartum illness as the entirety of the year following birth. Under the *DSM* definition, women who develop depression 31 to 365 days postnatal are excluded entirely. As a result, its conclusion is 3 to 6 percent of women suffer, rather than the accepted incidence of 10 to 15 percent. Under the broader, commonly accepted definition, as many as 800,000 women suffer this illness annually in the US. Under the *DSM*, the number is as low as 120,000. That number is still huge, but it allows the *DSM* to treat it under terms similar to seasonal affective disorders. It is obvious the treatment of postpartum illness in the history of *DSM* to date is at best inadequate; at worst, it is entirely wrong and unhelpful to its comprehensive understanding.

It should be obvious as well to the contributing authors of *DSM*-5. That document states, "The postpartum period is unique with respect to the degree of neuroendocrine alterations and psychosocial adjustments, the potential impact of breast-feeding on treatment planning, and the long-term implications of a history of postpartum mood disorder on subsequent family planning."[23]

Postpartum illness affects a larger population than any other class of diseases other than infectious diseases. It is unique in its population; almost exclusively female;[24] is specific in the timing of its onset, within a year after a pregnancy; and like the diseases in the preceding paragraphs, it is not contagious or spread by casual contact. Unfortunately, its distinctiveness is not reflected in that critical piece of the universal language of the treating doctor. Imagine how delayed the discovery of the cause and cure of Legionnaires' disease would be if no one noted that the population suffering from it acquired it shortly after all were attendees at a particular American Legion convention. Imagine too how delayed the discovery and treatment of AIDS would be if no one noted the population suffering from it acquired it within months of having unprotected homosexual sex. In the face of this, the refusal of the authors of *DSM* to recognize the disease is unique because of its fundamentally distinctive characteristics is incomprehensible. It is emblematic of how widespread the refusal to recognize this illness is as special. Merging its investigation and treatment with all other forms of depression is harmful to advancing its prevention and cure. Only in 2018 did the first certification of perinatal specialists begin,[25] reinforcing the need for unique knowledge and treatment.

The *DSM*'s refusal to recognize this disease and the more limited number of sufferers pursuant to their definition could be part of the reason that it was not until 2019 that the first specific medicine for postpartum depression was welcomed. Imagine trying to get the board of directors of a major pharmaceutical company to research drugs to treat 120,000 annually versus 800,000. Which volume of potential users would justify more research dollars? When the proponents of the research use the larger figure, regrettably the *DSM* stands in the way.

The future of treatment of this illness depends on a number of factors. The investigation of specialists may someday determine the cause or, more likely, causes of this disease. At this point, multiple risk factors are seen. These range from prior depression, especially bipolar illness in cases of postpartum psychosis, to trauma and other factors under investigation such as smoking, epidurals, hospital-based delivery, and formula feeding. The causes that have been investigated tended, quite reasonably, to focus on hormonal changes, lifestyle changes, and genetics. The influence of estrogen, progesterone, thyroid hormone, testosterone, corticotropin-releasing hormone, and cortisol has been studied.[26] The lifestyle factors considered include financial, loss of sleep, breastfeeding problems, and focus on the newborn instead of self. Other social factors may be influential. Most accept that a conflictual couple relationship is a contributing factor. Are these causes or merely influences on the severity of the illness? Researchers will have difficulty determining this chicken-or-egg issue. Examination of genetic and environmental effects can be influenced or subsumed by the effects of the new mother having been reared by a fellow postpartum sufferer.

WHY NOW IS THE TIME FOR THIS ISSUE TO BECOME LAW IN THE NATION, AFTER MANY MILLENNIA OF HUMAN EXISTENCE

If this issue is legitimate and the law workable, why hasn't it been law for all these years? The answer lies with human history and society itself. Relatively recent alterations in human society have changed completely the nature of family and village. Our industrial society is entirely different from its forebears. When the book *It Takes a Village* was published, the title was formerly a fundamental nature of life.[27] Even when tribal authority was questioned for the first times in recorded history, the tribal elders' authority was supplemented, not replaced, by the monarchy. Throughout the millennia, the spoken word passed on from the elders of each generation to the next. The elders were not as elderly as our elderly. Life was nasty, brutish, and short. The elders had no mark of authority upon them other than their grey hair. They had no armies or police to enforce their authority. It was government by consent or by fiat. The tribe, the family, and the village were the only source of assistance, security, and protection from aggression within or without the local group. Woe betide the individual forced outside of its protection. Imagine how defenseless and lacking in sustenance such a person would be, perhaps even barred from the only known watering hole. It would likely be wrong to assume this was truly and universally government by the consent of the governed, any more than present-day communities are under the thumb of mafiosi, warlords, or drug cartels. This form of governance may have been a part of the human, and perhaps universally mammalian, culture since prehistory and possibly before our species, or even our genus, existed.

This has much to do with the current state of childbearing and child raising, as well as the state of the law and the need to change it. Before the industrial revolution, even after the hunter-gatherers developed agriculture, child raising was a village affair. Even bereft of written records, the conclusion is inescapable. The physical limitations of maternity would be difficult, but possible, to overcome to some extent if circumstances demanded. But just as animal predators sought out the weak and slow as their prey, so too would life in the open for women with children be hazardous outside of the village's protection. Even within its protection, maternal death rates had to be equivalent to those prior to modern medicine, a calamitous effect on the locals. It is unreasonable to surmise orphaned children or those with mothers incapacitated by illness were abandoned to die for that reason alone. Even healthy mothers needed help. That help came from the village.

Our villages have been replaced with cities; an atomistic society is the result. Those changes in society as seen in our laws have not always been on the mark. Laws are written by legislators who are generally not mental health specialists. In our laws, consideration of mental illness often lacks empathy. Women are particularly affected by the absence of laws recognizing the difficulties of childbearing, the accompanying hormonal influences, and social changes. Only recently have women begun to take their rightful place in many professions. With respect to law, the US Senate has been called the world's most exclusive men's club. The membership was first opened to an elected woman in 1931.[28] The first woman to graduate from a US law school,

Ada Kepley, never actually became a lawyer. The court barred her from the practice of law for the sole reason she was female. This was in 1870, seven years after the Emancipation Proclamation. Much progress has been made since then. The US Senate has become about one-quarter female. The legal profession has become 50 percent female. This both reflects and causes modern attention to issues of women's rights.

Mental health treatment has gained much from science and the recognition of psychologists, psychiatrists, and therapists as worthy and respectable professions. Books are thick with laws regarding the ethical and legal treatment of the mentally ill, although by no means are all those laws admirable or consistent with the understanding of our medical professionals.

Whereas the field of medicine makes every effort to be science based, with its eyes aimed at the microscope, the field of law has its eyes to the windsock. Bill Ryan; then with Feingold, a rather private person who had been uncomfortable with public attention and dislikes any form of conflict; and last with help from me (Lewis), we created our own breeze. The windsock turned, just long enough. We won, if only the smallest of battles; it was the first and hopefully one of many victories as a group for the individual sufferers of postpartum mental illness.

I saw Bill Ryan, as selfless an individual as I have ever met. He did not stop to enjoy this first legislative victory. He moved without pause to his other efforts. As for me, my expectations rose. At first, I was just helping because of a personal request and my relationship with my life partner and coauthor. Feingold accepted the challenge and won for those postpartum survivors and sufferers and her cause. "What does winning look like? I know the answer. It looks like a woman who lets go of her demons and takes her strength into the world. . . . I was in the fight of my life and I was getting nothing but stronger . . . there was no self-doubt. No vacillation. No surrender. I was a flaming sword, honed and ferocious."[29]

NOTES

1. Charles Rosenberg, "Contested Boundaries: Psychiatry, Disease, and Diagnosis." In *Applied Ethics in Mental Health Care: An Interdisciplinary Reader* (Cambridge, MA: MIT Press, 2013).
2. *DSM-5* is the most recent addition to this manual of mental health nomenclature.
3. Referring to cancer treatment within conventional medicine rather than alternative medicine.
4. R. E. Kendall et al., "Diagnostic Criteria of American and British Psychiatrists," *JAMA Psychiatry*, August 1971, https://jamanetwork.com.

5. Stephen P. Hinshaw, "Historical Perspectives on Mental Illness and Stigma," in *The Mark of Shame: Stigma of Mental Illness and an Agenda for Change* (Oxford: Oxford University Press, 2007), 57.

6. Patrick W. Corrigan, "Empowerment and Serious Mental Illness: Treatment Partnerships and Community Opportunities," *Psychiatric Quarterly* 73, no. 3 (September 2002): 217–28, doi:10.1023/A:1016040805432.

7. Daniel 4:25–34.

8. James Neal Butcher, Susan Mineka, and Jill M. Holley, "Historical and Contemporary Views of Abnormal Behavior," in *Abnormal Psychology*, 16th ed. (Boston: Pearson, 2014), 30.

9. "History of Mental Disorders," Wikipedia, accessed July 31, 2019, https://en.wikipedia.org.

10. Steven A. Shimon, "Treatment of the Insane in Modern Great Britain: A Ship of Fools," written for the NEH Summer Seminar for School Teachers: The Dutch Republic and Britain, Lowell High School, San Francisco, 2011.

11. David H. Barlow and V. Mark Durand, *Abnormal Psychology: An Integrative Approach*, 7th ed. (Delhi, India: Cengage Learning, 2015), 13.

12. Ibid. See also "Francis Willis (physician)," Wikipedia, accessed July 31, 2019, https://en.wikipedia.org. Although straitjackets, coercion, and blistering of the skin were used, his patients' treatment included working outdoors, while well clothed. This was in marked contrast to the treatment in London's Bethlem, called Bedlam, with "patients" in chains, naked, in dark dungeons, and sitting in their own filth.

13. Barlow and Durand, *Abnormal Psychology*.

14. "*DSM-5*: Frequently Asked Questions," American Psychiatric Association, accessed July 31, 2019, https://www.psychiatry.org.

15. "The Majority of Children Live with Both Parents," US Census Bureau, July 17, 2016, https://www.census.gov. I (Lewis) consider this "single parent" figure low based on the number of examples I have seen.

16. D. T. Wong, K. W. Perry, and F. P. Bymaster, "Case History: The Discovery of Fluoxetine Hydrochloride (Prozac)," *Nature Reviews Drug Discovery* 4, no. 9 (September 2005): 764–74.

17. M. O'Neill, "The FDA Just Approved the First Drug for Postpartum Depression—but Can Anyone Afford It?" *Healthy Living Newsletter*, March 2019, http://www.health.com; H. Howard, "FDA Approves First Postpartum Depression Drug," CNN, March 20, 2019, https://www.cnn.com.

18. Lisa S. Segre and Wendy N. Davis, "Postpartum Depression and Perinatal Mood Disorders in the *DSM*," *Postpartum Support International*, June 2013.

19. M. S. McDonagh, A. Matthews, C. Phillipi, et al., "Depression Drug Treatment Outcomes in Pregnancy and the Postpartum Period: A Systematic Review and Meta-Analysis," *Obstetrics and Gynecology* 124, no. 3 (September 2014): 526–34. See also T. Pearlstein, M. Howard, A. Salisbury, and C. Zlotnick, "Postpartum Depression," *American Journal of Obstetrics and Gynecology* 200, no. 4 (April 2009): 357–64, doi:10.1016/j.ajog.2008.11.033.

20. K. Stuart-Parrigon and S. Stuart, "Perinatal Depression: An Update and Overview," *Current Psychiatry Reports* 16, no. 9 (September 2014): 468, doi:10.1007/s11920-014-0468-6.

21. Illinois PA 100-0574.

22. British Infanticide Act of 1938.

23. "Depressive Disorders, DSM-5 Selections," American Psychiatric Association, July 8, 2015, https://bit.ly/2KBhSQp.

24. It has recently been accepted that some males are afflicted with postpartum depression, although the prevalence is smaller than in the female population.

25. Postpartum Support International (PSI) has a program of certification of perinatal specialists, which can be found on their website: http://postpartum.net.

26. C. N. Soares and B. Zitek, "Reproductive Hormone Sensitivity and Risk for Depression across the Female Life Cycle: A Continuum of Vulnerability?" *Journal of Psychiatry and Neuroscience* 33, no. 4 (July 2008): 331–43.

27. H. R. Clinton, *It Takes a Village: And Other Lessons Children Teach Us* (New York: Simon & Schuster, 1996).

28. The first woman elected to the Senate was Hattie Caraway. "Women in the Senate," United States Senate, accessed October 5, 2019, https://www.senate.gov.

29. S. Hall, *Drawn to the Rhythm: A Passionate Life Reclaimed* (New York: Norton, 2002), 262–63.

Chapter Eight

The Origins of the Case against Recognition of Postpartum Mental Illness

> All others who have studied this problem are unanimous in the belief that there is no psychosis which may be designated "puerperal."
>
> —Edward A. Strecker and Franklin G. Ebaugh

THE RELEVANCY OF AN ANALYSIS OF THE STRECKER AND EBAUGH ARTICLE THAT IS ALMOST A CENTURY OLD

Dr. James Alexander Hamilton, an early pioneer in postpartum mental illness and one of the founders of the maternal mental health scientific organization, The Marcé Society, was adamant about the negative influence that Strecker and Ebaugh had on acceptance of the legitimacy of postpartum psychoses in the psychiatric medical community. That pernicious effect has ultimately led to the DSM's refusal to accept PPP and PPD as unique illnesses deserving a diagnostic classification and code. This can be traced back to the mid-1920s with Strecker and Ebaugh's seminal paper "Psychoses Occurring during the Puerperium" that contended there is no such thing as a specific postpartum mental illness.[1] In the previous chapter, we covered the unfortunate fact that postpartum illnesses have not been recognized as unique in the *Diagnostic and Statistical Manual of Mental Disorders (DSM)* or by some health care and mental health providers. Much of the basis of this is rooted in the erroneous argument by Strecker and Ebaugh.

AN OVERVIEW OF THE DUPLICITOUS STRECKER AND EBAUGH ARGUMENT

The Strecker and Ebaugh thesis on that subject is fraudulent. It cites nine articles and one book supporting their contention that there is no such thing as a specific postpartum illness. Two of the articles are in foreign languages, leaving only seven they could have understood in their native tongue. We have been unable to locate any English translation of either, so it is an open question whether Strecker and Ebaugh were able to actually understand the details of those. There is no reference in their work to a translator or any translation of the two foreign language sources.

Of the seven remaining, two *never existed.*

Evelyn Ballantine's article in the *New York State Journal of Medicine*, November 1919, does not exist in reality.[2] The November journal contains articles on treatment of facial injuries with a particular view toward helping injured soldiers, an article on the influenza pandemic, and an article on nutrition in childhood. There are also various reports on meetings and persons of note. There is no article or reference to pregnancy or lactation in any form. There is no article by Ballantine at all in that journal's index for the entire year of 1919. If that were the only error, perhaps it could be attributed to poor scholarship.

The *American Journal of Obstetrics and Gynecology* was also cited for articles by Oscar Harrison in 1894 and H. P. De Forest in 1918.[3] It can be established neither Strecker nor Ebaugh read Harrison's article in that journal. That article, again, does not exist.

De Forest's article does exist. It does not support the claim there is no such thing as postpartum illness. De Forest was a physician who had treated only three "well-marked" cases of "puerperal insanity." The article describes two, both victims of which had a macerated, deceased fetus within, causing a complete blockage of the anus and urethra. The physician naturally speculated what may cause postpartum psychoses: a "serious disturbance of the nervous system *may be caused* by a toxemia which is not sufficiently severe to produce the usual clinical symptoms" (emphasis added). The title of De Forest's article demonstrates he does not support the lack of existence of postpartum illness: "Complete Pelvic Obstruction Due to Fibromyomata as a Cause of Puerperal Psychosis." It is "a cause," not the sole and exclusive cause.

Representing an article citing two of three total events as conclusive of all the thousands of such events is inexcusably poor science. Considering the author of the article clearly states it is "a cause," not the sole and exclusive cause, establishes beyond doubt that their reference to this article (which by contrast with the others at least does exist) is not only poor scholarship but also something more sinister regarding Strecker and Ebaugh. Those authors claim "DeForest emphasizes illegitimate pregnancy as a determining factor . . . [with] greatest incidence . . . during the first two weeks of the puerperium." The actual article was about two cases of toxemia out of the three psychosis cases De Forest observed. There was no emphasis on illegitimate pregnancy. Why would Strecker and Ebaugh fabricate that? In fact, the real emphasis was on the complete pelvic obstruction in the two cases the article was about.

The R. R. Huggins article in the *American Journal of Obstetrics and Gynecology* (1914) also does exist. While its support for Strecker and Ebaugh's otherwise entirely fraudulent thesis is nonexistent, it does actually touch on the issues of causation. At page 245, Huggins states, "More attention should be given to the actual cause which precipitates the attack and to the early symptoms which often exist long before the final collapse." "What are the essential causes in the psychosis complicating the pregnant or puerperal state? A predisposition is an ill omen." Of course, it is entirely dishonest to change predisposition from an "ill omen" to "the cause." Huggins suggests at page 247 the psychoses associated with pregnancy and childbirth "may be caused by a toxemia which is not sufficiently severe to produce the usual clinical symptoms." In other words, Huggins, hindered by the absence of knowledge of hormones in 1914, speculated as to causation. If knowledge of hormones existed, would he not have speculated on that as a cause? Strecker and Ebaugh's paper contends that Huggins cites the danger of low-grade infection. That is not what the paper states.

Strecker and Ebaugh claim the Elliot Bishop article proves (page 249) "all others who have studied this problem are unanimous in the belief that there is no psychosis which may be designated 'puerperal.'" That is completely inaccurate. It is another conclusive instance of deliberate misrepresentation by Strecker and Ebaugh. Bishop in the article "Puerperal Insanity" in the 1916 *Long Island Medical Journal* reports the entirely opposite findings in the then-current literature. He reports (at pages 51–52)

> Williams, Hirst, Edgar, Webster, Dee Lee, Jones and Tweedy & Wrench refer to [puerperal insanity] as a disease. Wright of Toronto and the Englishmen Berry Hart, and Lea are more vague and only Lewis of Chicago [not the author Lewis] calls its occurrence a coincidence . . . we must feel that there is more than a coincidence and if we consider the large percentage who are confined to asylums suffering from it, I feel we have all the evidence needed.

Bishop's conclusions (page 55): "First, we have a definite clinical entity." It is appalling for Strecker and Ebaugh to have read that and claim unanimous support for the opposite viewpoint. It is completely contrary to the Bishop article itself.

Strecker and Ebaugh entirely overlook the work of Louis Victor Marcé. Marcé has exactly the opposite viewpoint of theirs and cites twice as many supporting references.

STRECKER AND EBAUGH PURPORTED TO QUOTE FROM THE ARTICLES THEY CITED

One might assume the authors Strecker and Ebaugh would have in their report used the language from the articles that most supported their viewpoint. From that assumption, the support ranges between woefully inadequate to nonexistent. Their article claims, "Ballantine . . . feels that schizophrenia may be precipitated by child-bearing . . . toxic-exhaustive psychosis is often determined by it . . . manic-depressive psychosis [is] incidental." Even if such a presentation was made somewhere, somehow, by Ballantine, feeling it is "precipitated by child-bearing" is entirely different from establishing childbearing is not a causation.

"Harrison reports . . . puerperal insanity" among 3 percent of 1,708 patients studied. The Harrison report does not exist. Even if in some other, unknown form Harrison said that, there is nothing at all in that statement indicative of any aspect of causation.

"Bossi believes that one third of all suicides in women are due to gynecological causes" and includes both pregnancy and puerperium among those causes. The Luigi Bossi article was in a foreign language.[4] We have been unable to locate a translation. Here, per Bossi as quoted by Strecker and Ebaugh, "gynecological causes" are present. There is no indication in the quoted language of a cause other than those directly related to pregnancy, childbirth, and lactation.

"Bishop recites nine subsidiary causes for puerperal psychoses." Actually, he does not. Bishop's article at page 53 quotes another article: "Tweedy & Wrench of Dublin give us nine subsidiary causes, drink, toxemia, post eclampsia, acute pain (the perineal stage), sepsis, severe hemorrhage, prolonged lactation, no marriage and heredity, laying emphasis on sepsis and hemorrhage in the puerperium." As we noted, Bishop found postpartum illnesses to be a distinct disease.

W. C. Sandy was quoted as claiming "heredity was tainted in 15 per cent; the personality deviated in 16 per cent." That leaves no explanation for the remaining group comprising greater than two-thirds of the total. However, unlike every other work cited by Strecker and Ebaugh, Sandy's work does not completely contradict them. It certainly does not support them. Sandy's conclusion was, "It seems as if *further study* of other cases *might result* in the discovery of causal factors other than childbearing" (p. 232; emphases added).[5] Of course, it might not and did not.

Rosanoff, in the authors' opinion, "properly stresses psychic factors, overwork," and so forth. "He is the only writer we have found who describes the toxic symptomatic character of some of the manic-depressive cases." Whatever that may have to do with the issues is unclear. The toxic symptomatic causes of some of one subclass of postpartum illness in no way, shape, or form shows childbirth is not a cause.

"Rosanoff" is apparently a reference to Aaron J. Rosanoff's *Manual of Psychiatry*. Since the Strecker and Ebaugh article was first presented in 1925, it can be assumed the fifth edition of 1926 was not the reference, but it is the fifth edition that we have located. Within the 684-page volume, words such as "puerperal" and "postpartum" do not appear in the index. Rosanoff gives some minimal support to Strecker and Ebaugh in his introductory chapter, but at page 256 Rosanoff states much to the contrary:

> The frequent appearance of the first symptoms [of "dementia praecox"] at the age of puberty, or in the female at the time of her first childbirth, and the occasional development of the disease in interrupted stages, each corresponding to a period of pregnancy, are arguments in favor of [the hypothesis that this disease is the "consequence of a disorder of the secretions of the genital organs"].

Rosanoff's other mention of pregnancy in that volume is on page 285. He notes the "causes [of what we now call bipolar disease] are not fully known." He points out the factors of inheritance and reports: "Quite frequently in women the disease appears with the onset of menstruation or with the first pregnancy." In short, Rosanoff favors the theory postpartum illnesses are a specific disease entity over the opposite hypothesis but is not conclusive as to either.

Strecker and Ebaugh note, "Langdon recognizes four types: melancholic, maniacal, demented, and confused." "Gregory gives the consecutive Bellevue Hospital statistics. . . . He emphasizes the mental hygiene of pregnancy." Clearly none of the quoted language supports a contention there is no such thing as a distinctive postpartum mental illness. The use of Menas Gregory in Strecker and Ebaugh's work, which has consequently caused the *DSM* to not recognize postpartum psychiatric illnesses as distinct, is ironic. Gregory plainly states, "The inadequacy . . . [of grouping] many dissimilar mental disorders . . . as one. . . . This attitude of mind became an obstacle to the growth of truth and harmful to the progress of psychiatry."[6]

Only F. W. Langdon supports Strecker and Ebaugh, who cite a *Lancet* article. That reference is to spoken remarks by Langdon before the Obstetrical Society of Cincinnati, December 17, 1914, which were printed in *Lancet* the next year. Langdon's speech contained no analysis, no citations of authority. His speech contains his conclusions bereft of evidence. By contrast with Langdon's sole support for Strecker and Ebaugh, Marcé cited seventeen supporting articles.

To the extent the "seminal" monograph by Strecker and Ebaugh, "Psychoses Occurring during the Puerperium," remains considered a serious, contemplative work, it is because its fraudulent nature has not been recognized. It is as though the infamous Wakefield immunization study, responsible for fear of vaccines and the reincarnation of dormant diseases, was accepted by the medical authorities. Both the Strecker and the Wakefield papers are appalling in their absence of verifiable fact and their reliance upon outright falsification. Even aside from the duplicitous representations of other works, which cannot be overlooked, these papers should be disregarded when examined for their own merits, or rather lack thereof.

SERIOUS METHODOLOGICAL PROBLEMS WITH THE STRECKER AND EBAUGH ANALYSIS

The Strecker and Ebaugh paper used a review of records of an extremely small number of subjects at a single hospital.[7] Their methodology is absolutely unacceptable according to any rational standard. Their article admits rejecting the conclusions of the actual treating professionals and replacing them with their own suppositions. They do not state the original conclusions in the patients' records. They also did not state to what degree and with what frequency they made changes. This was done without ever interviewing the treating professionals or the patients. It then draws conclusions from the newly created diagnoses of the authors, conclusions that are doubtless in favor of the authors' opinions. The century-old monograph is also based on certain medical knowledge known now, and possibly then, to be entirely wrong. While our comments are admittedly harsh, the harshness is justified.[8]

Their entire study includes a mere fifty cases from a single private hospital. This tiny group was then compared with a separate group from a public institution. Not only was the study so limited in scope, but also its methodology was designed, obviously purposefully, to obscure the effect of pregnancy, lactation, and the resulting hormonal changes in the course of the pregnancy and birth: "Scope. . . . The review looks somewhat beyond the usual symptomatic-diagnostic perspective, and considers such points as family history, personality, onset, previous physical and mental record, course, prognosis and treatment in their influential relationships to the types of psychoses." In other words, the identity of onset is rejected, replaced with the subjective analysis of family history, personality, previous physical and mental record, course, prognosis, and treatment.

The authors made the changes in an obscure, hidden fashion, to an unknown degree and in an unknown number of individuals, perhaps all fifty. They did this because they disagreed with the diagnosis of puerperium illness: "Diagnosis, which is usually dismissed with too much assurance, is in the puerperal psychotic reactions *beset with great difficulty*. . . . The diagnoses have all been subjected to the *retrospective consideration and revision* that come with from two to fifteen years of psychotic life history" (emphases added). In other words, the study rejected the diagnoses of the medical professionals who actually saw and treated these women.

Consequent to this revision, the diagnoses became eighteen events of "Manic-depressive psychoses, seventeen of Toxic-exhaustive psychoses (psychosis with somatic disease), thirteen of Dementia praecox, a single event of Paresis and a single event of Psychoneurosis with psychotic symptoms." At this point, the work of destroying the relevance of the unique onset of postpartum illness was completed. The remainder of the fourteen pages do nothing to justify, elucidate, or explain the extent of their "revision" of the actual medical records.

Summarizing what was shown on the first page alone of this strangely influential monograph, the authors were given unhindered access to medical records. These records were not presented even in a redacted format in their paper, although this was long before the restrictions of HIPAA required it. Their methodology was only summarized. They admit to changing diagnoses because the doctors who actually saw and treated these fifty women "had too much assurance" in their diagnoses, and the diagnoses "in the puerperal psychotic reactions is beset with great difficulty."

Consider that. If the treating physicians were "beset with great difficulty" in diagnosing (of that group none appear to have been interviewed or their experience, training, and talent evaluated, determined, or even considered), would not Strecker and Ebaugh suffer the same challenges? Would not those same challenges be exacerbated by their changing the diagnoses without interviewing the patients or the staff? Did Strecker and Ebaugh do anything more than to cross out one diagnosis and replace it with another, and then search for causes other than the hormonal influences of pregnancy and lactation to justify their conclusions?

In this context, please note hormonal science was in its infancy. The first hormone, secretin, was discovered only twenty-three years before the Strecker and Ebaugh paper.[9] In a very real sense, this paper belongs in the trash bin of history along with countless papers on countless subjects whose authors lacked the benefits of twentieth and twenty-first century science.

The paper continues with a brief and unfortunate digression on the fact that eighteen of the subjects, or 36 percent, were "Jews." Explaining this in the context of the authors' complete lack of knowledge of hormones and actual interviews, the authors conclude, citing Abraham Myerson, "From the angle of mental stability, Jewish women are prone to be upset by childbirth." Skipping the affront, the authors briefly, but significantly admit that childbirth is a cause of the illness. The authors are wrong about the susceptibility of Jewish women to postpartum illness.[10]

There is a brief reference to heredity as a factor. This factor made no reference at all to ancestors or relatives who may have had a prior or subsequent episode of postpartum illness, or any attempt to investigate this. In view of anecdotal reports of the heritability of mental illness existing for centuries, this omission is glaring.[11]

The next paragraph is directed to the issue of previous pregnancies. The authors note there were a total of seven subjects with "manic-depressive psychoses" and prior pregnancies. The authors state, "In the manic-depressive group there were eight earlier attacks in six patients (33 percent), all but one being associated with childbirth." Rather than conclude what we now call bipolar is a contributing factor to a unique disease, the authors state, "This is simply another way of expressing the constitutional and intrinsic character of manic-depressive." The only rational conclusion from the fact that all but one instance was associated with childbirth is that childbirth is *the cause of the observed illnesses*. Of eighteen diagnoses of bipolar disorder with related psychoses, only one had a discernible prior episode. That means only 5.5 percent of the bipolar subjects had an episode outside of the peripartum.

THE DATA FAIL TO SUPPORT THE STRECKER AND EBAUGH CONCLUSIONS

Strecker and Ebaugh's discussion of the effects of personality, had they chosen not to ignore the obvious conclusion, should have demonstrated to them the unique nature of postpartum illnesses: "In all, the personality was deviated in twenty-eight instances, thirteen occurring among the manic-depressive." The authors' conclusions:

> The high rate in the emotional psychoses is not difficult to understand, and naturally belittles the significance of childbirth as a precipitating factor. On the other hand, the personality defect was comparatively large in the toxic reactions. This throws some doubt on the validity of infection and exhaustion as sole specific etiologic agents. It is surprising that less than one half of the dementia praecox group were deviated as to their personal characteristics.

Again, consider that. The data did not match their conclusions. Nonetheless they infer there is no such thing as puerperium mental illness. Half of the subjects developed schizophrenia shortly after birth for no reason they could detect, even after manipulating the facts and the diagnoses to suit their suppositions. The obvious conclusion, that there is in fact such a disease as puerperium psychosis, was ignored.

The next portion of their monograph is called "Period of Incubation." The onset of the timing of diseases from the date of childbirth ranged from an average of two weeks in the case of bipolar to five weeks in the case of schizophrenia, with the toxic-exhaustive psychoses in between at just over three weeks.

> Whatever may be the nature of the chemical and pathologic processes [causing schizophrenia] which are taking place, it seems reasonable to believe that they must be intricate, complex and usually not rapidly consummated. Assuming that the psychologic mechanism is the resolution of a conflict by withdrawing from actuality, it is obvious, too, that such a situation cannot be quickly brought into operation. Childbirth probably has little or no direct effect. . . . With certain exceptions, labor can scarcely be credited with more than a precipitating influence. Sometimes even this is doubtful, and we seem to be dealing with pure coincidence.

This paragraph is full of assumptions and complete falsehoods, with no citations for its purported facts or support for its conclusions whatsoever. Schizophrenia is known to have a short incubation period. The literature describes the *gradual* onset of symptoms as "weeks to months," but also concludes it can come on "suddenly."[12]

One would expect the professionals in the field to have recognized these errors. The assumption that an event five weeks prior to the onset of a mental illness cannot be its cause is known to be wrong. The unsupported assumption that a longer "incubation period" was essential led to their limiting childbirth to "little or no effect" and labor merely a "precipitating influence." But this is only in the minds of Strecker and Ebaugh. They were ignorant of hormonal influences. Their paper lacked consideration of the effects of lactation in conjunction with the social changes of caring for an infant. Worse, they either lacked knowledge of the actual "incubation period" of the illnesses they diagnosed or entirely falsified the medical science thereof.

Under the heading of "Previous Organic Morbidity," the authors' recognition of good health prior to childbirth should have led to the conclusion that there is something about pregnancy, childbirth, and/or lactation that caused their mental illness. This fact is a direct contradiction of their conclusions. The significance of prior good health in the great majority of the subjects was noted but ignored, stating "As in both psychoses we are dealing with more far-reaching, deep-seated, intricate and profound physical and psychologic disorganizations." The absence of any precursor of any sort in the onset of the psychosis in twenty-one of thirty-one (68 percent) subjects other than peripartum was decreed of no significance and was dismissed by the authors.

In the section entitled "Mental Status During Pregnancy," commonplace matters were noted such as worries, phobias, apprehension, unhappiness, unwanted baby, and so forth, as well as a notation apparently one subject was of very low intelligence. Those authors dismissed the absence of significant symptoms in their tiny group during pregnancy by calling these issues "symptomatic premonitions." There is no such thing. There is no literature cited for those authors' unsupported conclusion that "symptomatic premonitions" exist that proved the illness was under way before or during pregnancy. Our research, limited to responsible publications, failed to find *any* matching Strecker and Ebaugh's unique opinion. The conversion of these ordinary worries into "symptomatic premonitions" led to their opinion that "the stress of labor is extremely likely to precipitate though not determine a frank psychosis." That conclusion is unsupported by anything beyond their imagination.[13]

In the section "Course of Outcome," the discussion of the duration of the dementia praecox was stated. No comparison of the duration of the symptoms in the study subjects to those of a control group was noted. The authors dismissed the fact the duration of symptoms in the "toxic-exhaustive group" was vastly different from controls without puerperium onset. Again they ignored the obvious conclusion: *This is a unique disease*. Instead, they explained this extended duration by noting the difference was the result of four such cases having a lengthy course of the illness. However, this meant that in one-quarter of the "toxic-exhaustive" cases, the course of the disease following pregnancy was different from cases not related to pregnancy. In three such cases, "patients have not yet recovered, after a course of two, three and four years, respectively."[14]

In the portion "Comparison with Public Hospital Group," the authors attribute the four groups of differences encountered: (1) the frequency of certain diagnoses; (2) the number of previous pregnancies; (3) the shorter interval between labor and mental illness symptoms in the public health group; and (4) especially notable, a mortality rate more than three times that in the public versus the private hospital that were all "largely [attributed] to social and economic reasons." It is unfortunate that poverty resulted in a 330 percent increase in mortality. Issues of medical care and insurance are exhaustively discussed elsewhere and are beyond the scope of this book. Sadly, even today, mortality among mothers remains too high.[15]

The diagnostic criteria the authors substituted were not discussed in their article. In the "Clinical Comments" section, they reported they used diagnostic criteria commonly employed at the time. These, they puzzlingly wrote, are not absolute, "and there is overlapping, perhaps particularly in the psychoses appearing during the puerperium." Strecker and Ebaugh do not further explore or explain this rather interesting phenomenon, which shows at minimum the difficulty of shoehorning this unique illness into others. It also raises the question if the diagnostic criteria were "commonly employed," why do their conclusions differ from those of the treating physicians?

A paragraph within that section of their article should be noted carefully by those who would refuse to recognize postpartum psychosis and postpartum depression as distinct illnesses. Their paper states,

> It will be seen at a glance that something has been added to the ordinary symptomatology. While manic-depressive is far from being a clear psychosis, yet a severely disturbed sensorium in 77 percent of the cases does go beyond the average. The high index of hallucinosis (39 percent) is even more distinctive and is about three times as great as is usually encountered. We cannot agree with those who feel that a manic-depressive psychosis during the puerperium is *always* and *entirely* a matter of coincidence.[16] While its occurrence may not be due to childbirth, yet the clinical picture is modified, perhaps by the intrusion of low-grade infection and exhaustion factors.

This is virtually an admission that postpartum mental illnesses are distinct. As stated by Bishop, "We have a definite clinical entity."

Interestingly, those authors, in possession of the medical records, did not test their low-grade infection hypothesis against the records or expressly search for "exhaustion factors." Perhaps the records did not disclose any infection, hence the authors speculated on the existence of a low-grade or undetected infection. Another hypothesis is apparent. There was no "low-grade infection." The cause instead is found in pregnancy, childbirth, or lactation.

We turn now to their "Conclusions." The authors admit, quite appropriately, "The number [50] is too small to permit accurate and final statistical conclusions . . . but has furnished certain clinical indications."

> The chief points of interest brought out in the clinical studies were that, although the occurrence of manic-depressive psychosis is not determined by childbirth, its clinical picture may be colored by it, and there is a greater likelihood of hypermanic states, disturbance of the sensorium and hallucinosis. In dementia praecox there is a greater frequency of manic-depressive features . . . the sensorium is more likely to be clouded.

In other words, an obvious conclusion should have been these psychoses of the "puerperium" are different.

OUR CONCLUSIONS ON THE CASE AGAINST RECOGNITION OF POSTPARTUM ILLNESS

"Science is based on fact, not opinion or preferences."[17] Only opinion, together with abundant misrepresentations, oppose the conclusion that postpartum illnesses are a separate entity. This is proven by all manner of distinctive features of the illnesses. The theorem of Strecker and Ebaugh is repeatedly disproven by their own results. The timing of onset, the differing course of the disease, and the fact a woman is twenty-five times more likely to have a psychosis in a given month of the time frame of the puerperium all point to a distinctive disease. While it is true that the psychoses resemble other psychoses, so too does a cough and fever resemble a huge host of diseases. The successful treatment of each of these involves addressing their distinctive nature, not their similarities.

Strecker and Ebaugh claim postpartum illness is an invented concept. Au contraire: They invented all their evidence—every last bit of it, save for the ramblings of one other doctor, F. W. Langdon.

Neither the papers cited by Strecker and Ebaugh nor their own work, after analysis, supports their conclusions. Their citations were fraudulent, their sample was an infinitesimal portion of the whole, their methodology was worse than suspect, and their conclusions were unsupported and contrary to much of the evidence. Science has advanced far beyond what was available to them.

One wonders if some of the admitted changes Strecker and Ebaugh made to the diagnoses included changing direct and specific diagnoses of postpartum (puerperal) psychosis into, for example, toxic-exhaustive psychosis. This certainly would explain their anomalies. A toxic-exhaustive psychosis does not persist years past the end of toxicity and exhaustion. That is not the normal course, except in the instance of the long-term effects of specific medications, such as fluoroquinolone. A particular and inexplicable absence in their report is any statement of what the original diagnoses were, or what—if anything—in the medical records prompted the abandonment of the diagnoses of the medical practitioners who actually evaluated the patients.

Much has been learned in medical science. One can search in vain for reports in and prior to 1925 for successful heart replacements, arthroscopic surgery, DNA, the causes and cures of cancer, Legionnaires' disease, most of the hormones, penicillin, and countless others. The function of hormones in pregnancy and lactation has been much explored since 1925. Even if we were to conclude, and we do not, the Strecker and Ebaugh article was the product of careful analysis and was without any attempt to support a preconceived notion, it is antiquated.

It is time to relegate it to the dustbin of history. The medical professionals should no more rely on the Strecker and Ebaugh conclusions than they should rely on their contemporaries to conclude there is no such thing as jet aircraft or a Second World War.

NOTES

1. Edward A. Strecker and Franklin G. Ebaugh, "Psychoses Occurring during the Puerperium," *Archives of Neurology and Psychiatry* 15, no. 2 (1926): 239–52. doi:10.1001/archneurpsyc.1926.02200200090006.

2. We believe this is a reference to Evelyn Ballantine. We cannot be certain in that there was no such article. An Evelyn Ballantine was elected to the Practitioner's Society in Rochester, New York, in 1906. The Strecker and Ebaugh article published in 1926 does not provide a first name or initial.

3. This may be a reference to Oscar George Harrison who practiced medicine and was referenced in 1870, yet we cannot be certain as the article does not exist. An Oscar George Harrison obituary gives his year of death in 1894.

4. This may be a reference to Luigi Maria Bossi who was a gynecologist and an Italian politician from 1859 to 1919 when he was assassinated by the husband of a patient due to an inappropriate personal relationship with said patient. Bossi per various articles in the English language believed in the physiological hysteria theory, that mental illness in women could be cured by gynecological surgery. This theory has been entirely rejected.

5. W. C. Sandy, *Journal of the Medical Society of New Jersey*, no. 10 (1913–1914): 230 et seq.

6. Menas Gregory, "Mental Disease Associated with Child-Bearing," *American Journal of Obstetrics and Gynecology* 8 (1924): 420.

7. An estimated 10 to 15 percent of women each year suffer postpartum illnesses. The estimated number of live births in 1925 was 2,909,000, which results in an estimate of 400,000 instances of postpartum mental illness. The study represents 0.000125 of a single year's sufferers. Since the study took place over the time frame of fifteen years or thereabouts, we arrive at a study involving an average of 3.3 women per year at a single hospital. Granted, they are purportedly consecutive cases, but over that period of time the percentage of women sufferers reviewed by Strecker and Ebaugh is cut to 0.000008.

8. The monograph was difficult to access. My request to reprint the work was rejected. I was seeking to analyze it for our book. Feingold was finally able to obtain an official copy for $30, with viewing eligibility for one day only. Having obtained, downloaded, printed, and studied a copy, it became more appalling with each reading.

It begins with a sarcastic introductory paragraph, which concludes with the sentence "This contribution is not merely another attempt to purify psychiatric nomenclature."

9. Ernest Starling and William Bayliss discovered it in 1902. J. H. Henriksen and O. B. de Muckadell, "Secretin, Its Discovery, and the Introduction of the Hormone Concept," *Scandinavian Journal of Clinical and Laboratory Investigation* 60, no. 6 (2000): 463–71, doi:10.1080/003655100448446.

10. In a study involving more than one thousand women in Israel, the rate of PPD among Jews was one-third of that of Arab women. N. Shwartz et al., "Postpartum Depression among Arab and Jewish Women in Israel: Ethnic Inequalities and Risk Factors," Midwifery Department of Public Health, Faculty of Health Sciences, Ben-Gurion University of the Negev, Beer Sheva, Israel, 2018, https://www.ncbi.nlm.nih.gov.

11. See, for example, Elizabeth J. Corwin et al., "The Heritability of Postpartum Depression," *Biological Research for Nursing* 12, no. 1 (July 2010), 73–83, doi:10.1177/1099800410362112, https://www.ncbi.nlm.nih.gov.

12. See, for example, J. Pierre, "Schizophrenia," *Healthy Women*, September 16, 2009, https://healthywomen.org.

13. A related concept, the "prodromal phase" has different symptoms and can last weeks to months. See, for example, Sarah Bromley, Monica Choi, and Sabiha Faruqui, *First Episode Psychosis: An Information Guide* (Toronto: Centre for Addiction and Mental Health, 2015), https://www.camh.ca. This in no way supports the concept of Strecker and Ebaugh that pregnancy, childbirth, and lactation never have a pernicious effect on the brain.

14. The authors did not note this in the "Course of Outcome" section. That information appears on page 247 of the magazine containing the article, in the "Clinical Comments" section. It is very unusual for a toxic event to cause such a persistent psychotic break once the toxin has been removed. Fluoroquinolone is one rare exception.

15. Mike Stobbe and Marilyn Marcione, "U.S. Pregnancy Deaths Up, and Report Shows Most Preventable," *Chicago Tribune*, May 8, 2019.

16. Italics were in the original Strecker and Ebaugh article.

17. Alina Bradford, "What Is Science?" Live Science, August 4, 2017, https://www.livescience.com.

Chapter Nine

The Steps for Professionals to Advocate and Enact Legal Change

Preparing Yourself for Advocacy

—session 2, Restore Justice

Recently we have found ourselves in the unique position of aiding and educating attorneys, legislators, and activists about postpartum psychosis. We have been assisting and advising them on how to advocate for new laws similar to, or more comprehensive than, PA 100-0574. Educating professionals, the media, and the public about the range of perinatal disorders, including postpartum psychosis, is natural for me. It has been a frequent occurrence in the course of my specialized professional career as a perinatal expert of two and a half decades. Yet my career took a definite turn in 2017 when I agreed to become involved in the legislative work of assisting with the passage of HB 1764.

Initially, I expected it to be a one-day commitment. Yet the decision to testify was based on both my commitment to perinatal issues and my inclination to assist when it is the right thing. It was a challenge. It led me down a path I never imagined. And to my delight, it has become the most significant as well as the most rewarding work of my career. Even more unexpectedly it has led to the shared goal and work with my life partner and coauthor. He has also become dedicated to the same cause. Neither one of us expected to find ourselves working together. After all, I am a clinical psychologist devoted to treating women's reproductive-related issues. Lewis has a longstanding career as a criminal defense attorney aiding and often representing the underdog.

In 2017 our career paths merged, and we have continued to work together. This has become a focal point of our professional careers and our personal life. Neither of us knew this would be the result when we first became involved in providing expert witness testimony in the Illinois legislature on HB 1764. We continued our work together, ushering that bill through many obstacles to become PA 100-0574. At the time of our decision to help with the legislative task of supporting the bill, we thought we were only aiding a small number of incarcerated women in Illinois. Many have served decades in prison following crimes committed during a brief psychotic episode related to childbirth. We never imagined the implications or the unique opportunity this one action would have.

THE NEW ILLINOIS LAW WAS JUST A BEGINNING

The law provided hope. It offered another chance for freedom to a group of incarcerated women in Illinois. It has also become the first step toward changing the law throughout the country. The Illinois law was just a beginning: a trajectory toward a crucial pivotal shift. It is changing the national climate surrounding maternal mental illness in the US.

THE NEED TO ACQUIRE ADVOCATE TRAINING AND EXPERIENCE

As we acknowledged in the prologue, we had no prior experience politically or as lobbyists, activists, or advocates prior to 2017. That changed. Following the passage of the law, we have found ourselves called upon to confer on specific postpartum criminal cases. We are being asked to provide aid to defense attorneys, as well as to consult with and advise others seeking to enact legislation in other states.[1]

Imagine our surprise on Memorial Day 2018 when we received a call with the request to consult with a small group in California about the tragic and sensationalized case of Carol Coronado. The state's supreme court had just rejected her appeal. The reader may recall that Coronado was given three consecutive life sentences with no chance of seeing freedom after her postpartum psychosis resulted in the death of her three children. Despite our doubts that we could provide much assistance to her, we agreed to participate with Carol's husband Rudy, her attorney, the expert witness for the defense, and Joy Burkhard, the director of the organization 2020 Mom. Unfortunately, as expected there was nothing much we could add or suggest after the California Supreme Court ruling.

JOINING WITH OTHER ADVOCATES TO CRAFT NEW STATE PERINATAL CRIMINAL LEGISLATION

We have joined with a small group of experts and advocates to help create broad, thorough postpartum criminal legislation in Massachusetts. This comprehensive bill, HD 1736, known as An Act Relative to the Well-Being of New Mothers and Infants,[2] sponsored by Representative James O'Day, is a model for other states. We anticipate the Commonwealth of Massachusetts will be the second state to enact a postpartum criminal law. That all-inclusive legislation addresses the defense of postpartum psychosis in criminal cases. Among other far-reaching advances, HD 1736 establishes that in cases of alleged crimes by persons suffering from mental illness related to a perinatal psychiatric complication, the following applies:

What this bill does:

- Section 1: Ensures that any defendant who gave birth within 12 months prior to the alleged crime is screened for perinatal psychiatric complications.
- Section 2: Ensures that when an examination is ordered following a positive screen, said examination is completed by a reproductive psychiatric expert within 48 hours.
- Section 3: Ensures that any person suffering from mental illness related to a perinatal psychiatric complication who is committed to a facility after being found not guilty by reason of mental illness is given a treatment plan made in consultation with an expert in reproductive psychiatry. Also ensures that additional services, like parent capacity building and parent-child dyadic therapy, are made available when appropriate.
- Section 4: Creates an outpatient conditional-release program for those found not guilty by reason of mental illness and for whom outpatient treatment is appropriate and poses no danger to the health and safety of others. Creates a hearing process, outlines an evaluation and treatment plan, specifies 90-day interval reporting, and creates revocation process for cases in which inpatient treatment becomes more appropriate.[3]

BUILDING OUR ADVOCACY KNOWLEDGE BASE

Often when we start on a new direction or field of knowledge there is a learning curve. We knew we needed to build our advocacy knowledge base. Aware of our limitations, we consulted with advocates and have learned skills from activists in Illinois through Restore Justice,[4] a nonprofit organization that provides advocacy training. The daylong training provided an instructional how-to for new advocates. The group instruction provided coaching and materials to help individuals learn to effectively speak with legislators, get sponsors, and take the steps needed to introduce a bill in Illinois. We recommend that all novice activists interested in pursuing a path of advocacy find training in their home state. We strongly endorse training through Restore Justice if you live in Illinois.

The Restore Justice workshop defined the key players in Illinois with simple vocabulary such as "state representatives (118) and state senators (59) are together called legislators." Terms such as *sponsors*, *cosponsors*, *proponents*, *opponents*, and *stakeholders* were clearly defined. The demographics of state decision makers in the general assembly in Illinois were addressed. This included a breakdown of race, gender, age, occupation, religion, geography of members (city, suburban, and rural), and party affiliation. It included teaching how and where to locate the sources of all of that information.

Next, there was a breakdown of the steps involved in advocating for a cause and trying to get a law passed including drafting an idea, getting sponsors in the house and senate, and introducing the bill in clear language. Once the bill is filed, it is given a number. Often amendments are made during the committee sessions. Before becoming law, the bill has to pass hearings and debates in the house and the senate committees. Thereafter the bill is voted on in the full house and the full senate. In Illinois, a "win" requires that there are 60 of 118 affirmative votes in the house and 30 of 59 votes in the senate. Following this progression of the bill, it moves to the governor for his signature in order to become a law.

As we learned in our training, there is a schedule that must be strictly adhered to, similar to a sports season. The general assembly kicks off the season and the first session in January. All bills are filed by mid-February, and most of the substance of debate, amending, and voting on new legislation takes place between February and May.

In the process of ushering HB 1764 through the legislature, it was pointed out that the number of the bill is only relevant for the session it is filed in. As you may recall this was a real concern with the bill in 2017. As the year was drawing to a close, we feared all would be lost and we would have to start all over again with a new Illinois General Assembly, a new number, and potentially new sponsors.

Restore Justice Advocacy Camp provided data on "2018 Illinois basics." This included the total number (40,872) incarcerated in twenty-five-plus state facilities in Illinois, broken down as 94 percent male, 56 percent African American, 47 percent from Cook County, and 62 percent having at least one child. The per capita cost of incarceration was stated to be $21,930,[5] not including Illinois Department of Corrections overhead and some programs in the criminal justice system. Restore Justice stated the US locks up more people, per capita, than any other nation. Prison Policy Initiative states there are many different types of correctional facilities and approximately 2.3 million people are confined throughout the country.[6]

A PROPOSAL BY #TEAM FREEDOM IN ILLINOIS

A #Team Freedom proposal reports that despite the overcrowding in Illinois prisons,[7] there is an understanding that "due to the seriousness of particular crimes a certain requirement of measures must be taken into account." However, article 1, section 11 of the Illinois Constitution states, "All penalties shall be determined both according to the seriousness of the offense and with the objective of returning the offender to useful citizenship." Truth in Sentencing implemented in 1999 requires murderers must serve 100 percent of their sentence. This removes the above-noted Illinois Constitution's stated objective of a sentence, "to be restored to useful citizenship." Prior to that statute under the determinative sentencing laws, those convicted of a violent crime were expected to serve at least 50 percent of their sentence. Thereupon they were eligible for release subject to review by prison authorities. It is known that recidivism is not likely to occur in offenders over the age of fifty, or in those who have served more than ten years no matter the age.[8]

The Illinois women who have committed crimes, such as infanticide or neonaticide, during their postpartum period are all incarcerated in Logan Correctional Center. This prison is seriously overcrowded according to #Team Freedom. The #Team Freedom proposal states that inmates transfer in from different counties with no bed space. This necessitated converting the gym of House Building 14 into a dorm. The gym sleeps seventy inmates who sleep on mattresses laid on the floor. In addition, other problems include inadequate health care services, education programs at an all-time low, small food portions that do not meet the Illinois Department of Corrections Food Service guidelines, and inadequate attire for inmates.[9]

GENERAL GUIDELINES FOR A DEVELOPMENTAL MODEL IN WRITING LEGISLATION

In constructing state postpartum criminal laws, some general guidelines of a developmental model follow. In creating legislation in your own home states, we highly recommend consulting with professional organizations and using any work already begun by sponsors, proponents, advocates, and stakeholders in other states. While we are an example of a successful two-member team with little professional organizational assistance, it is highly recommended to partner with legal committees and professional organizations. They can share the workload. They already possess advocacy experience and may have national influence. We are an example of the statement of Margaret Mead: "Never doubt that a small group of thoughtful and committed citizens can change the world. Indeed, it is all that ever has." We have volunteered an exhaustive amount of time and considerable personal expense. We have learned a lot. Our effort would have been more manageable if shared by a legal committee or a professional organization.

In chapter 12, we offer more recommendations for becoming effective advocates and suggestions for gaining sponsors and bipartisan support. A step-by-step roadmap for novice advocates is provided.

The three-step simple approach for beginning advocates we recommend is the following: (1) Start the process by finding out the schedule of when to introduce legislation in your state. (2) Begin to look for a sponsor in the house or senate committed to maternal mental health, someone with a voting history in favor of women's issues. (3) Try to find and take advocacy training, as it can help to guide novice advocates through the process.

A more comprehensive legislation to use as a model is provided in appendix D: HD 1736, An Act Relative to the Well-Being of New Mothers and Infants. Guidelines for a general model include the following:

A general developmental model in creating legislation:

- Identify the problem.
- Write out the new law clearly and understandably.
- Document the need for a new law.
- Attract a sponsor.
- Convince the legislature to act.
- Choose a name that will engender support rather than provoke opposition.[10]
- Act as a group, not as an individual.

Excerpts from an interview with Bill Ryan, the advocate who was responsible for HB 1764 being introduced in the Illinois General Assembly:

How and when did you get interested in prison relief and reform? How did you know how to get sponsors and how to be an advocate?

I'm from Kentucky originally. I got involved with volunteer work in child welfare. In Kentucky, I served as a counselor to juvenile delinquents. Eventually I moved to Illinois where I joined the Illinois Department of Children and Family Services (DCFS). I headed their child abuse system which was in shatters. We changed the way we tracked and investigated abuse and neglect.

My focus at that point was on the kids, not on perpetrators. I saw all the horrible things that people can do to kids. I didn't know about prisons.

This is what happened: My daughter in 1992 or 1993 sent me the book *Dead Man Walking* by Helen Prejean. [Sister Helen Prejean, a Roman Catholic nun, was a spiritual advisor to two convicted murderers on death row. The book is set largely at the Louisiana State Penitentiary. It examines moral issues related to the men's acknowledgment of their crimes and to the state's use of the death penalty.][11]

In some way that book did something to me. These people do horrible things, but there's some good in them.

So, I called Helen [Sister Prejean]. We got to be friends. She said you should visit somebody. So, eventually I went to a meeting of the coalition against the death penalty in Illinois. They told me a guy, Hernando Williams, was going to be executed on the following Tuesday. And his parents had never seen him for nineteen years. They were going to have a clemency hearing. . . . I found his parents and we went to Springfield the next day. It was a farce, the prison review board. I wound up taking the Williamses to visit their son at Pontiac. That was an interesting kind of execution, because to prove they weren't racist, they had both Jim . . . who was white and Hernando Williams executed at the same time. . . . After that was over, William Peeples . . . on death row called me to thank me for bringing Hernando's parents to the execution.

As a result we talked and he [Peeples] said why don't you come. And I went to death row to meet William. After that I met other guys who have gone to prison and it changed my whole perspective.

I know about prison. Illinois has undoubtedly the worst criminal justice system . . . if not in the world, certainly in the US. It's my opinion that it's racist. It's . . . against women. I've learned it's not right. OK maybe it's not the worst; it's in the top five.

My experience has been it is seriously infected with racism in the very core of it. And you can't hardly get away from that. Secondly, over the last twenty years, no the last forty years, they have continually added sentences so that people cannot get out.

As a taxpayer . . . the way they treat elderly people. Keep them in prison costing [taxpayers] $70,000 a year. There are seven thousand people who will eventually die in prison unless something happens. That will increase the budget by seven thousand people at $70,000 per year. . . . It's like a half a billion dollars a year. . . . The state should not spend my money on people who have changed and because of our "get tough on crime" thing, we let them die there. There is no reason for Janet Jackson [incarcerated woman at Logan Correctional Center] to die there.

Back to postpartum . . . along the way I had set up . . . a newspaper called *Stateville Speaks*. And Janet read that and wrote a piece about why not parole. . . . She called me and I started visiting her. It may have been fifteen years ago. And through Janet, I met Paulette and Paula Sims.

As we progressed I discovered that Jackson is brilliant . . . she's a paralegal. We began talking about cases with Paula Sims. Sims talked about her own psychotic postpartum and what had happened.

And they wrote the bill. And at that point I had talked to Linda Chapa La Via. . . . She was willing to take it and then you know we had your testimonies and Matt Jones of the state's attorney.

How did you pick Representative Linda Chapa LaVia as a sponsor? How did you go from working at DCFS to being an advocate? Any advice to us novice advocates?

I don't know. This is why I picked Linda. Many, many legislators are afraid to touch anything that would bring a little bit of justice to the men and women in prison, primarily because they would be labeled soft on crime and therefore risk their reelection. That's what all of them are about. That's what the politics are about.

I knew Linda a bit before. And she and I talked a little bit about some other legislation. . . . But Linda is a person who will do the right thing.

And . . . there is a piece from her in *Stateville* [*Speaks*]. And people tried to label her as being soft on crime. She took this because she believed it was wrong. People should be able to have the evidence, submitted with postpartum. . . . So, Linda took it. And it passed.

The reason why Linda was chosen [as a sponsor] was because . . . Linda believed very strongly in protecting people's rights, and she certainly is an advocate for women's issues. And so that's why I picked her.

Is it important to get an advocate who has a record of supporting women's issues when you are looking for a sponsor?

That's right. And is well respected in the legislature. . . . And then Linda was incidentally the one who referred it to [Senator] Toi Hutchinson. I never met Toi Hutchinson before. That was Linda. . . .

Here's an interesting little anecdote. After it passed the house—the committee in the house where you all were, I ran into Matt Jones. This was serendipity. I was just walking across the Capitol one day, and I ran across Matt [lobbyist for state's attorneys' office]. Matt had a piece of paper in his hand. He said, "You know we've changed your bill to make it not retroactive." I said, "What? The thing has to be retroactive." [There would be "no effect, no benefit" of a nonretroactive sentencing bill for the women incarcerated in Logan.]

Matt said, "Well, I just talked to Toi Hutchinson and Linda, and they agreed." I said, that's [BS]. . . . They wouldn't do that. So I went and talked to Linda, and . . . I told her, Linda, that kills the bill. She said, "Okay, we're not going to kill this bill. Not for the state's attorneys or anybody else."

She took it on and it went through. So, that's [what the lobbyists do]. . . . He snuck up and gave her some constitutional argument. . . .

The other thing you were asking, about the legislation . . . I learned how it works down there by trial and error. There were a few people out there I know and appreciated. . . . I had gone there and listened to them and [watched] what happened. . . . It's hard to understand exactly what goes on at that legislature.

There's this horrendous [fear] on criminal issues—that they would be seen as soft on crime . . . that cuts across both Democrats and Republicans. It is the undercurrent. And the state's attorneys frankly fuel that. They have a powerful lobbying group. I think the legislators, even those that aren't very good, do work hard when the legislature is in session. I think most of them try to do the right thing. But with criminal justice . . . because of media fears and their wanting to get reelected, that trumps everything else.

They pass important legislation during the veto session. [PA 100-0574 passed in the Illinois legislature veto session.] The veto session is after the two regular sessions. The death penalty was abolished during the veto session. Gay marriage was enacted in the veto session. The veto session is always heard in December. And the next one will come up and be important in 2020.

In the election in 2020 every legislator will be up for reelection; a third of the senate will be up for reelection. So come and see it. We have an election in November. A lot of the people . . . knew the death penalty should go, gay marriage should go [should be law], but they didn't vote for it. . . . It was the fear of not getting reelected. Some of them don't get reelected. They are free to vote the way they want to vote. And they did.

This is the first time I've seen things like the tax increase, gambling, marijuana being passed during the regular session. Those are all that would usually go to a veto session. . . . I don't know, I'm kind of fascinated by all the little shenanigans that go along in the legislature. . . . What I do I just take a position and say what it is and that's it. I don't get involved in political races so much.

It sounds like you are more involved in the issues.

Exactly, I am totally bipartisan.

It sounds like building relationships is important. And that, in that you have a relationship, people trust you and will carry the issue you are interested in.

Absolutely. Anyway, we got a bill passed [PA 100-0574] and you all are carrying it all over the United States.

NOTES

1. See webinars on perinatal legal advocacy through Postpartum Support International (2018) and 2020 Mom (2019). See Dr. Kat podcast: K. Kaeni, "157: Postpartum Psychosis, Changing the Law, Advocating for Women," *Moms and Mind* (2019), https://player.fm.

2. See precursors to the Massachusetts proposed law in Monica Bharel, "CY16 Summary of Activities Related to Screening for Postpartum Depression," Massachusetts Department of Public Health, 2017, http://www.archives.lib.state.ma.us.

3. HD 1736: Cate McAnulty, "The Ellen Story Commission on Postpartum Depression," Massachusetts Legislature, April 10, 2019, https://www.mass.gov.

4. Restore Justice Advocacy Camp, https://www.stridesforpeace.org.

5. #Team Freedom Proposal states it costs $24,655.75 to incarcerate a person for a year in prison.

6. P. Wagner and W. Sawyer, "Mass Incarceration: The Whole Pie 2018," *Prison Policy Initiative*, 2018, https://prisonpolicy.org.

7. E. Burnside, "Team Freedom Proposal Introduction," *Stateville Speaks* (Fall/Winter 2018), http://statevillespeaks.org. Overcrowding is a problem in Illinois prisons due to the crime rate and political gain.

8. Ibid. The author notes that the likelihood of recidivism has a sharp drop beginning from age thirty.

9. Ibid. #Team Freedom reports that currently there are no shoes for the inmates coming through Reception and Classification, and inmates are handed three pairs of socks to wear throughout the facility.

10. We strongly recommend legislation with a name like "The New Moms and Infants Well-Being Act" rather than an Infanticide Act.

11. See "*Dead Man Walking* (book)," Wikipedia, last updated September 16, 2019, https://en.wikipedia.org.

Chapter Ten

How to Partner with Like-Minded Advocates and Influential Organizations

This is the true meaning of "It takes a village."

Creating legislation is a very rewarding task that leads to new criminal laws. Once a law is enacted, there is an expectation that the law will have an effect in changing lives of specific people or affected organizations and stakeholders. This was definitely the case with the passage of the new Illinois law. We expected that the law would affect a small group of approximately twenty incarcerated women at Logan Correctional Center. As so often happens, there are effects of change that cannot be anticipated. So was the case with PA 100-0574.

In the last chapter we discussed how the Illinois law became a catalyst for other states' trajectory in proposing similar or more comprehensive postpartum criminal laws.[1] The likelihood is this will ultimately result in all states in the US having sensible sentences and treatment options. The US needs to join with many other countries that have fair criminal laws when the worst happens in cases of maternal mental illness gone awry.

We did not anticipate that twenty incarcerated women would contact us once they had a chance to have their sentences reduced. They were desperate for our assistance. Several wrote to us proclaiming how appreciative they were for our contribution to getting the new law passed. They inquired what the point is if no one's sentence was reduced. Without expert testimony and legal assistance in writing a viable petition for postconviction relief, the new law would not affect their sentence. Again, our work in advocacy took us down a path we never anticipated. It was clear we could no longer work only as a team of two. We needed the help of like-minded advocates and influential organizations.

LOCATING PERINATAL EXPERTS TO HELP THOSE INCARCERATED AT LOGAN

While the women at Logan were hastily preparing their own petitions for resentencing,[2] we began our own pursuit, searching through our professional contacts and various organizations for others who might be willing to help. Sometimes this met with a surprising dead end. Other times we found, to our delight, it led us to individuals and organizations interested in our cause. Some were willing to provide support and assistance. A problem we encountered was that all, including these authors, were to contribute their time and expertise pro bono. The women incarcerated at Logan for decades had no or limited financial resources. Another pressing concern was time. The Logan women were preparing their petitions for resentencing. They were concerned their petitions had to be filed between June 1, 2018, the time of the inception of the law, and December 1, 2018.

THREE STAGES OF A POSTCONVICTION HEARING PETITION

In Illinois, for a petition to be deemed sufficient at stage 1, it must state the "gist" of a valid claim. If it is deficient, the trial judge dismisses the petition. The only option then is to appeal. If the judge agrees the petition states the "gist" of a claim, the petition moves to stage 2. At stage 2, an attorney is appointed by the court to improve the petition. At this stage, at least one expert is needed to review records and submit an affidavit. The affidavit must explain what the expert would testify to on behalf of the incarcerated woman. This affidavit should be carefully prepared so it does not provide a basis for future cross-examination by the prosecutor. During stage 2 the prosecutor typically moves to dismiss the petition, claiming it does not state sufficient grounds to grant relief. If the court rules the petition sufficiently states a claim, it moves to the third stage. The third stage is a fact-finding hearing. Evidence is presented. The expert witness must be prepared by the defense attorney for cross-examination by the prosecutor.[3]

CONSIDERATIONS IN THE ILLINOIS CASES

The identified expert would need to travel to Logan Correctional Center to meet with the incarcerated woman. A good affidavit includes at minimum references to the interview of the petitioner, the review of all appropriate records (medical, legal, police, and prison), and other available information.

With our own time limitations, we were faced with the dilemma of identifying other perinatal and/or forensic experts for the defense attorneys assigned to the Logan women. With my longtime professional contacts in the perinatal professional community and psychological organizations,[4] I began the process of reaching out to like-minded individuals and those interested in our cause. I had many contacts in the perinatal professional community. Some were living in other parts of the country or abroad. There were only a few that had the right mix of availability, perinatal expertise, and forensic experience.

Several Postpartum Support International experts came forward. Some were from other states and even Canada. I felt it was unlikely that my colleagues would be able to serve as experts with minimal warning due to their own busy work schedules. Most likely their pro bono involvement would require them to be available to travel to Illinois at their own personal expense. This led to the realization that it was best to look for homegrown expertise.

This brought us to the Illinois Chapter of Postpartum Support International. We made an appeal for professional assistance to PSI-Illinois at a monthly meeting. One committee in particular was very interested in helping. This was the newly formed Legal and Justice Committee. Within a short time we began to hear from a few other professionals who felt a calling to work with us in aiding the Logan women. All committee members had perinatal clinical experience. A few had some additional proficiency in forensics. This led to several phone calls and Zoom meetings. We joined forces and became a like-minded group. It was clearly too much for any individual to take on with busy schedules filled with professional work and family commitments. Together we possessed various assets to contribute. It was clear we could work best by forming this team. We began developing a protocol to be used for both Illinois and other states. We anticipated a need when other states ratified postpartum criminal laws that advocates would face similar challenges in their own states.[5]

In our committee meeting, we shared our various backgrounds. We identified those who had forensic knowledge or experience as an expert witness. We considered how many years of clinical practice with perinatal expertise each of our members held. We then set out to develop a plan. What follows is our newly developed procedure of how to work together as a postpartum legal defense assistance team.

PROTOCOL OF POSTPARTUM LEGAL DEFENSE ASSISTANCE TEAM

The process begins with forming a cohesive group with the purpose of assisting the defense attorney in preparation for the case. The team meets in order to examine and discuss cases, to assign cases to individuals on the team, to review records, and to report back to the whole team. The team decides as a group who would be the best candidate to provide expert testimony from among the group members. Group meetings are held to receive forensic training with role-play exercises to prepare experts for testimony and cross-examination. Outside experts are engaged who can aid in training or assistance to team members to expand their forensic skills.

In addition to the Postpartum Legal Defense Assistance Team, influential organizations are used to support and help in any way possible. Remember, whatever legislation you are working on, you cannot do it alone! You need to get other influential organizations and interested individuals involved. In Illinois, the following groups have assisted in various ways: 2020 Mom, the Postpartum Psychosis Task Force, and Postpartum Support International.

NOTES

1. An example is HD 1736: An Act Relative to the Well-Being of New Mothers and Infants, Commonwealth of Massachusetts, 2019.
2. Coauthor Lewis provided a template of how to write a postconviction petition.
3. The postconviction procedures vary from state to state. See appendix B, "Stages of a Petition for Postconviction Hearing under the New Law."
4. I (Feingold) am a member of Postpartum Support International Advisory Council (PSI-AC), a member of the newly formed Postpartum Psychosis Task Force of PSI, a member of PSI's Legal and Justice Committee, a member of the American Psychological Association, and a member of the Illinois Psychological Association.
5. Although no exact numbers of incarcerated women who had PPP or PPD have been identified due to lack of research in this area, it is estimated that there are approximately a thousand such women in the US.

Chapter Eleven

Networking and Support for Postpartum Psychosis

Help from Our Friends

> It's five years [since my postpartum psychosis]—my family was able to talk to each other, but [not to me]. You go through it on your own.
>
> —anonymous patient describes the effect of stigma that silences sufferers

Women sufferers with postpartum psychosis, as noted by the above quote, are reluctant to discuss their experiences, even many years after the episode. Due to the stigma and lack of understanding about this severe maternal mental illness, they protect themselves with silence. The secretiveness of postpartum disorders has encouraged sufferers to develop online support where they can communicate anonymously. This is available through Facebook closed groups and subgroups within organizations such as Postpartum Support International and 2020 Mom.

It is no coincidence that this chapter follows one underscoring the phrase frequently used particularly among women of my generation and younger: "It takes a village." Both within as well as outside the perinatal community, women are joining together with their gender *sisters* to support each other in social action, issues of gender equality, and overall improvement for society both nationally and internationally.

A NEW FOCUS ON MATERNAL HEALTH AND MENTAL HEALTH IN THE US

In May 2019 a three-day gathering of moms from across the country was organized to talk with government leaders about what matters most in maternal and child health. This group, Mom Congress, set a policy agenda "anchored around improving maternal health—the care we receive during pregnancy, birth and the postpartum period."[1] The organizers' mission statement identifies the purpose: "To build on the momentum of the recent successful efforts addressing maternity care, including reversing the rising maternal mortality rates,[2] health disparities among African American mothers, and efforts to identify and treat maternal mental health disorders like postpartum depression." Proposed legislation named the "Momnibus" bill is meant to transcend party affiliations and address the comprehensive needs of expecting, birthing, and new mothers. The power to change outdated laws and government policies depends on the sheer numbers who attend and become a unified voice demanding change from their legislators. The time is right; the grassroots agenda to consider women's rights is focused on change happening now to affect our generation and those in the years to come.

MATERNAL WELLNESS HAS BECOME A POPULAR FOCAL POINT FOR THE PUBLIC AND HEALTH CARE PROVIDERS

In February 2018 I (Feingold) was invited to present on patient perspectives to PRGLAC, a national task force on research specific to pregnant and lactating women that met in Washington, D.C.[3] The purpose was to prepare and submit a report by September 7, 2018, to the secretary of Health and Human Services; the Committee on Health, Education, Labor, and Pensions of the Senate; and the Committee on Energy and Commerce of the House of Representatives. This report was the result of four two-day meetings and included the following:[4]

1. A plan to identify and address gaps in knowledge and research on safe and effective therapies for pregnant women and lactating women.
2. Ethical issues surrounding the inclusion of pregnant women and lactating women in clinical research.
3. Effective communication strategies for sharing with the public and health care providers information relevant to pregnant women and lactating women.
4. Identification of federal activities, including:
   a. The state of research on pregnancy and lactation;
   b. Recommendations for the coordination of, and collaboration on, research related to pregnant women and lactating women;
   c. Sharing with the public and health care providers information relevant to pregnant women and lactating women;

   d. Efforts and programs aimed at improving the scientific understanding of the health impacts on pregnant women, lactating women, and related birth and pediatric outcomes.
5. Recommendations to improve the development of safe and effective therapies for pregnant women and lactating women.

THE BEGINNING OF THE GRASSROOTS EFFORT TO RECOGNIZE ISSUES IN PERINATAL MENTAL HEALTH

Our current endeavors to recognize women's mental health issues around the postpartum period began in the US as a grassroots effort in the 1980s with two determined women, Nancy Berchtold and Jane Honikman.[5]

In 1983 Berchtold experienced a break with reality with psychotic symptoms following the birth of her daughter. Luckily, she was quickly hospitalized and responded to psychiatric medication. Yet her break with reality within two weeks of the birth of her first child left her indignant toward the medical community that had neither prepared her nor given any recognition to mental illness surrounding childbirth.

By 1985 within a few years of her own postpartum psychosis, Berchtold had organized fifty-two support groups around the country. As the years went on, Depression After Delivery, affectionately known as DAD, attracted mental health and health care professionals as well as lay women sufferers. The mission of the organization was to support, educate, and refer women and families suffering with mental health issues surrounding childbirth, during both pregnancy and postpartum. The nonprofit organization offered an easily recognizable toll-free phone line 1-800-944-4PPD for families and professionals, provided parent packs that included a list of nationwide volunteer phone support and national support groups, and supplied a national professional referral registry. Eventually a website presence was established along with a professional packet, including screening tools as well as publications and an educational video.

As the organization gained attention in a Phil Donahue show in 1985, and in various publications and media reports, the membership grew. More professionals joined, leading to a professional membership affiliation, a board of directors, and an executive board.[6] By 2004, DAD offered a website, http://www.depressionafterdelivery.com, which was estimated to receive more than fifty thousand visits a year. The DAD office was responding to more than five thousand requests annually for written information. The organization was becoming less grassroots, and disagreements broke out between Berchtold and the board of directors. Berchtold eventually stepped down from running the organization. Over the years, unfortunately, the organization suffered with various financial and fundraising problems and eventually closed its doors.[7] Many board members decided to put their energy into their sister organization. That nonprofit group incorporated DAD's phone line and materials and formed one large international organization, Postpartum Support International (PSI).

Depression After Delivery was founded by Berchtold in Pennsylvania in 1985. A few years later on June 28, 1987, on the West Coast, Jane Honikman of Santa Barbara, California, became the founder of Postpartum Support International. That organization was formed as a result of the first annual conference on Women's Mental Health following Childbirth. The participants of that conference included representatives from the Pacific Post Partum Support Society in Vancouver, Canada; Postpartum Education for Parents in Santa Barbara;[8] the Post and Ante Natal Depression Association in Melbourne, Australia; and Depression After Delivery. The mission statement of the newly formed international organization was "promoting awareness, prevention, and treatment of mental health issues related to childbearing." PSI's vision, which was created by a global network of individuals and organizations, was "to establish a postpartum parent support network in every community worldwide."[9]

PSI became a legal nonprofit in 1989 and created its bylaws and articles of incorporation. Local, state, province, and country coordinators were established to provide a support and referral network linking callers from the PSI office back to their own community. A warm line using the DAD phone number 1-800-944-4PPD and a website were initiated increasing its visibility. Many thousands now had access to maternal mental health information through the internet.

Since the inception of PSI, it has held an annual conference uniting professionals and social support network leaders in the field of maternal mental health. The PSI board of directors initiated two award categories. The Jane Honikman Award recognizes outstanding contributions to increasing awareness of emotional health related to childbearing. The Susan Hickman Memorial Research Award includes a grant to promote maternal mental health research. In 2011, a third award, the Ilyene Barsky Memorial Coordinators Award, was established by Dr. Diana Lynn Barnes in cooperation with the PSI board, in memory of one of PSI's first state coordinators. This award recognizes the contributions of individual PSI coordinators who have worked to further the goals and vision of PSI.

By 2003 a two-day training conference was established, Perinatal Mood Disorders: Components of Care. This became the basis for the most recent training courses, which then led to a specialized certification in perinatal mental health in August 2018. PSI began working with the internationally known certification company, Pearson VUE. They developed a computer-based certification exam that professionals can take at one of the 250 testing centers in the US and nearly twenty thousand authorized testing centers globally. Candidates for the exam visit the PSI website for the educational, approved evidence-based training requirements.[10]

More recent developments include a Postpartum Support International Advisory Council (PSI-AC)[11] and the creation of the Perinatal Psychiatric Consult Line with no cost to professional users. As stated on the website, the consultation line is available for medical professionals only and serves those who have questions about the mental health care related to pregnant and postpartum patients and for preconception planning. The Perinatal Psychiatric Consult Line is staffed by reproductive psychiatrists who are members of PSI and specialists in the treatment of perinatal mental health disorders.[12]

While the US perinatal grassroots movement was spearheaded in the 1980s by Depression After Delivery and Postpartum Support International, around the same time the Marcé Society was launched in Europe.[13] That perinatal professional organization began when Ian Brockington in the UK called for an international conference on postpartum disorders. As a result of the conference, a US psychiatrist James Hamilton and UK psychiatrists Ramesh "Channi" Kumar and Ian Brockington and others formed the scientific arm that has become the Marcé Society. That society is an important contributor to the perinatal movement, focusing on professional affiliations and scientific literature and research.[14]

Over the years these early beginning perinatal organizations gave rise to other smaller professional groups throughout the country that have all helped to further perinatal awareness to the public and professionals. These early roots contributed to new statewide programs and legislation. New laws required screenings and treatment for perinatal mood and anxiety disorders. Efforts are continuing to focus scientific research on postpartum psychosis, a maternal mental illness long ignored, denied, and malevolently hidden by physicians such as Edward A. Strecker and Franklin G. Ebaugh and others.[15]

Another breakthrough that has helped to legitimize postpartum disorders and reinforce the uniqueness of this maternal mental illness was the introduction of Zulresso (brexanolone) injection in 2019 by Sage Therapeutics. This company received the approval of the US Food and Drug Administration for the very first drug developed specifically to treat postpartum depression.

The FDA approval of Zulresso was based on findings from three multicenter, randomized, double-blind, parallel-group, placebo-controlled trials. Women included were aged between eighteen and forty-five and were diagnosed as having moderate to severe postpartum depression with onset of symptoms no earlier than the third trimester of pregnancy and no later than the first four weeks following delivery. Reproductive psychiatrists and the primary investigator of the clinical trials stated, "Approval of Zulresso represents a game-changing approach to treating PPD. The potential to rapidly reduce symptoms in this critical disorder is an exciting milestone in women's mental health."[16] It was impressive to note that Zulresso was evaluated "under priority review by the FDA, generally reserved for investigational therapies that, if approved, may offer significant improvements in the treatment, prevention or diagnosis of a serious condition. And in 2016 it was granted breakthrough therapy designation status, underscoring the significant unmet need in women with PPD."[17]

New scientific research is currently being conducted at Massachusetts General Hospital in cooperation with Harvard Medical School and Ammon-Pinizzotto Center for Women's Mental Health to obtain and review stories of postpartum psychosis sufferers and to take DNA samples for analysis.[18] These researchers are examining the genetic contributions and risk factors associated with postpartum psychosis.

Postpartum psychosis survivors have banded together and organized the first meeting of the newly formed postpartum psychosis task force at the annual 2019 PSI conference in Portland, Oregon. This task force was requested by PPP sufferers and others interested in this illness. The hope of survivors was to have a safe place to share their stories and receive support. Others attending the meeting and participating in the task force hoped to further understand the severest form of postpartum illness. Task force members strived to facilitate research efforts and expand knowledge of this overlooked maternal mental illness.

NOTES

1. Mom Congress, https://www.mom-congress.com.
2. For more on maternal mortality, see chapter 14.
3. I presented in the February 26–27, 2018, PRGLAC meeting, addressing effective communication strategies with health care providers and the public on information relevant to pregnant women and lactating women, as well as a plan to develop therapies and identify and address gaps in knowledge and research regarding safe and effective therapies for pregnant women and lactating women. PRGLAC meeting, Washington, DC, February 26–27, 2018. See appendix K for my report to PRGLAC.
4. Materials from PRGLAC for February 2018 meeting agenda. See "Research Specific to Pregnant Women and Lactating Women (PRGLAC)," NIH, last updated March 26, 2018, https://www.nichd.nih.gov/about/meetings/2018/022618.

5. Berchtold is the founder of Depression After Delivery, Inc. Honikman is the founder of Postpartum Support International.

6. I was the president of Depression After Delivery from 1996 to 1998, and followed that period by serving on the executive board of DAD until it closed its doors in 2004.

7. A detailed history of DAD can be found at "Depression After Delivery (DAD) is a nonprofit, national postpartum depression education/support organization," *Depression Info* (blog), August 26, 2007, http://infoaboutdepression.blogspot.com/2007/08/depression-after-delivery-dad-is.html?m=1.

8. Honikman cofounded Postpartum Education for Parents (PEP) in 1977.

9. "History of PSI," Postpartum Support International, accessed October 9, 2019, https://www.postpartum.net.

10. "Certification in Perinatal Mental Health: PMH-C," Postpartum Support International, accessed October 9, 2019, https://www.postpartum.net.

11. I became a member of the Postpartum Support International Advisory Council (PSI-AC) in 2017.

12. "Perinatal Psychiatric Consult Line," Postpartum Support International, accessed October 9, 2019, https://www.postpartum.net.

13. The Marcé Society was named after the French physician Dr. Louis Marcé.

14. T. Twomey, *Understanding Postpartum Psychosis: A Temporary Madness* (Westport, CT: Praeger, 2009).

15. See detailed account of Strecker and Ebaugh's 1926 article covered in chapter 8.

16. "Sage Therapeutics Announces FDA Approval of ZULRESSO™ (Brexanolone) Injection, the First and Only Treatment Specifically Indicated for Postpartum Depression," Sage Therapeutics, March 19, 2019, https://investor.sagerx.com.

17. Ibid.

18. "Massachusetts General Hospital Postpartum Psychosis Project (MGHP3)," MGH Center for Women's Mental Health, accessed July 31, 2019, https://www.mgho3.org, https://womensmentalhealth.org.

Chapter Twelve

Working with Local Issues and State and Federal Laws for Change

It takes a village, part 2.

It takes a village. Each village has its leaders. Some are leaders in general. Others lead on more limited issues, such as members of a historical preservation society or the PTA. With respect to postpartum leadership, specifically targeted professional and responsible organizations exist, such as Postpartum Support International, 2020 Mom, Marcé of North America (MONA), and the International Marcé Society for Perinatal Mental Health. These organizations have inspired and influenced the development of knowledge, understanding, and treatment for maternal mental illness in the US and internationally.

Shakespeare wrote in his dramatic fashion about the time and place to move for change. It was just before the seventeenth century. Aspects of his statement are hopefully never to recur. Others should continue to inspire:

In Julius Caesar, Brutus speaks:

> There is a tide in the affairs of men
> Which, taken at the flood, leads on to fortune;
> Omitted, all the voyage of their life
> Is bound in shallows and in miseries.
> On such a full sea are we now afloat,
> And we must take the current when it serves,
> Or lose our ventures.
>
> —act 4, scene 3, lines 217–23

This was written in England in "an era of intense and mutating political and religious turmoil." That should sound familiar. Our previous century had the bloodiest wars in all history. In this century, bloodbaths are erupting all around, most commonly led by men. Caesar's chief protagonist, Brutus, was misled by forgeries and his emotions, resulting in a cascade of events culminating in the downfall of the republic his ancestors created.

The tide is rising. Increasingly, but not yet, "tide in the affairs of *men*" is becoming an anachronism. The previous century has seen wholesale changes in the authority and rights of women. This was all a consequence of what Margaret Mead noted. It will not take massive numbers to effect change. Indeed, Illinois's PA 100-0574 was the consequence of barely a handful of people. It changed the law in a state of more than twelve million citizens.

A principal problem with current law regarding postpartum illness is its arbitrariness. Sound and careful discussion presented by a small group of concerned citizens will result in consistency and fairness in dealing with the tragedies of mental illness. The laws of murder and child harm were written in past decades without an understanding of maternal mental illness, for many reasons discussed in this volume. Instead, they were written to deal with the evil and malignant heart of the criminal. The application of laws designed around the latter group is wrong for the former. Indeed, the consequences of this misapplication are obvious.

"Heather" plotted the death of several of her children in an altruistic filicide. She was untouched by the criminal laws, because she did not take the "substantial step" to fruition of the crime.[1] Carol Coronado was sentenced to serve three lifetimes in jail; that was the consequence of a single judge's decision in response to laws that just do not fit.[2] Cynthia Wachenheim's tragedy also demonstrates the arbitrariness and unfairness of current law.

While PA 100-0574 is a limited law, as a result change was initiated.[3] The first public defender's act was in Illinois and was limited to murder cases. The first law in the United States authorizing married women to control their own property came from Maine in 1821, *provided their husbands were incapacitated.* Countless examples exist of a very limited law's enactment that spread throughout the nation, after its application showed its merits. What begins as a law limited in scope is powerful in changing the tide and ultimately the state of the nation.

BECOMING AN EFFECTIVE ADVOCATE: A ROADMAP AND STEP-BY-STEP INSTRUCTIONS FOR NOVICE ADVOCATES

What can you do, and how do you begin the process? The tide is rising. You too can become a "village leader" and an effective advocate. You only need to learn your subject, prepare to meet your local and state representatives, and connect with the legislature. Introduce yourself and get to know your legislative leaders, educate them about perinatal issues, and explore how they can help. Make them aware that the US is far behind other developed countries in our laws concerning maternal mental illness. There is an overwhelming volume of literature on the subject matter that you can make available to them. Be familiar with your topic and the current literature to respond to the inevitable questions with citations. Present yourself and bring a briefcase full of books and articles on the issue supportive of your contentions. Be prepared and willing to obtain others if needed to address any questions or concerns.

Where do you go to get the references, recognizing that your budget does not allow you to purchase every single book? Any number of potentially favorable, even critically important, volumes are not found on the internet. Sometimes even articles on the internet whose copyrights have expired still require payment of a fee to obtain them.

If you have access to a university, medical school, or law school, start with its library. The staff there has access to countless journals, articles, and books. They are usually prepared to help you locate articles they have. They are usually willing to order those not available in their own library. Even if the university lacks a medical school, it doubtless has a psychology department. It likely also has an interlibrary loan agreement. Your state-supported community college or university likely has some provision for access by state citizens to their library. Often libraries are enhanced by interlibrary loan agreements.

A few minutes spent on your computer will help you locate your best contacts in the legislature. Google "legislative liaisons" in your state. Google "legislative advocacy training," and sign up for a course, online or, preferably, in person. More information on advocacy training is included and available in chapter 9.

During that course, take the opportunity to discuss your interests and concerns with other like-minded advocates or those in your professional organization. They will likely have suggestions and can provide support. If you have common interests, it is best to work together.

HOW TO MAKE YOUR PRESENTATION TO POTENTIAL SPONSORS IN YOUR LEGISLATURE

A written presentation should accompany any in-person meeting and should include, in three pages at most, a written prospectus. Request help writing the prospectus, especially if you are not an accomplished writer. Edit it with "fresh eyes" after letting it sit a few days; you may spot content and grammatical errors that way. Have a fellow advocate or experienced writer read it.

The written presentation should include the following:

1. An introductory paragraph of who, what, and two whys. This should convincingly establish the overwhelming support, including whatever group or organization is supportive of your effort (who), the change in the law (what), and why the change is desirable to the citizenry (first why) and why the effort to change the law (second why) will enhance the representative's career, speaking opportunities, and reelection chances.
2. A description of the illness including
   the state's attitude to mental illness;
   the specific mental illness involved; and
   the incidence or prevalence of that mental illness
3. Examples of persons who suffered
4. The arbitrariness of the resulting trial outcomes
5. The path to a solution
6. Cite responsible journals, and add an appendix available for further reading. These should be one-sentence summaries of a large number of high-quality references.

The proposed law must be written in simple, easy-to-understand language. If it is a change to an existing law, it should include the entire relevant portion of the current law. Include any deleted portions with strikethroughs. Highlight all additional language, and identify its placement. It is said to be easier to change an existing law than to create a new one.

THE CONTENT OF THE PROPOSED LAW

At the present time there are three legislative models to present. There is the successful Illinois law. There is a more comprehensive law modeled on the British Infanticide Act of 1938, which has been proposed in Massachusetts. Both are in the appendix of this book. There is also a conditional-release program in California, which is available in certain limited circumstances.

We would propose a fourth model, simple and clear, as an addition to any state's sentencing act:

> When a person, by reason of pregnancy, lactation, or childbirth becomes mentally disturbed, and her mental equilibrium had not yet returned as of the date of the alleged offense, the following applies: Even if that person is not adjudicated insane, any mandatory minimum sentence greater than "X" years for murder or "Y" years for any offense other than murder does not apply to any such person. This applies to any offense within a year of childbirth.

Remember, the proposed legislation may have to start with a limited rather than comprehensive law. You can introduce more far-reaching legislation at some future time.

Once you are sufficiently trained in advocating to the legislature, and have made copies of your compelling written prospectus, you will need the proper approach and the suitable initial contact. The model for the nature of the approach is multifold. You can combine as many approaches as are useful. Like all successful lobbyists, you must be personable, likeable, and courteous, yet determined.

If possible align your efforts with a respected sponsor and a professional organization. For partners in your effort, consider Marcé of North America (MONA), Postpartum Support International, the American Psychological Association, the American Psychiatric Association, the American Medical Association, and the American Bar Association. Do not forget state or local organizations or branches of the above. Be persistent. Assume more partners are better than fewer. Legal committees with their own agenda exist within each of these and other professional organizations. Find them. Let them refine your work. Use their help to hone your presentation to legislative representatives. In conjunction with the committees and in view of what you learned at your local advocacy workshop, decide whether to make "cold calls," cold visits, or scheduled appointments with legislators, or some combination of these approaches.

Be Positive and Persistent, and Don't Get Discouraged

Can you do this? Yes, you can. HB 1764 was written by Janet Jackson and Paula Sims. Jackson and Sims were inmates serving life sentences. They had severely limited opportunities to visit the law library, and minimal legal training. With only minor modifications, HB 1764 became the first postpartum criminal law in the nation.

How to Find a Sponsor for the Bill

No law gets enacted, or even presented to the legislature, without at least one "sponsor." Bipartisan support is demonstrated by having sponsors from both parties. This often is key. In getting a sponsor, your presentation is likely critical. This presentation must ultimately be made in person and must be accompanied with your written prospectus and persuasive argument. With that preparation completed, and having considered the suggestions of your fellow advocates and stakeholders for your proposed law or laws, it is time to identify the members to approach. There is no harm in providing alternatives in case one or another proposal is more likely to succeed. Consider the interests of particular members. There are bound to be many women's rights or mental health advocates in your legislature. Who are the legislative representatives that are particularly influential in getting affirmative votes and bills passed? Which legislators are particularly approachable? Identify the track record of those representatives who may be particularly influential. Did your advocacy training group identify anyone particularly useful in your endeavor? Which members would like this compelling issue for their reelection?

What About Potential Opponents?

Among your likely opponents, who can be neutralized or appeased? Perhaps a member who has voted against women's issues such as abortion legislation would like to prove he is not misogynistic. Remember it takes research and commitment. Keep trying. The history of law has countless examples of laws succeeding after several attempts. "You miss 100 percent of the shots you don't take."[4]

THE LEGISLATIVE PROCESS

Once you have your first sponsor, it is essential to consult with your sponsor to further work on the bill. Your sponsor will most likely be able to obtain others' support and identify others to cosponsor the bill.

It will likely become essential to gain a general knowledge of the legislative process. Each body of a typical bicameral legislature (house and senate) has numerous committees or subcommittees. For our purposes, the committees likely involved will have such names as "justice committee," "criminal law committee," "health and science committee," "medical science committee," and critically as well, "assignment committee" or "rules committee." One of the last two is a committee that decides which of the many committees will be assigned the fate of your law. You can have some influence in this selection by the title of the prospectus you write, together with the title of the proposed law. The title "A Law Respective of Mental Illness" is more likely to be sent to the "health and science committee" with some risk the committee may conclude it is improperly placed.

Unanimous approval by the committee greatly enhances the chance of the bill becoming law. It is more likely debate will occur in the subcommittee than the full house or senate. The sponsor may testify and may also identify experts to testify on behalf of the bill, even if the sponsor is not a member of the assigned committee.

A Long Day When You Present Expert Testimony on Your Bill

Expect at some point, you will be a speaker or at least an observer of the halls of the state legislature in action. The bill will be submitted for hearing and voting at the assigned committee on a given date with advance, but oftentimes limited, notice. The committee will have several bills before it on that date. The committee's time for their meeting may be scheduled for first thing in the morning, or at a particular time, or upon adjournment of its respective legislative body. You may desire to testify yourself, or to present another person as the expert witness. The bill's sponsor and your local branch of the professional organization that you have been working with can aid you. Be prepared for opposing lobbyists or witnesses. Most likely these opponents will be well known to the subcommittee. Your sponsor may be able to advise you on how best to prepare and respond to their objections. Contact the professional organizations you worked with to help you prepare your responses to any objections.

Before you present to the legislature or a subcommittee, you will likely have to submit your credentials, and possibly your request, in a specific format to a specific liaison. Oftentimes this process must be completed in advance.

If the vote by the subcommittee is favorable, the bill will be sent to the legislature (house or senate) to be reviewed through the usual process. Typically, this will involve routines such as scheduling, multiple "readings," and finally a vote. Then the bill gets sent according to the procedural rules to the other half of the legislative body, assigned to a subcommittee, reviewed, discussed, and voted upon. If the subcommittee recommends it, the bill will be sent according to the local procedural rules to the entire house or senate. At this final stage, there are legislative rules regarding readings, dates and times of presentation, arguments pro and con, and voting. Once the bill passes both houses, there are rules determining who must send the bill to the governor for his or her signature. At this point, congratulations are in order, as your bill just became a new state law.

Why Is It Important to Know These Rules?

Can you defer to the legislators and let the process play out? Not necessarily. What you don't know can hurt you. At each step, there are rules that must be followed. Overlooking deadlines and procedures may be disastrous.

Pitfalls that Might Have Caused Our Efforts to Fail

In the case of PA 100-0574, certain pitfalls were potentially fatal. The house created the bill. By the time it got to the senate, the calendar permitted only two of the three mandatory readings. Concerned this could result in the bill dying procedurally, we were watching the bill. We became involved again. We learned our best option was to have the bill presented at the "veto session" instead of the procedural default of having it appear at the next year's session of the legislature. The sponsor informed us of the options. She told us the law could be presented at the veto session, with the concurrence of the senate president and the senate sponsor. With help from Lewis, I prepared a new prospectus and hand-delivered it to the senate president's office. We persisted. We made sure that President John J. Cullerton actually received the prospectus. He came to the senate with our prospectus. The third reading, and a near-unanimous favorable vote, brought the bill to passage.

The bill had to be sent to the governor for his signature. With near-total unanimity, the only impediment to his signature was procedural. As the time for its submission approached expiration, we became concerned. We were afraid it was overlooked because of the adjournment of the legislature and the uncommon procedure used to pass it. A few phone calls resulted in the necessary action. The new ground-breaking bill was signed by the governor and became the first such law in our nation.

The following are excerpts from interviews with the Illinois House and Senate sponsors of HB 1764. Representative Linda Chapa LaVia is now the director of the Illinois Department of Veterans' Affairs. In 2019, she retired from the house to accept an appointment to the cabinet of Illinois governor J. B. Pritzker.

We wanted to discuss HB 1764, your part in the legislation that you sponsored that has become PA 100-0574, the first postpartum criminal law in the country.

I just played a small part; it wasn't a big part, it was a small part.

About three weeks ago we went to the prison to meet with Paula Sims and Janet Jackson who initially wrote up that legislation.

How are they doing? They [Sims and Jackson] are pretty powerful. I tried to explain that to them. It doesn't matter where you sit on the planet. You can be an advocate, and they showed that. They showed this can be done and duplicated throughout the United States within the female prison system with the right mix of people.

We have to find a willing heart to listen. Sometimes that's the hardest thing is just finding somebody just to listen, open minded, without judgment . . . and hear the story or the stories.

There is mistreatment of women that do that; they are like lepers. Like people want to kill them in their own tribe . . . in the prisons 'cause they look at people that kill babies in a different light. But once they're educated on what exactly transpired, then empathy opens up because it is a mental breakdown.

It is interesting because I did talk to my colleagues before we got into committee where you came and so gracefully spoke . . . and it seems to land on the female legislators a bit quicker and with more power.

We [women legislators] legislate totally differently. Women come in from the mother nurturer side. . . . Women create legislation to correct issues which mankind has placed on the system. Education, health care, senior citizen issues, posttraumatic stress, postpartum stress. . . . I noticed right off the bat when I came in the general assembly, probably because I was from the military, I was treated like one of the guys.

Women coming into the legislature are treated differently. We even raise funds differently. . . . You know even the way we conduct ourselves in the general assembly is just totally different. We are bridge builders. And we try to fix the issues within the system that are systemic. These are not going to make us rich but are going to allow generations to survive.

So that piece of legislation [HB 1764] that was tough because people on the other side of the table want to incarcerate our women because of the issues that they deal with, postpartum depression. They didn't like our legislation . . . they bartered . . . they would not oppose it, they would stay neutral, if [it was changed]. . . . I totally let it go because it's perfect the way it is.

It could be better. Right. But we took what we could get. It is a phenomenal start. Now we need . . . to have a campaign of awareness on what that looks like and how many women are incarcerated for that issue. . . . In all other countries . . . they don't punish the women, incarcerate them; they get the help they need.

Any way that you can work with other departments of social workers throughout the country to take this up . . . for the other forty-nine states.

The senate sponsor of HB 1764 was Senator Toi Hutchinson. Excerpts from her interview follow:

We wanted to discuss the new Illinois postpartum law PA 100-0574 which began as HB 1764, and your part as the sponsor in the senate. It is a groundbreaking law and the first postpartum criminal law in the country. How did you become the sponsor?

Sometimes when bills get involved in either chamber the originating sponsor will have an idea of who they want to carry it.

Linda [Representative Chapa LaVia] asked if it was something I wanted to work on because I do a lot in the niche of women's reproductive health. Because I'm in this arena, it's not uncommon for my house counterparts, my colleagues, or I call them my house sisters, to tap me on the shoulder and ask me to work on things. And I'm grateful for that. This topic evolved because we had a small group of women that it was impacting currently . . . and there was no relief for them.

Women in my position understand all the nuances and the difficulties with describing what postpartum psychosis is. And the term prior, postpartum depression didn't really give voice or show the full complexity of what psychosis actually is . . . and it wasn't really surprising to me that the law didn't answer it . . . this wasn't used in determining what a sentence should be.

The law had not caught up with what we understand psychologically and medically as to what this condition is, the time frame it is, and when it's gone, it's gone. It's not going to stay this way until the end of your life. It is a crisis born of acuteness, that happens quickly. . . . We know more now than we did when we would just call it baby blues or postpartum depression, which doesn't give the full color of what it is.

How I got involved . . . I was interested in the full spectrum of all that from the time you get pregnant to the time you deliver a baby and what happens in that year to two years after you have a baby and the response of the whole health care community to women and to women of color.

I'm a mother of three myself and I had two home births . . . my kids are now nineteen, twenty-one, and twenty-three. That's how I got involved, and I think the work is so compelling.

Every single decision in the midst of those things [the lifespan of a woman] is painted with politics. And a whole bunch of opinions . . . that don't belong there.

There are all sorts of folks listening when we don't want them to and all sorts of folks turning a deaf ear when we need them to hear. It's an incredible irony in the health and life of a woman.

From the time puberty starts until it literally ends, there is no part of our lives in that part of our bodies that is not tainted with all kinds of policy and political stuff. . . . It just does not exist in any respect, in any form, in a man's life.

And when you get to the point where the most tragic things of all can happen, and now you are talking about the mental health, the mental well-being, and the psychological health of the woman in question . . . all tied up into the politics . . . you have a woman who does something unthinkable to their child and it gets layered on top of all that.

I think that's why for so long we didn't attach the word *psychosis* to this because people really didn't understand how not only prevalent but acute it is to pin it down when you don't study it. You can't solve something you don't see. You can't fix something you don't understand, and we didn't study it. We don't talk about it, and when we do talk about it, it's only either in places [or in] cases where it's way extreme.

This small group of women who had no relief in the state of Illinois who were incarcerated for something that happened during an acute mental break phase of their lives, with no indication that they would ever be like that before or ever be like that again, just this small group of women . . . ended up being like the intersection of all kinds of really big policy debate . . . that is happening all across the country in multiple baskets.

My job as a senator [is] to give a voice to those who don't have one. . . . As I grew in my position, it became clear to me that I have an incredible opportunity to do more than just wish it was different. I have an incredible opportunity to make it different.

NOTES

1. More detail on the case of "Heather" is provided in appendix H.
2. I (Lewis) contacted numerous principal actors in this case. To distinguish this query from the merely or morbidly curious, I attached to the letter my article on postpartum illness in the *Champion* and our invitations to speak at the Biennial Perinatal Conference, Postpartum Support International, and the American Psychological Association. Aside from Coronado's defense counsel, only the judge responded. His response, he stated, was prohibited by judicial ethics.
3. See appendix C: "The Benefits and Limitations of Illinois's Postpartum Criminal Law PA 100-0574."
4. This statement is usually attributed to Wayne Gretzky.

Chapter Thirteen

Expert Witness Training and Educating Attorneys and Judges

> In no class of cases is the law as out of touch with reality, as it is with respect to mothers suffering from postpartum illnesses.
>
> —Barry M. Lewis, JD

The effort to provide legal training within Postpartum Support International (PSI) has been revived recently, perhaps inspired in part by the passage of PA 100-0574 in Illinois. Other states are proposing legislative initiatives concerning postpartum screening and treatment guidelines. 2020 Mom, Postpartum Support International, and MONA, the North American chapter of the International Marcé Society for Perinatal Mental Health, as well as other organizations, have partnered to help build a legal knowledge base by offering legal advocacy webinars[1] and breakout sessions at conferences. Their goal: working to change postpartum laws at the national and statewide level throughout the US.

LEGISLATIVE EFFORTS FOCUSED ON POSTPARTUM PSYCHOSIS

Attention has recently become focused on postpartum psychosis and the crimes committed by a small number of those mothers suffering from that severe maternal mental illness. Legislative efforts are making headway in changing outdated criminal laws in the United States. This highlights the need to develop a niche of mental health professionals who have reproductive-related expertise in perinatal mood and anxiety disorders and postpartum psychosis, and also possess a proficiency in forensics. There are currently only a handful of perinatal specialists who testify as expert witnesses in cases of infanticide and neonaticide. Training in this specialty area is badly needed and seriously overdue.

> Words spoken by a physician in 1783: "The insane are not held to be responsible for their actions."

It was more than two hundred years ago when a physician spoke to the British Medical Society about the need to inquire about and understand the state of mind of those responsible for the death of children. On July 14, 1783, William Hunter, MD, FRS, spoke these words to the members of the British Medical Society:

> In those unhappy cases of the death of . . . children, as is every action indeed that is either criminal or suspicious, reason and justice demand an enquiry into all the circumstances; and particularly to find out from what views and motives the act proceeded. For, as nothing can be so criminal but that circumstances might be added by the imagination to make it worse; so nothing can be conceived so wicked and offensive to the feelings of a good mind, as not to be somewhat softened or extenuated by circumstances and motives. In making up a just estimate of any human action, much will depend on the state of the agent's mind at the time; and therefore the laws of all countries make ample allowance for insanity. The insane are not held to be responsible for their actions.[2]

Still today we struggle to understand or accept the concept of insanity as a defense. "Yet, many infanticides are committed *not* by women intent on callously ridding themselves of their children but rather by women who are experiencing a psychosis precipitated by gross postpartum mental illness."[3]

A 2018 journal article on filicide in the twenty-first century and the 2019 topic of the Marcé Society's special edition reported,

> [Margaret] Spinelli recounts her work providing expert testimony for women who committed neonaticide and the realization that, in the USA, the definition of insanity used by the criminal justice system was established in 1843. Spinelli makes the case that this reliance on outdated notions about mental health, added to the lack of clarity of the *DSM*, are systematically disadvantaging women who are severely mentally ill and facing a murder charge.[4]

In the US, the public and those attorneys and judges in the judicial system are much more likely to conclude that the motives for this type of criminal behavior are a consequence of an evil or wicked person, than someone mentally ill. This leads to harsh sentences. In England and many other countries, prosecution under *specific statutes* has resulted in lenient sentencing or the defendant being charged with a lesser crime. "The British statute has been replicated in slightly varying forms in at least 22 nations around the world. . . . Many nations have statutes specific to infanticide; all but one of these make infanticide a less severe crime than ordinary homicide (Oberman 1996)."[5]

THE CHALLENGE OF THE DEFENSE ATTORNEY IN CRIMINAL CASES

Judith Macfarlane, JD, describes the current guideline in the US for the insanity defense in cases of infanticide or neonaticide for a mentally ill mother. Macfarlane reports,

> A woman accused of killing her newborn or infant is typically charged with some gradation of homicide. All homicide statutes contain a criminal intent requirement (*mens rea*) that the prosecution must prove beyond a reasonable doubt in order to obtain a conviction. . . . Depending on the facts of her case, her defense attorney may raise a number of defenses, such as involuntary act, diminished capacity, or insanity, in fighting the prosecution's intentionality claim. These defenses are used to show that at the time of the killing, the woman did not possess the level of intent to kill specified by the statute under which she is prosecuted . . . because her mental facilities were undermined by mental illness, namely a postpartum mental disorder.[6]

Perinatal Forensic Experts Face the Challenge of an Unsympathetic Justice System and Cross-Examination in the Criminal Courts

The difficulties for the legal defense team in these criminal cases of maternal mental illness are described by Spinelli: "Scant literature is available for the mental health professional who is facing the challenges of the criminal court system or for the attorney who must understand the implications of psychiatric diagnoses as defenses for infanticide and neonaticide."[7] Macfarlane emphasizes, "In reviewing the facts of any given case of infanticide or neonaticide, a defense attorney must take extreme care to ascertain whether his or her client was suffering from any mental illness at the time of the killing so that he or she may consider asserting a suitable defense to the crime."[8] Furthermore, the limited number of forensic and psychiatric experts who possess expertise in postpartum psychiatric syndromes adds to the challenge, leading to problems with testimony and cross-examination.

The Need for Experts to Educate the Attorneys and Judges

In order to, as stated above, "ascertain whether his or her client was suffering from any mental illness" at the time of the crime, it is imperative that the defense attorney has extensive knowledge of postpartum mental illnesses.

A psychiatric evaluation in the case of an Illinois woman currently incarcerated for the death of her child during the postpartum period cleverly inserted crucial educational information about psychosis in her report to educate the woman's attorney and the judge assigned to the case (it is also possible to insert information about maternal mental illness into an affidavit, in order to educate the presiding judge about the relationship of postpartum disorders to a specific case). In order to establish a case for altruistic filicide, the evaluating psychiatrist included a section in the body of the report on delusions and bipolar disorder, stating,

> Religious preoccupations, delusion and grandiose fantasies that one can save the afflicted through one's benevolent, godly actions can be symptoms of bipolar disorder. Bipolar disorder was previously referred to as manic depression. It has historically been recognized as an incurable but highly treatable disease, with appropriate medications and psychotherapy. A hallmark of bipolar illness is mood cycling from very depressed, despondent, tearful and hopeless states (depression) to elevated, irritable, impulsive, and highly energized states (mania). Extremely poor judgment, disorganization, racing thoughts, spending sprees, risk-taking behavior, paranoia and grandiose thoughts may accompany mania. Psychosis, or a derangement in one's ability to accurately perceive reality, can accompany either state.[9]

The Uniqueness of Maternal Mental Illness, Evaluation and Expert Testimony

In chapters 7 and 8, we discuss "the uniqueness of maternal mental illnesses" such as perinatal (pregnancy and postpartum) depression and psychosis. It is critical to emphasize the distinctive attributes of these illnesses to attorneys and judges in trials and sentencing. These psychiatric illnesses need to be distinguished from the common understanding of depression, as used by the public, jurors, attorneys, and judges.

Louis Victor Marcé, James Hamilton, and many other early pioneers of this specialized field of maternal mental illness indicate there is "compelling evidence that postpartum psychiatric illness is a distinct entity, or group of entities" and that "many unique qualities of postpartum illness reflect deficits and imbalances in the endocrine system, as this system moves rapidly from the hyperactivity of pregnancy down to, and sometimes beyond, the levels of the nonpregnant state. Superimposed upon, but secondary to, the organic factors are stresses that are unique to the responsibilities and the anxieties of new motherhood."[10]

It is crucial that expert witnesses are proficient in perinatal mental illness. Otherwise some *may not* understand the unique symptoms of these psychiatric illnesses, a product of the physiological events of the reproductive process.[11] In the scope of our book we were not able to cover the extensive amount of new scientific research that demonstrates the importance of neurobiology, genetics, and the immune system as precipitants on maternal mental illnesses such as perinatal depression and psychosis. However, we strongly encourage expert witnesses to become familiar with that body of knowledge to explain the basis of maternal mental illness to attorneys, judges, and juries. An extensive background in the treatment of perinatal mental illnesses, including a certification of expertise in this specialty, will do much to deflect cross-examination and increase the acceptance of the expert's testimony.

In our earlier chapters, we discussed the works of psychiatrists Edward A. Strecker and Franklin G. Ebaugh, and others[12] who provided support for "the doctrine that psychiatric illnesses after childbirth have little or no relationship to the physiological events of the puerperium."[13] It was this attitude that influenced psychiatry in the first through the third editions of the *Diagnostic and Statistical Manual of Mental Disorders* (*DSM*), wherein the word "postpartum and its synonyms were expunged from the official diagnostic terminology."[14] This psychiatric policy was expressed in the *DSM-III* with the following statement: "There is no compelling evidence that postpartum psychosis is a distinct entity."[15] It continues to be an uphill battle to distinguish perinatal psychiatric illnesses in each edition of the *DSM*, which finally added a peripartum specifier to *DSM* editions IV and 5.

An example of the devastating consequences of the *DSM*'s refusal to recognize perinatal illness is not allowing a defendant to use psychiatric evidence, expert testimony, or a psychological summary report in the 2003 case *People of the State of Illinois v. Hulitt* (99 CR 16597). In the public records of the transcripts, the state made a motion to bar the testimony of an expert witness because "as far as the symptoms of antepartum and post-partum depression, they are the basic symptoms of depression. It's not something that an average person can also not understand. It's sadness, guilt, anxiety, tiredness." The state's prosecutor further justified this position: "If the defendant got up on the stand and testified to all of these things, the jury would be able to understand that just as well as if a doctor did."

It is evident that the state's attorney and judge were not aware of the uniqueness of postpartum psychiatric illnesses and thus regarded it as any other depression, even indicating that everyone knows what depression is. *This is absolutely wrong*. Postpartum depression and psychosis are unique illnesses, and professionals who specialize in these illnesses now receive specialized training and need to pass a certification exam demonstrating proficiency. The result of assuming "everyone knows what depression is" was that evidence was barred from trial; the judge determined that the testimony of the medical expert as well as his report would not be allowed to be presented to the jury.

It is also an example of why it is critical that the "medical expert" possess specialization in perinatal psychiatric illnesses, as the state in the above-mentioned case maintained the expert possessed no special knowledge and therefore should be barred from testifying. This was explicitly stated by the prosecutor in the public records:

> Judge, first of all, we believe that the doctor should not be allowed to testify about anything in regards to this case because, first of all, what he is testifying to or what his proffer is not something that's beyond the scope of what most people could understand. . . . If you read through this report, there's absolutely nothing in here that indicates any sort of expertise at all, expert opinion on anything.[16]

The other compelling aspect of the Hulitt case is this: In 2003 antenatal depression was not recognized in the *DSM-IV*. The state used the lack of an official diagnostic terminology in the *DSM* to invalidate the psychiatric state of the defendant. As stated in the records, "And I understand post-partum depression is certainly a recognized mental disorder, but antenatal depression is not."

Science has progressed since 2003. We now understand the continuum of maternal psychiatric disorders that often begin in the antepartum period and progressively worsen following delivery. Hormones plummet following childbirth, causing further deterioration of the mother's mental state. In fact, antepartum depression and anxiety disorders are considered significant risk factors, along with family genetics for postpartum psychiatric illnesses. However, this is not something attorneys, judges, and jurors are aware of and exemplifies the importance of educating legal professionals.

Critical Aspects Needed by Experts

Sometimes in retrospect we learn what is important for the expert to include in the report and testimony, by finding out what was problematic. In the Hulitt case, the expert's opinion was discounted for various reasons, including the following: The expert failed to report what records he had reviewed. He never reviewed or attempted to obtain any psychiatric or medical records of the defendant's siblings, although he indicated other relatives reported to him that they had psychiatric problems. The most concerning and damaging criticisms were that the expert did not quote the defendant's own description of her symptoms at the time of the offense. Instead, he only described her behavior changes reported by distant relatives and her ex-boyfriend. He did not use any objective measures or tests to validate her mental state. Finally, his conclusions were unclear. It made it difficult for the defendant to receive an insanity defense: he summarized, while he believed she had postpartum depression, he does not believe she fit the guilty but mentally ill or the insanity defense.[17]

The Need for a Prompt Evaluation

The sooner the medical expert is able to evaluate the defendant, the better. As postpartum psychosis waxes and wanes, symptoms may begin to remit with time and with the use of psychotropic medications. This is problematic in the defense of these women. The absence of observable symptoms at the time of the examination is grist for the cross-examiner's mill. A medical expert may see a very different presentation of the defendant as time passes. A woman who has been incarcerated for months or years may no longer resemble the woman who committed the crime.

The defense of a mother who has been charged with taking the life of her child or children depends on noting her symptoms and clinical presentation and diagnosis at the time of the offense, or as close to that time as possible. In many of the sensationalized cases, the experts for the defense and the state evaluated the woman months or even years later. The defendant has often been on some psychotropic medications for a period of time and therefore is no longer floridly psychotic. The judge and jury are also seeing a different woman than the woman who committed the crime. It is up to the expert to present the "then and now" difference as clearly and descriptively as possible. The expert must portray the picture of the woman who committed the crime accurately and in as much detail as possible for the judge and jury.

An example of this "then and now" visual image is apparent in the film footage and photographs of Andrea Yates of Texas. In the photos of Andrea at the time of her arrest, she exhibited a disheveled look and an unresponsive faraway stare, whereas when she was on trial, she resembled a completely different woman after being on psychotropic medication.

There are laws in many states requiring the videotaping of police questioning, especially regarding homicide cases. These videotapes are useful for the defense, not just the prosecution. Behavior that is observable on the video can support the defense. The expert witness can explain behavior the lay person or legal professional would likely overlook. For example, Andrea Yates was videotaped early on while still symptomatic. The professional witness can note her rigid posture and faraway stare are common in those with mental illness and often observed when individuals are responding to command hallucinations or voices in their head.

An Expert Must Go to the Prison and Evaluate the Defendant

Even in our own work helping the defense team in the resentencing hearing of the women incarcerated in Illinois, we have found it is necessary to interview the incarcerated women in person at Logan prison. Other advocates will likely need to do the same. We have added in the appendix of our book a copy of our letter to gain permission to interview, evaluate, and tape the defendants.[18] Use this as a sample or make alterations as you see fit when requesting visitation. You will likely need advance permission from the warden's office to visit an inmate and to bring any form of electronics into the prison.

A Request for Guidance from Prominent Perinatal Experts Doing Forensic Work

We have drawn on the expertise of Dr. Diana Lynn Barnes, a prominent expert witness who has experience in testifying in postpartum criminal cases in the US. Barnes generously agreed to provide some insights, as well as recommendations and guidelines, for those perinatal professionals who will testify and be faced with cross-examination.

As a perinatal and forensic expert, Barnes's contribution follows:

> The courtroom presents an intellectual challenge for the women's reproductive mental health expert given that the court's assertions about insanity bear almost no resemblance to what we, as clinicians, understand to be true about psychosis. In addition, while there are consistent themes that run through most cases, no two cases are exactly alike. Consequently, there is a frequent clash between mental health and the criminal justice system.
>
> Attorneys usually initiate a call to a woman's reproductive mental health expert because they sense that maternal mental illness may be at issue in a critical incident where a mother and her baby/children are involved. As an expert, I am generally asked to establish a woman's state of mind at the time of the commission of the act. Because a woman's reproductive history is so delicately intertwined with her mental health, creating a reproductive timeline, especially when there has been more than one child, becomes essential in explaining the cumulative impact of reproductive events on mental state and mood. Because psychosocial history, namely, early trauma, has an extraordinary effect on women's moods during the childbearing years, an in-depth and detailed accounting of a woman's life narrative may also act as mitigation during sentencing given our knowledge about the neurobiological effects of trauma on cognition as well as on mental illness. Particularly in cases of altruistic filicide, where a mother takes

the life of her child believing it is in the child's best interests, testifying to the jury about her own history of trauma is crucial. Because women who kill their babies are inevitably demonized, sharing her story through direct examination is critical in order to humanize her. In doing so, the fact of her illness becomes more obvious. Your evaluation of the young woman who is being charged and your interviews with any relevant family members or friends are part of that narrative. Every document that exists as part of overall discovery and is made available to the expert is essential in crafting the story of a woman's downward spiral. That includes, but is certainly not limited to, police reports which demonstrate observable behaviors at the scene, psychosocial histories, obstetric records, additional medical records including mental health records from the jail where she is incarcerated along with any other evaluations and assessments are important as you complete a report which is generally asked of the expert, particularly in cases where sanity is being argued.

The mental disease or defect that must exist in order to assert insanity as a defense must also exist in the *Diagnostic and Statistical Manual of Mental Disorders* (*DSM-5*). Postpartum psychosis is not recognized as a distinct category of mood disorder. Pregnancy denial and neonaticide also does not exist as an officially recognized disorder. As a result, the expert is tasked with finding a diagnosis that fits the particular symptoms, circumstances, and actions of the mother who is generally charged with intentional murder. With regard to an insanity defense, the M'Naghten statute, commonly referred to as the "right and wrong test," is commonly used to determine a woman's culpability. In cases of infanticide, postpartum psychosis is commonly described as a bipolar I disorder with psychotic features with peripartum onset. Diagnoses of major depression with psychotic features, with the peripartum specifier, schizophrenia, or schizoaffective disorder can also be used. With respect to pregnancy denial, depersonalization disorder, or in certain cases, a brief psychotic disorder can be used to explain a woman's inability to control her own actions because of her mental state.[19]

Another perinatal mental health professional who has been making a significant impact in conducting research and has gained prominence in the perinatal expert witness field is Canadian psychologist Dr. Gina Wong. Her research findings from her qualitative investigation into the experience of becoming an expert witness in infanticide and filicide cases in Canada and the United States were presented at the 2019 Postpartum Support International Conference in Portland, Oregon. Her preliminary results are provided, as well as some information on competency for expert witness testimony. These competency areas underlie the impetus of a forthcoming book that is coedited by Dr. Wong and George Parnham, who was the defense attorney for Andrea Yates. Results of Wong's study will be published in their book in 2020.[20]

As a perinatal and forensic expert, Dr. Wong's preliminary results found novice and veteran expert witnesses, as defined by the number of maternal filicide cases they have participated in, experienced a sense of satisfaction and meaning in their role and participation in these cases. Participants were asked to share their most memorable moments working with these cases, the impact on their personal lives, if any, and how they prepared for their role as an expert witness. They were queried about their comfort level being in the media when they were involved in high-profile cases.

The research "expert witness" subjects reported on the most challenging and rewarding aspects of this work. Specific competency areas were identified for training professionals interested in becoming a maternal mental health expert witness. All participants in the study had formal training in one or more forensic areas; they were either self-taught or sought out mentorship in the other competency areas. Some of the participants reported that they needed greater competency in the area of maternal mental health. Veteran expert witnesses such as forensic psychologists or psychiatrists indicated maternal mental health awareness and training is paramount in the competency of an expert witness in maternal filicide cases.

Podcasts, Webinars, and Educational Seminars to Learn about Perinatal Mental Illness

Learn from experts and build your knowledge base by listening to podcasts and webinars, and by attending skill-building seminars. The podcast *Mom and Mind* with Dr. Kat has several informative programs, including one with us.[21] Among the other excellent podcasts, see podcast 150: "Postpartum Psychosis and the Law" with Parnham.[22] We highly recommend you listen to these podcasts to get some pointers for all interested in working or advocating in the area of maternal mental illness and criminal law. As Dr. Kat states, postpartum psychosis is "a sensitive topic but the more we understand, the better foundation we have for advocacy."

The Beginnings of an Educational Skill-Building Seminar

Postpartum Support International and other organizations were receiving an increasing number of requests to provide information to assist attorneys and educate judges when legal charges were brought up in criminal cases related to postpartum depression and psychosis. Years before the passage of the new Illinois law was even contemplated, there was evidence within the perinatal professional community of the growing need to educate attorneys, judges, and medical and mental health experts about perinatal illnesses. In October 2015, I (Feingold) received a request from Ann Smith, the president of Postpartum Support International. PSI was creating an educational seminar, "Maternal Mental Illness and the Criminal Justice System." Smith requested that I present at that seminar. The main purpose of the event was to train and develop educational skills for attorneys, judges, and expert witnesses and other perinatal experts. Along with the presentations, a documentary film-maker attended to record and produce an educational video for legal training purposes.

Presenters included attorney George Parnham,[23] Margaret Spinelli, MD,[24] Shoshana Bennett, PhD, and others with specialized knowledge and skills in legal and forensic matters. I was requested to describe my testimony to the prison review board in the case of Debra Gindorf for executive clemency in 2002. In 2009 Gindorf finally received clemency from Illinois governor Pat Quinn after serving twenty-four years in prison for the deaths of her two children in a postpartum altruistic filicide in 1985.

What follows is the Gindorf case and my narrative of the experience testifying in front of the prison review board that was presented at that PSI seminar.

Rough Times: The Story of Debra Gindorf

As I wait for my turn to speak, I look around the crowded courtroom, filled with spectators, some supporters of Debra, a few journalists, and others there to present petitions on behalf of other prisoners.

Debra is not there, nor are any other prisoners.

I am an expert witness, there to testify on her behalf. My heart is beating against my chest, as I confess silently, we have more in common than I want to openly admit, and yet we have never met.

"Dr. Feingold, please stand up and come forward to take the oath, we are ready to hear your testimony."

Obediently, I comply. I raise my hand to take the oath, and look up at the thirteen-member prison review board sitting several feet higher than me, appointed to decide the continuing fate of Debra Gindorf.

"Do you swear to tell the truth, the whole truth, and nothing but the truth so help you God?"

"I do."

The words of Kathleen Hamill, the assistant state defense attorney who has represented Debra since her trial, ring true.

"The board members will be mostly male. Just so you know, they are hardened to sob stories, and not what you would consider a bleeding-heart crowd."

I stand before the largely male judicial board hoping to influence them to make a favorable recommendation to Governor Ryan for a pardon.

My mind quickly reviews the facts of the case that I studied extensively as I prepared for this day.

Debra was only twenty years old at the time of the event in 1985. She had reported severe depression after the birth of her first child but assumed it was because of the violence she endured by her abusive, alcoholic husband.

After Christina's birth, Debra became pregnant again but miscarried following a beating by her husband.

She eventually divorced her husband on grounds of physical cruelty, after she became pregnant a third time with her son.

Alone with no job, no car, no phone. and lacking a support network of family or friends, her depression worsened. and she started hearing voices and had uncontrollable crying spells.

At that time, experts were of the same opinion that she was a depressed and battered wife but couldn't agree what was wrong with her when she attempted to kill herself and then decided to kill the children as well.

Her attorney Hamill said, "She saw death as a mode of transportation to heaven. They would all be together in heaven. In a weird, warped way, this was something she thought she was doing for her children."

In her depressed, psychotic state, she swallowed lethal doses of alcohol and sleeping pills but worried about her children when they woke up crying. So, she spiked formula and juice with crushed sleeping pills and got into bed with her children.

During the night Debra vomited part of the medication and woke the next day to find the children dead. She spent the next several hours trying various ways to kill herself, cutting herself and placing her head in the old gas stove in her tiny apartment.

After a time, the desperate, hopeless Debra finally walked the few blocks to the Zion Police Department and turned herself in.

In 1986, the twenty-year-old Gindorf was found guilty but mentally ill of a double homicide in Lake County, Illinois, which led to her being sentenced to the mandatory *life in prison without parole*.

At that time, I had been living only thirty minutes away from Debra, but I might have easily been living on the other side of the world, as our lives were so different. I was married and living in the suburbs, had a three-year-old daughter, and was finishing my first year of a graduate program toward a doctorate in clinical psychology.

I had no idea at that time that our paths would merge and that we would eventually share an experience of postpartum hell.

My mind replays the memories of my own postpartum experience and the agony of despair and hopelessness, intense anxiety, and depression that went on for months after my son was born.

Now, I visibly shudder and feel myself breaking into a sweat, aware that I could have been *that woman* who lost her sanity and ended up in prison. My thoughts drift to the quote "There but for the grace of God, go I."

I remember the torment of sleeplessness for weeks on end as I laid awake shaking, with racing, scary thoughts of never getting well, while my infant son was sleeping peacefully in his crib.

At times, I considered taking my own life, as I was filled with fears that I would never be back to myself, nor capable of taking care of my own children, much less returning to my work helping others as a psychologist at the VA and Naval Hospital where I was employed.

But in contrast to Debra, I was one of the lucky ones, as I used my resources as well as friends, family, and colleagues to find the help I needed and eventually recovered.

When I received the call from Hamill in 2002, I had been specializing in the treatment of perinatal depression for nine years, having left the military environment to help other women with maternal mental illness, a mission that was dear to my heart after my own gut-wrenching experience. The memories of the past are temporarily interrupted.

My mind returns to the courtroom. I gaze up at the thirteen members on the prisoner review board, appointed with the task of reviewing Debra's petition. I'm hoping for compassion and a plea for mercy. This is Debra's third request to the governor of Illinois.

The hearing is brief, only about thirty minutes or less. It consisted of her attorney opening with a summary of the grounds for requesting clemency.

Then, Carol Blocker, the advocate and mother of Melanie Blocker Stokes, who jumped from a Chicago high rise hotel in 2001, walked up to the stand and spoke briefly about the tragedy of untreated postpartum illness that resulted in the death of her own daughter.

My own testimony was only ten minutes at most. I described the prevalence and the differences between the various postpartum mood disorders. Most of my time testifying was spent responding to questions and clarifying misconceptions and myths about postpartum mental disorders.

"What would happen if she was released and gets pregnant or if she has other children? Could she do this again?"

"Debra did not plan to have any more children, and toward that end, she has even volunteered sterilization."

"Did she have any history of violence?" (I take a breath, to avoid showing my irritation and frustration.)

"No, she had no criminal history prior to the convictions of homicide that were a direct consequence of her postpartum mental disorder." I informed them, "These are temporary psychiatric illnesses connected to childbirth."

A few members wanted clarification on the distinction between women who abuse their children and how that is different from women with postpartum mental illness.

I explain that perinatal mood disorders are a group of mental disorders surrounding childbirth that can include depression, severe anxiety, panic attacks, obsessive-compulsive disorder, and for some women the rare and severe postpartum psychosis. Even the most loving mothers can be affected, as it is largely hormonal and biochemical in nature, although other psychological and social stressors contribute to the likelihood of a woman being affected.

Several members approached after the hearing. They were friendly and seemed grateful for the understanding and clarification of their concerns. They gave the overall impression that they would be supporting a recommendation to the governor for a pardon.

Then we waited and waited and waited for some word from the governor.

Although we all anticipated a favorable recommendation, Debra was unfortunately not released at this time.

Years passed without any word, and I'm embarrassed to admit that I forgot about Debra's plight after a while. Despite the good intentions of her attorneys and others there at her clemency hearing, we all eventually returned to our own lives, while Debra remained incarcerated.

It was seven years after I testified as an expert witness, on a day not much different than any other. I was in my Skokie office with a full day planned seeing patients for therapy. At one point, while I waited for my next patient to arrive as I characteristically do, I went on my computer to scan the online news. Something caught my eye: a brief reference tucked in between other news stories, apparently not very important or newsworthy. Did I imagine it?

The sound of a buzzer went off, letting me know that my patient had arrived. My heart pounded as I scanned the online paper.

I needed to see if it was true. It took a few more seconds, but I found it: "Governor Pat Quinn finally releases Gindorf."

It was hard to keep my mind focused during my session. But as soon as it was lunchtime, I scoured the paper for more information.

The *Chicago Tribune* wrote: "She was sentenced to life in prison without the possibility of parole in 1986. But that sentence was a miscarriage of justice that needed a humanitarian touch to correct given the justice system's poor understanding of post-partum illness at that time."[25]

Sadly, although Debra's mental illness was temporary, she spent twenty-four years at Dwight Correctional Facility and then eventually, at age forty-five, was released by Governor Quinn, who commuted her life sentence to forty-eight years. With credit for good conduct, she qualified for immediate release on parole after serving more than two decades.

I wish I could inspire the reader with a happy ending.

From a mental health perspective, in 1985 there was a general lack of knowledge that surrounded postpartum disorders. This led to lack of agreement by the experts about what was wrong with Debra, as well as contributed to her failure to get adequate diagnosis and treatment.

After hearing about Debra's release, I made contact with the *Chicago Tribune* reporter who covered her story. He told me, once released, Debra's life again fell on rough times.

She had a hard time finding work because she had to register as a danger to children since her crime was not expunged. She again appealed to Governor Quinn for a pardon but never got it.

The reporter said that Debra sometimes misses the routine and security of prison, as it was the life she had known for many of her adult years.

As I hang up the phone, after thanking him for the update, I glance at my computer and notice a few inspirational quotes have appeared in my email feed.

One quote caught my eye by John Bradshaw, the sixteenth-century English evangelical preacher, "There but for the grace of God, go I."[26]

NOTES

1. Susan B. Feingold and Barry M. Lewis, "Legal Issues and Advocacy in Perinatal Mood Disorders: Innovation Awards Webinar for 2020 Moms" (recording), Postpartum Support International, February 12, 2019.
2. Judith Macfarlane, "Criminal Defense in Cases of Infanticide and Neonaticide," in *Infanticide: Psychosocial and Legal Perspectives on Mothers Who Kill*, ed. M. Spinelli, 133–66 (Washington, DC: American Psychiatric Publishing, 2003), 133.
3. Ibid, 134.
4. C. Klier, J. Fisher, P. Chandra, and M. Spinelli, "Filicide Research in the Twenty-First Century," *Archives of Women's Mental Health* 22, no. 1 (2018): 136.
5. M. Oberman, "A Brief History of Infanticide and the Law," in *Infanticide: Psychosocial and Legal Perspectives on Mothers Who Kill*, ed. M. Spinelli (Washington, DC: American Psychiatric Publishing, 2003), 9. Note: The number has by now increased to approximately thirty countries.
6. Macfarlane, "Criminal Defense," 134.
7. Spinelli, *Infanticide*, xvi.
8. Macfarlane, "Criminal Defense," 134.
9. L. Rone, "Psychiatric Evaluation Report," Submitted in the Circuit Court of Cook County, 2011.
10. Ibid.
11. James A. Hamilton and Patricia Neel Harberger, eds., "The Issue of Unique Qualities," in *Postpartum Psychiatric Illness: A Picture Puzzle* (Philadelphia: University of Pennsylvania Press, 1992).

12. D. A. Boyd Jr. was prominent in American psychiatry in the 1950s and has been cited as misquoting Marcé; he presented a position exactly opposite of what Marcé really held (Hamilton and Harberger, "Issue of Unique Qualities").

13. Hamilton and Harberger, "Issue of Unique Qualities," 18.

14. Ibid.

15. American Psychiatric Association, *Diagnostic and Statistical Manual of Mental Disorders*, 3th ed. (*DSM-III*) (Arlington, VA: American Psychiatric Publishing, 1980), 373; Hamilton and Harberger, "Issue of Unique Qualities."

16. State of Illinois, County of Cook, *People v. Hulitt*, 361 Ill. App. 3d 634, 638–39 (1st District, 2005).

17. The parallel between Hulitt and Sims is remarkable. In Hulitt, the attorneys were aware of the deficiencies but were helpless to correct them, likely because of budgetary obstacles in obtaining an expert with perinatal expertise. In Sims, the attorney was aware of the issue but did not act upon it in any discernable way. We hope attention to the issues of postpartum and the law will prevent such a travesty of justice from ever occurring again.

18. See appendix I for a sample letter when requesting visitation.

19. Diana Lynn Barnes, contribution to this manuscript, 2019.

20. Gina Wong and George Parnham, eds., *Infanticide and Filicide: Foundations of Maternal Mental Health Forensics* (Washington, DC: American Psychiatric Publishing, 2020); we have contributed a chapter for that book.

21. Katayune Kaeni, Susan Feingold, and Barry Lewis, "157: Postpartum Psychosis, Changing the Law, Advocating for Women," *Mom and Mind* (podcast), August 5, 2019, http://momandmind.libsyn.com.

22. Katayune Kaeni and George Parnham, "150: Postpartum Psychosis and the Law," *Mom and Mind* (podcast), May 20, 2019, https://drkaeni.com.

23. Parnham was the defense attorney in the infamous 2001 Texas case of Andrea Yates, who killed her five children in a psychotic episode.

24. Spinelli, a psychiatrist and professor at Columbia University of New York, had served as an expert witness in a multitude of cases of postpartum psychosis.

25. Eric Zorn, "Quinn Brave Where Blago Was Cowardly—Announces He Will Release Debra Gindorf," *Chicago Tribune*, May 1, 2009.

26. S. B. Feingold, "Rough Times: The Story of Debra Gindorf," Maternal Mental Illness and Criminal Justice Seminar, Postpartum Support International, New Jersey, November 2015.

Chapter Fourteen

Maternal and Infant Mortality Linked to Postpartum Illness

> An American mom today is 50 percent more likely to die in childbirth than her own mother was.
>
> —Neel Shah, obstetrician

How many maternal or infant deaths in the US are related to a mother who has a mental illness such as postpartum depression or postpartum psychosis? The Centers for Disease Control and Prevention (CDC) national pregnancy-related mortality surveillance service was established thirty-three years ago. Despite that, there are still no statistics stating how many pregnant and postpartum women were suffering with maternal mental illness at the time of their death. Nor are there statistics classifying maternal death related to suicide, or infant death due to infanticide or neonaticide.

PREGNANCY-RELATED MORTALITY RATES IN THE US

Recently published maternal, infant, and pregnancy-related mortality rates in the US are a cause for concern. There is alarm and trepidation as the numbers have been rising for decades, particularly among black women. The CDC states, "Black and American Indian/Alaska Native women were about 3 times as likely to die from a pregnancy-related cause as White women."[1] Neel Shah, an obstetrician at Harvard Medical School, reports a frightening statistic: "An American mom today is 50 percent more likely to die in childbirth than her own mother was." A report by the CDC affirms that about seven hundred women die each year as a result of pregnancy or delivery complications. As stated, more US women are dying from pregnancy-related causes, and more than half of those are preventable.[2] The CDC relates that about one-third of deaths happen during pregnancy, a third were during or within a week of delivery, and the rest were in the first postpartum year.[3]

THE DISCREPANCY IN MATERNAL MORTALITY BETWEEN THE US AND OTHER COUNTRIES

The CDC report released May 7, 2019, indicated that the US rates are soaring (and now in double digits) compared to other countries (in single digits). The World Health Organization (WHO) states that globally maternal mortality fell 44 percent between 1990 and 2015. Yet nationally, maternal mortality is up to a rate of 26.4 out of every one hundred thousand live births. That is a significant increase from a quarter century ago. Despite more technological advances in medicine and obstetrics, US women, and black women in particular, are faced with dread at the frightening thought (and perhaps reality) that *childbirth may lead to their death*. Organizations like the American College of Obstetricians and Gynecologists (ACOG) and the CDC are attributing a combination of factors, such as high C-section rates, high rates of obesity, heart-related problems, diabetes, and racial bias causing a lack of adequate prenatal care and less attention to complaints by black and minority women.[4]

NPR and ProPublica teamed up for a six-month investigation on maternal mortality in the US with the following findings:[5]

- More American women are dying of pregnancy-related complications than in any other developed country. Only in the US has the rate of women who die been rising.
- There's a hodgepodge of hospital protocols for dealing with potentially fatal complications, allowing for treatable complications to become lethal.
- Hospitals—including those with intensive care units for newborns—can be woefully unprepared for a maternal emergency.
- Federal and state funding show only 6 percent of block grants for "maternal and child health" actually go to the health of mothers.
- In the US some doctors entering the growing specialty of maternal-fetal medicine were able to complete that training without ever spending time in a labor-delivery unit.

In 2017, an NPR special series reported,

> American women are more than three times as likely as Canadian women to die in the maternal period (defined by the Centers for Disease Control as the start of pregnancy to one year after delivery or termination), and six times as likely

> to die as Scandinavians. In every other wealthy country, and many less affluent ones, maternal mortality rates have fallen. In Great Britain, the journal *Lancet* recently noted, the rate has declined so dramatically that "a man is more likely to die while his partner is pregnant than she is." But in the US, maternal deaths increased in the years from 2000 to 2014.[6]

In countries such as the UK, Germany, France, Finland, Canada, Portugal, the Netherlands, Spain, Ireland, Sweden, Australia, Finland, Italy, and Denmark, maternal mortality rates are within a single digit. Compare that with the US mortality rate of 26.4.[7]

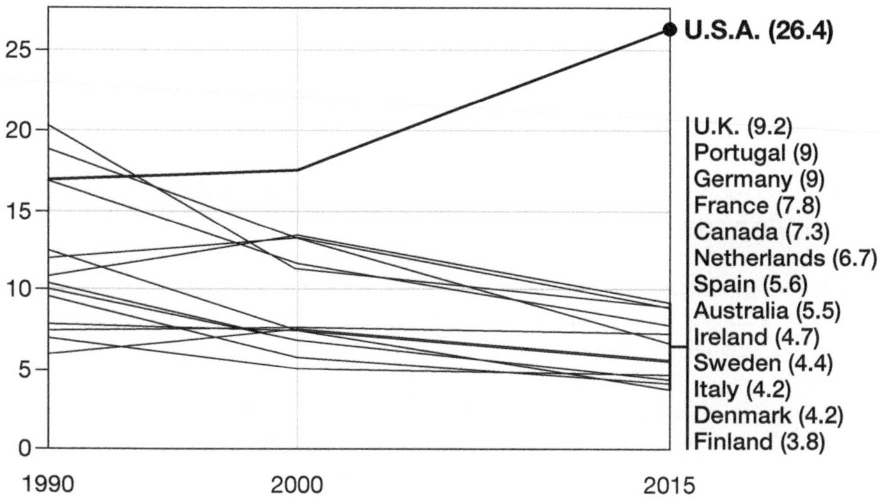

Figure 14.1. Maternal mortality, 1990–2015. ***Courtesy of the authors***

THE HIGH RATE OF PREGNANCY-RELATED DEATHS IS NOT A NEW PROBLEM

The CDC began conducting a national surveillance of pregnancy-related deaths in 1986 to fill in data gaps about what causes maternal death. The data are analyzed by scientists. Information about causes of pregnancy-related deaths and risk factors associated with these deaths is released periodically through CDC's *Morbidity and Mortality Weekly Report*. Findings are also regularly released in the scientific literature and on their website. This information aids clinicians and public health professionals to better understand circumstances surrounding pregnancy-related deaths. It allows professionals to take appropriate action toward prevention.

The government program, Healthy People 2020, of the Office of Disease Prevention and Health Promotion provides further evidence of the importance of decreasing the rates of maternal mortality: "Improving the well-being of mothers, infants and children is an important public health goal for the United States. Their well-being determines the health of the next generation and can help predict future public health challenges for families, communities and the health care system. The objectives of the Maternal, Infant and Child Health topic area address a wide range of conditions, health behaviors, and health systems indicators that affect the health, wellness, and quality of life of women, children and families."[8]

Healthy People 2020 reports their objective: 11.4 maternal deaths per one hundred thousand live births in 2019. What is remarkable is that their baseline data was from 2007 when the maternal mortality rate was 12.7 per one hundred thousand live births.[9] Instead of decreasing, it has more than doubled since 2007.

There are many other factors that affect mortality related to pregnancy and childbirth, such as preconception health status, access to appropriate health care, and poverty.[10]

> The risk of maternal and infant mortality and pregnancy-related complications can be reduced by increasing access to quality preconception (before pregnancy), prenatal (during pregnancy), and interconception (between pregnancies) care. . . . Infant and child health are similarly influenced by sociodemographic and behavioral factors, such as education, family income, and breastfeeding, but are also linked to the physical and *mental health of parents and caregivers*.[11]

WOMEN OF COLOR ARE AT HIGHER RISK OF DEATH AT CHILDBIRTH

According to the Centers for Disease Control and Prevention, mothers, particularly those of color, have a much higher rate of racially related and ethnic health disparities. According to healthypeople.gov, "A health disparity is a health difference that is closely linked with social, economic, or environmental disadvantage." Maternal and infant mortality and morbidity appear to be highest for African American women due to several factors that lead to increased complications during pregnancy and childbirth, and result in a higher risk of maternal death.[12]

At the 2019 Mom Congress held in Washington, D.C., a speaker and the cofounder of Motherly, Liz Tenety, stated, "Giving birth in America is shockingly dangerous: Discrimination against women, and women of color in particular, has led to an appalling maternal health crisis—where women's voices are not heard, women's needs are not met, and they, as well as their children and families, suffer."[13]

MATERNAL DEATH LAW ENACTED IN THE US

In 2018 the Preventing Maternal Deaths Act was signed into law, a first of many needed steps to eliminate preventable maternal deaths in the US and decrease the maternal mortality rates. An overview of HR 1318 (115th) states the following purpose: "To support States in their work to save and sustain the health of mothers during pregnancy, childbirth, and in the postpartum period, to eliminate disparities in maternal health outcomes for pregnancy-related and pregnancy-associated deaths, to identify solutions to improve health care quality and health outcomes for mothers, and for other purposes."[14]

Hopefully, future research and federal and state programs will continue to address the issues of maternal, infant, and pregnancy-related deaths. In addition, more awareness of the racial and ethnic disparities in the US may help to develop prevention programs and new progressive laws.

SPECIFIC CAUSAL FACTORS IN INFANT MORTALITY

It is essential to distinguish between infant deaths from various causes such as premature birth, genetic abnormalities, fetal malformations, sudden infant death syndrome (SIDS), and so forth in order to effectively lower the mortality rate. The CDC reported that the infant mortality rate in 2017 in the US was 5.8 deaths per one thousand live births. Infant mortality is defined as the number of deaths for every one thousand live births before the child's first birthday. Information on the CDC website reports the five leading causes of infant mortality identified in 2017 as birth defects, preterm birth, pregnancy complications, SIDS, and injuries (e.g., suffocation). It is unclear how many of these accidents, injuries, or SIDS deaths have been associated with maternal mental illness. This information may help to boost the incentive for close monitoring and better prenatal care, as well as screening and evaluation of women during the perinatal period.

In cases of infant mortality that are associated with the mother, such as fetal alcohol spectrum disorder or postpartum illnesses, the focus on prevention and interventions during pregnancy and postpartum would be critical to lower mortality rates. One might expect a better prognosis for mother-infant attachment and healthy families as a result of greater awareness and prompt treatment of postpartum depression and psychosis. That will likely also decrease the incidence of infanticide or neonaticide-related deaths.

MINIMAL ATTENTION TO MENTAL HEALTH IN THE PERINATAL PERIOD

There is insufficient research and limited attention to the prevalence of specific causal factors associated with maternal and infant death in the US. There is even less information on mortality rates linked with maternal mental illness, such as postpartum depression and psychosis. While this data appears to be either unavailable or unknown, the CDC information and materials state, "The rate of infant mortality provides key information about maternal and infant health, as well as being a marker for the overall health of a society."[15]

Our assumption is that greater awareness and an emphasis on prevention and prompt treatment will lower the maternal and infant mortality rates that may be an outcome or consequence of a postpartum depression or postpartum psychosis.

A BETTER FUTURE FOR CHILDBEARING WOMEN

Health care reform must continue to be addressed as a nationwide priority. Health disparities must be corrected. When and if that is done, there is a greater likelihood that all mothers and families presently and in generations to come will experience healthy pregnancy, delivery, and postpartum well-being and health.

All women need to be listened to when they complain about pregnancy or postpartum concerns, distressing symptoms, or complications. Black and Latina women need to be treated with the same *high-quality prenatal care* and attention as are all other women. *No woman should be concerned that pregnancy increases her risk of a shortened life.*

The hope for the future is there will be greater focus on prevention, early identification, and intervention for those at risk. Prompt treatment of mothers who experience maternal mental illness, such as postpartum depression and psychosis, will produce better health outcomes for mothers and families. Destigmatizing postpartum disorders and making available better education will encourage more openness and promote prompt and successful evidence-based treatment.

In catastrophic cases when the worst tragedy ensues, new state laws such as Illinois PA 100-0574 will lead to better outcomes. Greater understanding of mental illness, including perinatal mental illness, will generate progressive laws throughout the US. Our goal is to change criminal laws state by state, to foster humane laws throughout the nation, and to transform the national climate.

NOTES

1. R. C. Robin, "Huge Racial Disparities Found in Deaths Linked to Pregnancy," *New York Times*, May 7, 2019.

2. "Pregnancy-Related Deaths Happen Before, During, and Up to a Year after Delivery; *3 in 5 Pregnancy-Related Deaths Could Be Prevented, No Matter When They Occur," Centers for Disease Control and Prevention,* May 7, 2019, http://cdc.gov.

3. T. Crawford, "Report: US Pregnancy Deaths Up, and Most Are Preventable," *Chicago Tribune*, May 8, 2019.

4. Ibid.

5. R. Montagne and T. Martin, "Many Women Come Close to Death in Childbirth," NPR and ProPublica, March 11, 2018, https://www.npr.org.

6. "Lost Mothers: Maternal Mortality in the U.S.," NPR Morning Edition, May 12, 2017, https://www.npr.org.

7. Rob Weychert and ProPublica, "Global, Regional, and National Levels of Maternal Mortality, 1990–2015: A Systematic Analysis for the Global Burden of Disease Study," *Lancet* 388, no. 10053 (October 8, 2016): 1775–1812, https://www.thelancet.com.

8. Healthypeople.gov, "Maternal, Infant, and Child Help," Office of Disease Prevention and Health Protection, accessed October 19, 2019, https://www.healthypeople.gov.

9. Ibid.

10. Healthy People 2020 of the CDC provides science-based, ten-year national objectives for improving the health of all Americans. One of the Healthy People 2020 objectives is to reduce the rate of all infant deaths. In 2017, twenty-six states met the Healthy People 2020 target of six infant deaths per one thousand live births. Geographically, infant mortality rates in 2017 were highest among states in the South. Rates were also high in some states in the Midwest.

11. Healthypeople.gov, "Maternal, Infant, and Child Help."

12. Centers for Disease Control and Prevention, "Identifying Infants with Hearing Loss—United States, 1999–2007," *Morbidity and Mortality Weekly Report* (*MMWR*) 59, no. 8 (2010): 220–23; M. S. Watson, M. Y. Mann, M. A. Lloyd-Puryear, et al., "Newborn Screening: Toward a Uniform Screening Panel and System; Executive Summary," *Pediatrics* 117, no. 5 (May 2006): 296–307; M. J. Tucker, C. J. Berg, W. M. Callaghan, et al., "The Black-White Disparity in Pregnancy-Related Mortality from 5 Conditions: Differences in Prevalence and Case-Fatality Rates," *American Journal of Public Health* 97, no. 2 (February 2007): 247–51.

13. Heather Marcoux, "At Mom's Congress, Mothers Are Making Their Voices Heard," Motherly, May 3, 2019, https://www.mother.ly.

14. "HR 1318 (115th): Preventing Maternal Deaths Act of 2018," Govtrack, accessed August 10, 2019, http://www.govtrack.us.

15. "Infant Mortality," CDC, accessed July 31, 2019, https://www.cdc.gov.

Epilogue

Legal Advocacy and Changing Postpartum Laws

> One of my prayers when I first arrived in prison and I saw what I saw, "Lord, make me a better person not a bitter person."
>
> —Paula Sims, Logan Correctional Center

Transformation can come both on an individual level and on a societal level. In my book *Happy Endings, New Beginnings: Navigating Postpartum Disorders*, I describe and tell the stories of many women who have experienced personal growth and constructive changes following their postpartum illness. Happily, these are the majority of cases. Likewise, most women with postpartum psychosis recover, yet not without significant scars from that serious mental disorder. It is a unique illness that society continues to stigmatize and does not understand.

My own patients who have suffered from this severest form of postpartum illness often report fears of the psychosis returning. They are sometimes crippled with self-doubt when odd thoughts come to mind. They are quick to ask for reassurance that their thinking has not become delusional. Despite a complete remission of symptoms, women who have experienced postpartum psychosis (PPP), and their partners and families, are often left with a silent traumatization that perseveres well beyond the illness. Society at the present time does not encourage these families to speak up. This leaves survivors and families with shame, guilt, and a feeling of humiliation. And these are the lucky ones.

Yet there are those other PPP survivors whom we cannot forget or ignore. Women whose lives were devastated. Women whose lives were forever altered by their postpartum illness. There are also families, spouses, parents, siblings, and children who were left tragically distraught and traumatized after a loved one ended their own life or took the life of their infant or children. Women like Cynthia Wachenheim, Carol Coronado, and Andrea Pia Yates and their families come to mind. These are the sad stories. They have no happy endings. These are the women that we as a society have failed.

Andrea Yates was sentenced to life in prison with eligibility for parole in forty years, after the Texas jury rejected the insanity defense and found her guilty of first-degree murder. A few years later the Texas Court of Appeals reversed the conviction. That allowed a retrial. Yates was then found not guilty by reason of insanity. She was still committed to North Texas State Hospital. She eventually was transferred to Kerrville State Hospital to serve her time in a state mental hospital rather than a prison.

Andrea Yates, Carol Coronado, and other women serving decades or a lifetime in prison do not give rise to a sense of optimism. They do not give rise to a sense that justice has been served. Once the illness is treated and symptoms remit, some postpartum women are not left with the proverbial happily ever after. A large number of women and families are unfortunate. These women are those that we have focused on in this book. These are the women, often not diagnosed promptly, not diagnosed correctly or at all, who did not receive appropriate and timely treatment from a perinatal mental health specialist.

Various genetic, biochemical, hormonal or endocrine, and psychosocial risk factors have been identified that increase the probability of maternal mental illness. Prevention and being proactive with a perinatal treatment plan may aid to lower the potential risk. Women with a personal or family history of bipolar disorder, depression, obsessive-compulsive disorders, or anxiety disorders need to be monitored closely. Their risk is higher than those without prior episodes of a mood disorder. This *does not* guarantee a woman with no history of mental health problems *will not* experience a first episode of a mood disorder surrounding childbirth. Many perinatal women do.

This is an illness that needs to be taken seriously. Early intervention is optimal to reduce the incidence of the depression worsening, the potential for tragedy, or the possibility of depression becoming a chronic, lifelong condition. In cases of postpartum psychosis, the need to act quickly is critical for the sake of the woman as well as her child and family. The possibility of tragedy, although not always an outcome, is too great to risk by delaying hospitalization and medication.

On a societal level there is a global need for recognition of maternal mental illness as a serious disease that responds well to prompt identification and treatment. The World Health Organization (WHO) reports that 15 to 57 percent of women in developing countries experience symptoms of depression. WHO cites maternal mental health problems are likely a risk factor for poor growth in young children.[1] "Currently, unipolar depressive disorder is the third leading cause of disease burden accounting for 4.3% of the global burden of disease."[2]

All too often women resist treatment for depression due to the shame that has been associated with emotional problems. This is even more common for women during pregnancy and the postpartum period. At this vulnerable time, women are adjusting to this major change in identity and their new role of being a mother. They can be self-critical and feel inadequate in their mothering duties, and oftentimes fear the wrath of others judging them as a bad mother. Combine these normal stressors with the stigma of a mental illness, and it becomes evident why new mothers would resist getting treatment.

A collaborative care model has been missing from prevention and treatment models of maternal mental illness in the US, leading to perinatal women failing to know whom to turn to for help. A multidisciplinary model of care for women with perinatal illnesses should include providers from relevant fields, such as obstetricians, specialized perinatal mental health providers in psychiatry and psychotherapy, doulas, lactation consultants, midwives, nurses and primary care physicians, pediatricians, child-birth educators, nutritionists, and sleep specialists. Including specialists from various fields can address the complicated, multifaceted needs of a new mother and family suffering with maternal mental illness while adjusting to the most stressful period for a new mom and family.

Until 2001, only two states, New Jersey and New York, required educational materials on postpartum emotional disorders be provided to new parents at hospitals. In 2006, mandatory screening for postpartum depression (PPD) was passed by the state legislature in New Jersey.[3]

In 2001 Melanie Blocker Stokes, a new mother battling postpartum psychosis, jumped to her death from the twelfth floor of a Chicago hotel. Melanie's mother, Carol Blocker became an advocate to change the law.[4] The result was The Mother's Act, sponsored by US senator Robert Menendez (D-NJ) and Representative Bobby Rush (D-IL), which established a comprehensive federal commitment to combating postpartum depression through new research, education initiatives, and voluntarily support service programs.[5] Eventually, the Mother's Act passed after it was tied to the Affordable Care Act.

In 2015, Representative Katherine Clark of Massachusetts introduced H.R. 3235, the Bringing Postpartum Depression Out of the Shadows Act, to provide grants to states to create, improve, or maintain programs around maternal mental health and help women who are pregnant or recently gave birth. Clark stated, "No mom should feel alone while suffering from the pain, isolation, and frustration that comes with postpartum depression. The health and success of families include—the whole health of our moms. The passage of the *Shadows Act* means we're taking active steps to break down the stigmas that have kept moms from getting the care they need and deserve."[6] The bill passed the US House on November 30, 2016.[7] The Shadows Act passed in the House and Senate as part of HR 34, the 21st Century Cures Act.[8] It includes a section addressing screening and treatment for maternal depression.[9]

The only glimmer of hope for the most serious cases in which women find themselves involved with the criminal justice system comes with changes to our laws. With legislative change, women currently incarcerated finally have a realistic chance of freedom after years of prison and the traumatization and shame that follow stories of postpartum psychosis with the worst possible outcome. While the past decade has seen changes in national and state laws for postpartum screening and treatment, it is only recently that *criminal laws* have addressed the issue of postpartum depression and psychosis.[10] Only by education and changing laws can the national consciousness transform old medieval views of mental illness and those who suffer with these maladies. Some women, many reported on in this book, narrowly escaped decades in prison by a twist of fate. Too many throughout the nation continue to serve decades or even a lifetime.

Within a week of our visit to Logan Correctional Center to interview Janet Jackson and Paula Sims, the two friends who had first written the draft for HB 1764 that would become the nation's first postpartum criminal law, we heard the first glimmers of hope.[11] Sims sent a letter the day of our interview to let us know that the first of the women at Logan had negotiations opened for a sentence reduction by agreement with the prosecutor, based on the new law, PA 100-0574.

And so, we along with other advocates will continue to work to change the criminal laws state by state to have maternal mental illness considered an exception to the current homicide laws in the United States.

NOTES

1. P. J. Surkan, "Maternal Depression and Early Childhood Growth in Developing Countries: Systematic and Meta-Analysis," *Bulletin of the World Health Organization*, May 2011.

2. "ECOSOC Meeting Discussion Paper: Mental Health, Poverty and Development," World Health Organization, July 2009, 2, accessed October 19, 2019, http://www.who.int/nmh/discussion_paper_en.pdf.

3. J. Belsito, "Legislation," Postpartum Support International, 2018, accessed August 1, 2019, https://www.postpartum.net.

4. Carol Blocker, "It's Like My Daughter Was Killed by a Faceless Murderer and No One Is Helping Me Look for Him," Speech to the US House of Representatives, September 29, 2004.

5. "Mother's Act Becomes Law," MGH Center for Women's Mental Health, March 29, 2010, https://womensmentalhealth.org.

6. "House Passes Clark Postpartum Depression Legislation" Katherine Clark, Press Releases, November 30, 2016, https://katherineclark.house.gov.

7. Belsito, "Legislation."

8. On December 13, 2016, President Obama signed the 21st Century Cure Act after it had passed the House and Senate.

9. Caroline Bologna, "Congress Passes Groundbreaking Postpartum Depression Legislation 'Our Moms Need to Know They Matter,'" *Huffington Post*, December 8, 2016, https://www.huffpost.com.

10. PA 100-0574, the first postpartum criminal law, was enacted in Illinois in January 2018.

11. Visit and interview with Jackson and Sims was on June 4, 2019.

Appendix A

Illinois PA 100-0574: The First in the Nation Postpartum Criminal Law

PA 100-0574 was written as a modification to a previous law that did not reference postpartum illness. The changes to the previous law are specified by use of strikethroughs and underlines to indicate deletions and additions. In 2019, the portion of the law placed in the Post-Conviction Act (725 ILCS 5-122-1) was moved to 735 ILCS 5/2-1401 (b-10).

Public Act 100-0574
HB 1764 Enrolled
LRB100 04687 RLC 14693 b
AN ACT concerning criminal law.
Be it enacted by the People of the State of Illinois, represented in the General Assembly:

Section 5. The Code of Criminal Procedure of 1963 is amended by changing Section 122-1 as follows:

(725 ILCS 5/122-1) (from Ch. 38, par. 122-1)

Sec. 122-1. Petition in the trial court.

(a) Any person imprisoned in the penitentiary may institute a proceeding under this Article if the person asserts that:

(1) in the proceedings which resulted in his or her conviction there was a substantial denial of his or her rights under the Constitution of the United States or of the State of Illinois or both; ~~or~~

(2) the death penalty was imposed and there is newly discovered evidence not available to the person at the time of the proceeding that resulted in his or her conviction that establishes a substantial basis to believe that the defendant is actually innocent by clear and convincing evidence; or.

(3) by a preponderance of the evidence that each of the following allegations in the petition establish:

(A) he or she was convicted of a forcible felony;

(B) his or her participation in the offense was a direct result of the person's mental state either suffering from post-partum depression or post-partum psychosis;

(C) no evidence of post-partum depression or post-partum psychosis was presented by a qualified medical person at trial or sentencing, or both;

(D) he or she was unaware of the mitigating nature of the evidence or if aware was at the time unable to present this defense due to suffering from post-partum depression or post-partum psychosis or at the time of trial or sentencing neither was a recognized mental illness and as such unable to receive proper treatment; and

(E) evidence of post-partum depression or post-partum psychosis as suffered by the person is material and noncumulative to other evidence offered at the time of trial or sentencing and it is of such a conclusive character that it would likely change the sentence imposed by the original court.

Nothing in this paragraph (3) prevents a person from applying for any other relief under this Article or any other law otherwise available to him or her.

As used in this paragraph (3):

"Post-partum depression" means a mood disorder which strikes many women during and after pregnancy which usually occurs during pregnancy and up to 12 months after delivery. This depression can include anxiety disorders.

"Post-partum psychosis" means an extreme form of post-partum depression which can occur during pregnancy and up to 12 months after delivery. This can include losing touch with reality, distorted thinking, delusions, auditory and visual hallucinations, paranoia, hyperactivity and rapid speech, or mania.

(a-5) A proceeding under paragraph (2) of subsection (a) may be commenced within a reasonable period of time after the person's conviction notwithstanding any other provisions of this Article. In such a proceeding regarding actual innocence, if the court determines the petition is frivolous or is patently without merit, it shall dismiss the petition in a written order, specifying the findings of fact and conclusions of law it made in reaching its decision. Such order of dismissal is a final judgment and shall be served upon the petitioner by certified mail within 10 days of its entry.

(b) The proceeding shall be commenced by filing with the clerk of the court in which the conviction took place a petition (together with a copy thereof) verified by affidavit. Petitioner shall also serve another copy upon the State's Attorney by any of the methods provided in Rule 7 of the Supreme Court. The clerk shall docket the petition for consideration by the court pursuant to Section 122-2.1 upon his or her receipt thereof and bring the same promptly to the attention of the court.

(c) Except as otherwise provided in subsection (a-5), if the petitioner is under sentence of death and a petition for writ of certiorari is filed, no proceedings under this Article shall be commenced more than 6 months after the conclusion of proceedings in the United States Supreme Court, unless the petitioner alleges facts showing that the delay was not due to his or her culpable negligence. If a petition for certiorari is not filed, no proceedings under this Article shall be commenced more than 6 months from the date for filing a certiorari petition, unless the petitioner alleges facts showing that the delay was not due to his or her culpable negligence.

When a defendant has a sentence other than death, no proceedings under this Article shall be commenced more than 6 months after the conclusion of proceedings in the United States Supreme Court, unless the petitioner alleges facts showing that the delay was not due to his or her culpable negligence. If a petition for certiorari is not filed, no proceedings under this Article shall be commenced more than 6 months from the date for filing a certiorari petition, unless the petitioner alleges facts showing that the delay was not due to his or her culpable negligence. If a defendant does not file a direct appeal, the post-conviction petition shall be filed no later than 3 years from the date of conviction, unless the petitioner alleges facts showing that the delay was not due to his or her culpable negligence.

This limitation does not apply to a petition advancing a claim of actual innocence.

(d) A person seeking relief by filing a petition under this Section must specify in the petition or its heading that it is filed under this Section. A trial court that has received a petition complaining of a conviction or sentence that fails to specify in the petition or its heading that it is filed under this Section need not evaluate the petition to determine whether it could otherwise have stated some grounds for relief under this Article.

(e) A proceeding under this Article may not be commenced on behalf of a defendant who has been sentenced to death without the written consent of the defendant, unless the defendant, because of a mental or physical condition, is incapable of asserting his or her own claim.

(f) Except for petitions brought under paragraph (3) of subsection (a) of this Section, only ~~Only~~ one petition may be filed by a petitioner under this Article without leave of the court. Leave of court may be granted only if a petitioner demonstrates cause for his or her failure to bring the claim in his or her initial post-conviction proceedings and prejudice results from that failure. For purposes of this subsection (f):

(1) a prisoner shows cause by identifying an objective factor that impeded his or her ability to raise a specific claim during his or her initial post-conviction proceedings; and (2) a prisoner shows prejudice by demonstrating that the claim not raised during his or her initial post-conviction proceedings so infected the trial that the resulting conviction or sentence violated due process.

(Source: P.A. 93-493, eff. 1-1-04; 93-605, eff. 11-19-03; 93-972, eff. 8-20-04.)

Section 10. The Unified Code of Corrections is amended by changing Section 5-5-3.1 as follows:

(730 ILCS 5/5-5-3.1) (from Ch. 38, par. 1005-5-3.1)

Sec. 5-5-3.1. Factors in mitigation.

(a) The following grounds shall be accorded weight in favor of withholding or minimizing a sentence of imprisonment:

(1) The defendant's criminal conduct neither caused nor threatened serious physical harm to another.

(2) The defendant did not contemplate that his criminal conduct would cause or threaten serious physical harm to another.

(3) The defendant acted under a strong provocation.

(4) There were substantial grounds tending to excuse or justify the defendant's criminal conduct, though failing to establish a defense.

(5) The defendant's criminal conduct was induced or facilitated by someone other than the defendant.

(6) The defendant has compensated or will compensate the victim of his criminal conduct for the damage or injury that he sustained.

(7) The defendant has no history of prior delinquency or criminal activity or has led a law-abiding life for a substantial period of time before the commission of the present crime.

(8) The defendant's criminal conduct was the result of circumstances unlikely to recur.

(9) The character and attitudes of the defendant indicate that he is unlikely to commit another crime.

(10) The defendant is particularly likely to comply with the terms of a period of probation.

(11) The imprisonment of the defendant would entail excessive hardship to his dependents.

(12) The imprisonment of the defendant would endanger his or her medical condition.

(13) The defendant was a person with an intellectual disability as defined in Section 5-1-13 of this Code.

(14) The defendant sought or obtained emergency medical assistance for an overdose and was convicted of a Class 3 felony or higher possession, manufacture, or delivery of a controlled, counterfeit, or look-alike substance or a controlled substance analog under the Illinois Controlled Substances Act or a Class 2 felony or higher possession, manufacture or delivery of methamphetamine under the Methamphetamine Control and Community Protection Act.

(15) At the time of the offense, the defendant is or had been the victim of domestic violence and the effects of the domestic violence tended to excuse or justify the defendant's criminal conduct. As used in this paragraph (15), "domestic violence" means abuse as defined in Section 103 of the Illinois Domestic Violence Act of 1986.

(16) At the time of the offense, the defendant was suffering from a serious mental illness which, though insufficient to establish the defense of insanity, substantially affected his or her ability to understand the nature of his or her acts or to conform his or her conduct to the requirements of the law.

(17) At the time of the offense, the defendant was suffering from post-partum depression or post-partum psychosis which was either undiagnosed or untreated, or both, and this temporary mental illness tended to excuse or justify the defendant's criminal conduct and the defendant has been diagnosed as suffering from post-partum depression or post-partum psychosis, or both, by a qualified medical person and the diagnoses or testimony, or both, was not used at trial. In this paragraph (17):

> "Post-partum depression" means a mood disorder which strikes many women during and after pregnancy which usually occurs during pregnancy and up to 12 months after delivery. This depression can include anxiety disorders.
>
> "Post-partum psychosis" means an extreme form of post-partum depression which can occur during pregnancy and up to 12 months after delivery. This can include losing touch with reality, distorted thinking, delusions, auditory and visual hallucinations, paranoia, hyperactivity and rapid speech, or mania.

(b) If the court, having due regard for the character of the offender, the nature and circumstances of the offense and the public interest finds that a sentence of imprisonment is the most appropriate disposition of the offender, or where other provisions of this Code mandate the imprisonment of the offender, the grounds listed in paragraph (a) of this subsection shall be considered as factors in mitigation of the term imposed.

(Source: P.A. 98-463, eff. 8-16-13; 99-143, eff. 7-27-15; 99-384, eff. 1-1-16; 99-642, eff. 7-28-16; 99-877, eff. 8-22-16.)

Effective Date: 6/1/2018

Appendix B

Stages of a Petition for Postconviction Hearing under the New Law

Stage 1. With or without counsel, a petition is prepared by the incarcerated woman. The petition is verified by a sworn affidavit saying the contents are true. In the initial stage of the petition, the judge reviews the petition without input from the prosecutor or the defense. The judge decides on his/her own whether the petition states the "gist" of a valid claim. If so, the judge sets the petition for stage 2.

Details: *Gist* is not well defined, but it is a low standard. It is intended to be an objective standard. The attorney should not treat *Gist* as the standard for any successive or second petitions. These should be fully fleshed out.

If the petition is denied at stage 1, typically an appellate attorney is appointed if the petitioner chooses to appeal.

Stage 2. An attorney is appointed. His job is to fix up the petition. Experts may review the records and sign an affidavit that they believe to a reasonable degree of medical certainty that the incarcerated woman was suffering from postpartum depression (PPD) or postpartum psychosis (PPP) at the time of the crime. The expert needs to relate the crime to the illness in a manner that will convince the judge that justice was not served in the prior sentencing. Once that is done, the prosecutor moves to dismiss the petition as being deficient and not stating a valid claim. If the judge determines the petition states a valid claim, it moves to stage 3.

Stage 3. A hearing at which the prisoner has the burden of proving her case factually. At this point, experts come in to testify on behalf of the incarcerated woman and will be cross-examined by the prosecutor.

If in stage 3 the judge rules that the incarcerated has a valid claim for a resentencing hearing, a hearing date is set.

Appendix C

The Benefits and Limitations of Illinois's Postpartum Criminal Law PA 100-0574

WHAT IT DOES

It's a beginning. Since it wasn't too ambitious, it was able to gain support in the Illinois House and Senate and passed the General Assembly! It is a ground-breaking law. It is the first criminal law in any state of the US that identifies postpartum depression and postpartum psychosis as "mitigating factors" that need to be considered in trial and sentencing.

It recognizes postpartum depression and postpartum psychosis as forms of maternal mental illness that are unique. In the US infanticide is considered just like every other homicide.

It is retroactive so women currently incarcerated have an opportunity to file for resentencing. This affects approximately twenty women in Illinois's Logan Correctional Center.

It creates a model to build upon that may allow Illinois and other states to introduce more comprehensive legislation in the near future.

It's gotten the attention of legislators and the postpartum community and has led to others advocating and working on legislation. In addition it may have contributed to the development of a postpartum psychosis task force at Postpartum Support International (PSI). It is also the focus of the legal committee in the chapter of PSI-IL to help the incarcerated women in Illinois with their resentencing hearings.

WHAT IT DOESN'T DO

PA 100-0574 limits relief to incarcerated women by these conditions: it stipulates that postpartum depression and postpartum psychosis was not addressed in trial, nor was it diagnosed or treated, and it was not addressed in sentencing.

It is not as comprehensive as the British Infanticide Act of 1938. Yet in 2009 when Texas tried to introduce a bill like the British act, it gained no traction.

It doesn't allow a reduction of the minimum sentence, so if a postpartum psychosis (PPP) woman has a minimum sentence of twenty years, PA 100-0574 would not likely help her. It doesn't allow a judge to issue a below-minimum sentence.

SHORTCOMINGS

The bill fails to be tied to treatment or a mental health conditional-release program once a woman is no longer a danger to herself or others.

It does not eliminate imposing a mandatory life sentence with no parole.

It does not necessarily help a mother in the event that the occurrence was the death of more than one child. In Illinois like many states the death of more than one person results in a life sentence with no parole.

It does not provide a name, such as the New Moms and Infants Well-Being Act, that engenders the support of the public, legislatures, or many professionals and professional organizations.

Appendix D

A Sample Comprehensive Postpartum Legislation in Massachusetts

This is the actual bill as it was presented to the Commonwealth of Massachusetts. The function of the line numbers is to easily focus on changes in order to make additions or deletions in changing the law.

HOUSE DOCKET, NO. 1736 FILED ON: 1/17/2019
To the Honorable Senate and House of Representatives of the Commonwealth of Massachusetts in General Court assembled:
The undersigned legislators and/or citizens respectfully petition for the adoption of the accompanying bill:
An Act Relative to the Well-Being of New Mothers and Infants.
The Commonwealth of Massachusetts
In the One Hundred and Ninety-First General Court (2019–2020)
An Act relative to the well-being of new mothers and infants.
Be it enacted by the Senate and House of Representatives in General Court assembled, and by the authority of the same, as follows:

SECTION 1. Section 15 of chapter 123 of the General Laws, as so appearing, is hereby amended by inserting after the word "psychologists," in lines 7 and 8, the following words; provided however, that a defendant who gave birth within 12 months prior to the crime for which the defendant has been charged shall undergo a screening for perinatal psychiatric complications by a treating physician, psychiatrist, or psychologist or other qualified physician or psychologist.

SECTION 2. Subsection (a) of section 15 of chapter 123 of the General Laws, as so appearing, is hereby amended by inserting at the end thereof the following new sentence; When an examination is ordered for a female defendant who suffers or suffered, at the time the crime for which the defendant has been charged with occurred, from mental illness related to a perinatal psychiatric complication such as postpartum psychosis, said examination shall be conducted by an expert in reproductive psychiatry within 48 hours of such order.

SECTION 3. Section 16 of chapter 123 of the General Laws, as so appearing, is hereby amended by inserting at the end thereof the following new subsection;

(g) Any person committed to a facility under the provisions of this section who suffers from mental illness related to a perinatal psychiatric complication such as postpartum psychosis shall receive a diagnosis and treatment plan made in consultation with an expert in reproductive psychiatry. Additional services, including but not limited to parenting assessment, parenting capacity building, and parent-child dyadic therapy shall be made available if deemed appropriate by the consulting expert.

SECTION 4. Chapter 123 of the General Laws, as so appearing, is hereby amended by adding the following section;

Section 37. (a) The department shall appoint a community program director to coordinate the department's role provided for in this section in a particular county or region.

(b) Any person committed to a state hospital or other treatment facility under the provisions of section 16 may be placed on outpatient status, from that commitment subject to the procedures and provisions of this section.

(c) In the case of any person charged with and found incompetent to stand trial or not guilty by reason of mental illness or mental defect in such proceedings of murder, a violation in which the victim suffers intentionally inflicted great bodily injury, or an act which poses a serious threat of bodily harm to another person, outpatient status under this section shall not be available until that person has actually been confined in a state hospital or other treatment facility for 180 days or more after having been committed under the provisions of law specified in section 16, unless the court finds a suitable placement, including, but not limited to, an outpatient placement program, that would provide the person with more appropriate mental health treatment and the court finds that the placement would not pose a danger to the health or safety of others, including, but not limited to, the safety of the victim and the victim's family.

(d) In the case of any person charged with and found incompetent to stand trial or not guilty by reason of mental illness or mental defect of any misdemeanor or any felony other than those described in subsection (c), or found not guilty of any misdemeanor by reason of mental illness or mental defect outpatient status under this section may be granted by the court prior to actual confinement in a state hospital or other treatment facility under the provisions of law specified in section 16.

(e) Before any person subject to the provisions of subsection (d) may be placed on outpatient status, the court shall consider all of the following criteria:

In the case of a person who is an inpatient, whether the director of the state hospital or other treatment facility to which the person has been committed advises the court that the defendant will not be a danger to the health and safety of others while on outpatient status, and will benefit from such outpatient status.

(ii) In all cases, whether the community program director or a designee advises the court that the defendant will not be a danger to the health and safety of others while on outpatient status, will benefit from such status, and identifies an appropriate program of supervision and treatment. In the case of a female defendant who suffers from mental illness related to a perinatal psychiatric complication such as postpartum psychosis, an appropriate treatment program shall be identified in consultation with an expert in reproductive psychiatry. Additional services, including but not limited to parenting assessment, parenting capacity building and parent-child dyadic therapy shall also be made available if deemed appropriate by the consulting expert.

(f) Prior to determining whether to place the person on outpatient status, the court shall provide actual notice to the prosecutor and defense counsel, and to the victim, and shall hold a hearing at which the court may specifically order outpatient status for the person.

(g) The community program director or a designee shall prepare and submit the evaluation and the treatment plan specified in paragraph (ii) of subsection (e) to the court within 15 calendar days after notification by the court to do so, except that in the case of a person who is an inpatient, the evaluation and treatment plan shall be submitted within 30 calendar days after notification by the court to do so.

(h) Any evaluations and recommendations pursuant to paragraphs (i) and (ii) of subsection (e) shall include review and consideration of complete, available information regarding the circumstances of the criminal offense and the person's prior criminal history.

(i) Before any person subject to subsection (c) of this section may be placed on outpatient status the court shall consider all of the following criteria:

(i) Whether the director of the state hospital or other treatment facility to which the

72 person has been committed advises the committing court and the prosecutor that the defendant
73 would no longer be a danger to the health and safety of others, including himself or herself,
74 while under supervision and treatment in the community, and will benefit from that status.
75 (ii) Whether the community program director advises the court that the defendant will
76 benefit from that status, and identifies an appropriate program of supervision and treatment. In the
77 case of a female defendant who suffers from mental illness related to a perinatal psychiatric
78 complication such as postpartum psychosis, an appropriate treatment program shall be identified
79 in consultation with an expert in reproductive psychiatry. Additional services, including but not
80 limited to parenting assessment, parenting capacity building, and parent-child dyadic therapy
81 shall also be made available if deemed appropriate by the consulting expert.
82 (j) Prior to release of a person under subsection (c), the prosecutor shall provide notice of
83 the hearing date and pending release to the victim or next of kin of the victim of the offense for
84 which the person was committed where a request for the notice has been filed with the court, and
85 after a hearing in court, the court shall specifically approve the recommendation and plan for
86 outpatient status. The burden shall be on the victim or next of kin to the victim to keep the court
87 apprised of the party's current mailing address.
88 (k) In any case in which the victim or next of kin to the victim has filed a request for
89 notice with the director of the state hospital or other treatment facility, he or she shall be notified
90 by the director at the inception of any program in which the committed person would be allowed
91 any type of day release unattended by the staff of the facility.
92 (l) The community program director shall prepare and submit the evaluation and the

93 treatment plan specified in paragraph (ii) of subsection (i) to the court within 30 calendar days
94 after notification by the court to do so.
95 (m) Any evaluations and recommendations pursuant to paragraphs (i) and (ii) of
96 subsection (i) shall include review and consideration of complete, available information
97 regarding the circumstances of the criminal offense and the person's prior criminal history.
98 (n) Upon receipt by the committing court of the recommendation of the director of the
99 state hospital or other treatment facility to which the person has been committed that the person
100 may be eligible for outpatient status as set forth in paragraph (i) of subsection (e) or (i) of this
101 section, the court shall immediately forward such recommendation to the community program
102 director, prosecutor, and defense counsel. The court shall provide copies of the arrest reports and
103 the state summary criminal history information to the community program director.
104 (o) Within 30 calendar days the community program director or a designee shall submit
105 to the court and, when appropriate, to the director of the state hospital or other treatment facility,
106 a recommendation regarding the defendant's eligibility for outpatient status, as set forth in
107 paragraph (ii) of subsection (e) or (i) and the recommended plan for outpatient supervision and
108 treatment. The plan shall set forth specific terms and conditions to be followed during outpatient
109 status. The court shall provide copies of this report to the prosecutor and the defense counsel.
110 (p) The court shall calendar the matter for hearing within 15 business days of the receipt
111 of the community program director's report and shall give notice of the hearing date to the
112 prosecutor, defense counsel, the community program director, and, when appropriate, to the
113 director of the state hospital or other facility. In any hearing conducted pursuant to this section,

114 the court shall consider the circumstances and nature of the criminal offense leading to
115 commitment and shall consider the person's prior criminal history.
116 (q) The court shall, after a hearing in court, either approve or disapprove the
117 recommendation for outpatient status. If the approval of the court is given, the defendant shall be
118 placed on outpatient status subject to the terms and conditions specified in the supervision and
119 treatment plan. If the outpatient treatment occurs in a county other than the county of
120 commitment, the court shall transmit a copy of the case record to the superior court in the county
121 where outpatient treatment occurs, so that the record will be available if revocation proceedings
122 are initiated pursuant to subsection (w) or (x).
123 (r) The department shall be responsible for the supervision of persons placed on
124 outpatient status under this title. The commissioner shall designate, for each county or region, a
125 community program director who shall be responsible for administering the community
126 treatment programs for persons committed from that county or region under the provisions
127 specified in subsection (b).
128 (s) The department shall notify in writing the chief justice of the trial court, the district
129 attorney of each county, and the executive director of the committee on public counsel services
130 as to the person designated to be the community program director for each county or region, and
131 timely written notice shall be given whenever a new community program director is to be
132 designated.
133 (t) The community program director shall be the outpatient treatment supervisor of
134 persons placed on outpatient status under this section. The community program director may
135 delegate the outpatient treatment supervision responsibility to a designee.

(u) The outpatient treatment supervisor shall, at 90-day intervals following the beginning of outpatient treatment, submit to the court, the prosecutor and defense counsel, and to the community program director, where appropriate, a report setting forth the status and progress of the defendant.

(v) Outpatient status shall be for a period not to exceed 1 year. At the end of the period of outpatient status approved by the court, the court shall, after actual notice to the prosecutor, the defense counsel, and the community program director, and after a hearing in court, either discharge the person from commitment under appropriate provisions of the law, order the person confined to a treatment facility, or renew its approval of outpatient status. Prior to such hearing, the community program director shall furnish a report and recommendation to the medical director of the state hospital or other treatment facility, where appropriate, and to the court, which the court shall make available to the prosecutor and defense counsel. The person shall remain on outpatient status until the court renders its decision unless hospitalized under other provision of the law. The hearing pursuant to the provisions of this section shall be held no later than 30 days after the end of the 1 year period of outpatient status unless good cause exists. The court shall transmit a copy of its order to the community program director or a designee.

(w) If at any time during the outpatient period, the outpatient treatment supervisor is of the opinion that the person requires extended inpatient treatment or refuses to accept further outpatient treatment and supervision, the community program director shall notify the superior court in either the county which approved outpatient status or in the county where outpatient

157 treatment is being provided of such opinion by means of a written request for revocation of
158 outpatient status. The community program director shall furnish a copy of this request to the
159 defense counsel and to the prosecutor in both counties if the request is made in the county of
160 treatment rather than the county of commitment.
161 Within 15 business days, the court where the request was filed shall hold a hearing and
162 shall either approve or disapprove the request for revocation of outpatient status. If the court
163 approves the request for revocation, the court shall order that the person be confined in a state
164 hospital or other treatment facility approved by the community program director. The court shall
165 transmit a copy of its order to the community program director or a designee. Where the county
166 of treatment and the county of commitment differ and revocation occurs in the county of
167 treatment, the court shall enter the name of the committing county and its case number on the
168 order of revocation and shall send a copy of the order to the committing court and the prosecutor
169 and defense counsel in the county of commitment.
170 (x) If at any time during the outpatient period the prosecutor is of the opinion that the
171 person is a danger to the health and safety of others while on that status, the prosecutor may
172 petition the court for a hearing to determine whether the person shall be continued on that status.
173 Upon receipt of the petition, the court shall calendar the case for further proceedings within 15
174 business days and the clerk shall notify the person, the community program director, and the
175 attorney of record for the person of the hearing date. Upon failure of the person to appear as
176 noticed, if a proper affidavit of service has been filed with the court, the court may issue a capias
177 to compel the attendance of such person. If, after a hearing in court conducted using the same

178 standards used in conducting probation revocation hearings pursuant to section 3 of chapter 279,
179 the judge determines that the person is a danger to the health and safety of others, the court shall
180 order that the person be confined in a state hospital or other treatment facility which has been
181 approved by the community program director.
182 (y) Upon the filing of a request for revocation under subsection (w) or subsection (x) and
183 pending the court's decision on revocation, the person subject to revocation may be confined in a
184 facility designated by the community program director when it is the opinion of that director that
185 the person will now be a danger to self or to another while on outpatient status and that to delay
186 confinement until the revocation hearing would pose an imminent risk of harm to the person or
187 to another. The facility so designated shall continue the patient's program of treatment, shall
188 provide adequate security so as to ensure both the safety of the person and the safety of others in
189 the facility, and shall, to the extent possible, minimize interference with the person's program of
190 treatment. Upon the request of the community program director or a designee, a peace officer
191 shall take, or cause to be taken, the person into custody and transport the person to a facility as
192 described in subsection (z) and designated by the community program director for confinement
193 under this section. Within 1 business day after the person is confined in a jail under this section,
194 the community program director shall apply in writing to the court for authorization to confine
195 the person pending the hearing under subsection (w) or subsection (x). The application shall be
196 in the form of a declaration, and shall specify the behavior or other reason justifying the
197 confinement of the person in a jail. Upon receipt of the application for confinement, the court
198 shall consider and rule upon it, and if the court authorizes detention in a jail, the court shall

actually serve copies of all orders and all documents filed by the community program director upon the prosecuting and defense counsel. The community program director shall notify the court in writing of the confinement of the person and of the factual basis for the opinion that the immediate confinement in a jail was necessary. The court shall supply a copy of these documents to the prosecutor and defense counsel.

(z) The facility designated by the community program director may be a state hospital, a local treatment facility, a county jail, or any other appropriate facility, so long as the facility can continue the person's program of treatment, provide adequate security, and minimize interference with the person's program of treatment. If the facility designated by the community program director is a county jail, the patient shall be separated from the general population of the jail. A county jail may not be designated unless the services specified above are provided, and accommodations are provided which ensure both the safety of the person and the safety of the general population of the jail. Within 3 business days of the patient's confinement in a jail, the community program director shall report to the court regarding what type of treatment the patient is receiving in the facility. If there is evidence that the treatment program is not being complied with, or accommodations have not been provided which ensure both the safety of the committed person and the safety of the general population of the jail, the court shall order the person transferred to an appropriate facility, including an appropriate state hospital.

(aa) Nothing in this section shall prevent hospitalization pursuant to the provisions of section 12.

(bb) A person whose confinement in a treatment facility under subsection (w) or

220 subsection (x) is approved by the court shall not be released again to outpatient status unless
221 court approval is obtained under subsection (e) or subsection (i).
222 (cc) No person who is on outpatient status pursuant to this section shall leave this state
223 without first obtaining prior written approval to do so from the committing court. The prior
224 written approval of the court for the person to leave this state shall specify when the person may
225 leave, when the person is required to return, and may specify other conditions or limitations at
226 the discretion of the court. The written approval for the person to leave this state may be in a
227 form and format chosen by the committing court.
228 (dd) In no event shall the court give written approval for the person to leave this state
229 without providing notice to the prosecutor, the defense counsel, and the community program
230 director. The court may conduct a hearing on the question of whether the person should be
231 allowed to leave this state and what conditions or limitations, if any, should be imposed.
232 (ee) Any person who violates subsection (dd) is guilty of a misdemeanor and upon
233 conviction shall by punished by imprisonment for not more than 6 months in a house of
234 correction or by a fine of not more than $1,000.
235 (ff) The department shall be responsible for the community treatment and supervision of
236 judicially committed patients. These services shall be available on a county or regional basis.
237 The department may provide these services directly or through contract with private providers.
238 The program or programs through which these services are provided shall be known as the
239 forensic conditional release program.
240 (gg) The department shall contact all regional mental health programs by January 1,
241 2021, to determine their interest in providing an appropriate level of supervision and treatment of

judicially committed patients at reasonable cost. Regional mental health programs may agree or refuse to operate such a program.

(hh) No later than January 1, 2022, and by January 1 of each subsequent year, all state hospitals or other treatment facilities participating in the forensic conditional release program shall report to the commissioner the following information: (i) the cost of the program to the facility; (ii) the demographic profiles of persons receiving supervision and treatment in the program; and (iii) the rates of adherence to treatment under the program.

(ii) No later than January 1, 2022, and by January 1 of each subsequent year, the chief justice of the trial court shall report to the commissioner the following information: rates of re-offense while these persons are served by the program and after their discharge.

(jj) The department shall conduct yearly evaluations of the forensic conditional release program. An evaluation of the program shall determine its effectiveness in successfully reintegrating these persons into society after release from state institutions. This evaluation of program effectiveness shall include, but not be limited to, a determination of the rates of re-offense while these persons are served by the program and after their discharge. This evaluation shall also address the effectiveness of the various treatment components of the program and their intensity.

(kk) The department shall ensure consistent data gathering and program standards for use statewide by the forensic conditional release program.

(ll) The department of correction, and the executive office of public safety and security shall cooperate with the department in conducting this evaluation.

(mm) The administrators and the supervision and treatment staff of the forensic

264 conditional release program shall not be held criminally or civilly liable for any criminal acts

265 committed by the persons on parole or judicial commitment status who receive supervision or

266 treatment.

267 (nn) The court retains jurisdiction over the person until the end of the period of the

268 assisted outpatient treatment established under this section or until the court finds that the person

269 no longer meets the criteria in this section.

Appendix E

British Infanticide Act of 1938

Section 60, mentioned toward the end, is a procedural law applicable in England.

1938 CHAPTER 36
An Act to repeal and re-enact with modifications the provisions of the Infanticide Act, 1922.
[23rd June 1938]

Be it enacted by the King's most Excellent Majesty, by and with the advice and consent of the Lords Spiritual and Temporal, and Commons, in this present Parliament assembled, and by the authority of the same, as follows:

Offence of infanticide.

(1) Where a woman by any willful act or omission causes the death of her child being a child under the age of twelve months, but at the time of the act or omission the balance of her mind was disturbed by reason of her not having fully recovered from the effect of giving birth to the child or by reason of the effect of lactation consequent upon the birth of the child, then, notwithstanding that the circumstances were such that but for this Act the offence would have amounted to murder, she shall be guilty of felony, to wit of infanticide, and may for such offence be dealt with and punished as if she had been guilty of the offence of manslaughter of the child.

(2) Where upon the trial of a woman for the murder of her child, being a child under the age of twelve months, the jury are of opinion that she by any willful act or omission caused its death, but that at the time of the act or omission the balance of her mind was disturbed by reason of her not having fully recovered from the effect of giving birth to the child or by reason of the effect of lactation consequent upon the birth of the child, then the

jury may, notwithstanding that the circumstances were such that but for the provisions of this Act they might have returned a verdict of murder, return in lieu thereof a verdict of infanticide.

(3) Nothing in this Act shall affect the power of the jury upon an indictment for the murder of a child to return a verdict of manslaughter, or a verdict of guilty but insane, or a verdict of concealment of birth, in pursuance of section sixty of the Offences against the Person Act, 1861, except that for the purposes of the proviso to that section a child shall be deemed to have recently been born if it had been born within twelve months before its death.

(4) The said section sixty shall apply in the case of the acquittal of a woman upon an indictment for infanticide as it applies upon the acquittal of a woman upon an indictment for murder.

Appendix F

Amendments to the Infanticide Act of 1938

CHAPTER 36 1 and 2 Geo 6
An Act to repeal and re-enact with modifications the provisions of the Infanticide Act 1922.

Offence of infanticide.

(1) Where a woman by any wilful act or omission causes the death of her child being a child under the age of twelve months, but at the time of the act or omission the balance of her mind was disturbed by reason of her not having fully recovered from the effect of giving birth to the child or by reason of the effect of lactation consequent upon the birth of the child, then, [F1if] the circumstances were such that but for this Act the offence would have amounted to murder [F2or manslaughter], she shall be guilty of felony, to wit of infanticide, and may for such offence be dealt with and punished as if she had been guilty of the offence of manslaughter of the child.

(2) Where upon the trial of a woman for the murder [F3or manslaughter] of her child, being a child under the age of twelve months, the jury are of opinion that she by any wilful act or omission caused its death, but that at the time of the act or omission the balance of her mind was disturbed by reason of her not having fully recovered from the effect of giving birth to the child or by reason of the effect of lactation consequent upon the birth of the child, then the jury may, [F4if] the circumstances were such that but for the provisions of this Act they might have returned a verdict of murder [F3or manslaughter], return in lieu thereof a verdict of infanticide.

(3) Nothing in this Act shall affect the power of the jury upon an indictment for the murder of a child to return a verdict of manslaughter, or a verdict of guilty but insane, . . . F5

(4) F6

Annotations:

Amendments (Textual)

F1Word in s. 1(1) substituted (4.10.2010) by Coroners and Justice Act 2009 (c. 25), **ss. 57(2)(a)**, 182(5) (with s. 180, Sch. 22 para. 7); S.I. 2010/816, art. 5(c)

F2Words in s. 1(1) inserted (4.10.2010) by Coroners and Justice Act 2009 (c. 25), **ss. 57(2)(b)**, 182(5) (with s. 180, Sch. 22 para. 7); S.I. 2010/816, art. 5(c)

F3Words in s. 1(2) inserted (4.10.2010) by Coroners and Justice Act 2009 (c. 25), **ss. 57(3)(b)**, 182(5) (with s. 180, Sch. 22 para. 7); S.I. 2010/816, art. 5(c)

F4Word in s. 1(2) substituted (4.10.2010) by Coroners and Justice Act 2009 (c. 25), **ss. 57(3)(a)**, 182(5) (with s. 180, Sch. 22 para. 7); S.I. 2010/816, art. 5(c)

F5Words repealed by Criminal Law Act 1967 (c. 58), **Sch. 3 Pt. III**

F6S. 1(4) repealed by Criminal Law Act 1967 (c. 58), Sch. 3 Pt. III

F1S. 2(3) repealed by Statute Law Revision Act 1950 (c. 6)

Appendix G

The New Law in Illinois: PA 100-0574—Ground-Breaking Legislation

Susan Benjamin Feingold, PsyD
Barry Michael Lewis, JD

As of 2018, there is a new law in Illinois, PA 100-0574, formerly known as HB 1764, that recognizes postpartum illnesses as a factor in criminal cases. The law is groundbreaking because it is the first criminal law in the nation to reference in any way postpartum illnesses. It makes postpartum depression and postpartum psychosis a mitigating factor in sentencing. It also, for the very first time in Illinois provides for a new sentencing hearing after a valid sentence has been imposed.

Most often, postpartum depression and anxiety disorders (incidence of 10–20 percent) are extremely responsive to treatment when recognized early and treated by specialists in perinatal mental health. Yet, there are those atypical cases when women have severe postpartum depression or the rare postpartum psychosis (1–2 of 1000 childbearing women), and become involved in the criminal justice system (1 to 4 percent of women with postpartum psychosis commit infanticide/neonaticide).

There are approximately twenty Illinois women who were convicted and sentenced to life or decades in prison before the effects of this disease were well-known in the legal community. Now that Illinois has passed this new law, these women serving long or life-time sentences will be entitled to a new hearing that allows for re-evaluation and the possibility of a reduced sentence.

This new Illinois law, PA 100-0574[1] will not only correct a known wrong, but in addition it will be a model for other states in the US to follow. These women need mental health treatment, not long prison sentences or life imprisonment without parole.

Historically, "common law" jurisdictions were not favorable for appeals.[2] Only in the 1500's did it become possible to challenge an erroneous factual finding on appeal. It was not until the middle of the 20th century in the US that it first became constitutionally required for a state to allow a challenge to a conviction after appeals were completed, known as a "Post-Conviction Petition." In many states, including Illinois, only one such petition is generally allowed. The Supreme Court's mandated petition is limited to challenging trial errors that amount to a violation of the constitution. In most states, this specifically meant a sentence could not be changed or challenged. Only a few states have a law permitting reconsidering a validly imposed sentence. In Illinois, this is the first and only law allowing for such a resentencing.

The only prior attempt in the entire US to enact a postpartum illness criminal law was an abject failure. In 2009, the Texas legislature refused to pass a bill modeled after the British Infanticide Act of 1938. Although eighty years have passed since The British Act became law, and it has been adopted in over twenty countries, nothing even approaching it has become law in any state in the US until January 8, 2018.

In England and more than 20 [this has since been updated to 37] other countries (including Australia, Austria, Brazil, Canada, Colombia, Finland, Germany, Greece, Hong Kong, India, Italy, Japan, Korea, New Zealand, Norway, Philippines, Sweden, Switzerland, Turkey and Wales), a woman who causes the death of her child, in the twelve months following delivery, is assumed to be mentally ill. In lieu of prison or the death sentence, these women receive psychiatric treatment and rehabilitation. The majority of nations that have infanticide laws have followed the British precedent (The British Infanticide Act of 1938) and decrease[d] the penalty for mothers killing children under one year old (Friedman, SR and Resnick, PR. World Psychiatry, 2007 Oct; 6(3): 137–141).

Illinois PA 100-0574 specifically names postpartum depression and postpartum psychosis as a mitigating factor. It specifies that a Post-Conviction Petition can be filed even if a prior Petition was filed. If the facts are proven at the Petition stage, a new sentencing hearing results. The sentence can be reduced or remain the same, but not increased.

The door, shut tight for eight decades, has finally been opened by Illinois. Other states have expressed interest in this legislation with plans to follow our lead.

Articles related to PA 100-0574:

Barry Lewis, "Postpartum Disorders: A New Law Offers Hope," *Champion* (National Association of Criminal Defense Lawyers) (March 2018): 20–25.

Teme Ring, "Illinois Postpartum Law Will Be the First in the Nation! Call Your State Senator!" *Everything's Political* (blog), May 21, 2017, http://www.chicagonow.com/everythings-political/2017/05/illinois-postpartum-law-will-be-the-first-in-the-nation-call-your-state-senator.

NOTES

This is an article for the International Marcé Society for Perinatal Mental Health Newsletter, December 2018 issue.

1. HB 1764 was signed by the governor and became Public Act 100-574 on January 8, 2018.

2. "Common law" jurisdictions include the United States (except Louisiana) and numerous countries with an English historical background.

Appendix H

The Champion *Article (NACDL), March 2018*

A NEW MODEL LAW OFFERS HOPE: POSTPARTUM DISORDERS AND THE LAW

by Barry M. Lewis, JD

For most women, the pain of childbirth is rewarded with the delight of parenting an infant. For a significant percentage of young mothers, the pleasure does not arrive. Instead, postpartum depression (PPD) or postpartum psychosis (PPP) is the debilitating accompaniment of what usually is called a bundle of joy. A small number of such mothers under the overwhelming stress of caring for the infant and their postpartum illnesses commit horrible crimes. Many civilized nations specifically account for this illness in their criminal laws, but this is not the case in the United States. No U.S. law made any accommodation for such mothers who faced either a murder sentence or an uphill battle to be found not guilty by reason of insanity. The first law in the United States specifically establishing the mitigating factor of PPP and PPD, Illinois' Public Act 100-0574, was signed by the governor on January 8, 2018. While the law is limited in its scope (when compared to laws in many other countries), it is a breakthrough that deserves to be the stepping stone for similar or broader laws throughout the United States.

The purpose of this article is to inform the criminal defense bar of the nature of the disease with the objective that no new defendants will have this issue overlooked or misconstrued. With an eye toward Illinois PA 100-0574 or a constitutional argument,[1] the hope is that defense lawyers will find an avenue to approach justice for those presently incarcerated in other states.

Postpartum disorders have in recent years gained attention in the medical community and in popular culture. Different and far more serious than the "baby blues," postpartum depression affects about one in seven new mothers, about 800,000 women each year in the United States alone. The much rarer postpartum psychosis affects a much smaller group, about 0.05 percent to 0.1 percent of pregnancies.[2] Of that smaller group, about 4 percent commit infanticide or neonaticide.[3] Infanticide by new mothers is far more common than the occasional news story would lead us to believe.[4] Postpartum illnesses can be severe, yet despite their severity, are extremely responsive to early treatment. The sufferer is no more responsible for her condition than if she had cancer.

WHAT ARE PPD AND PPP?

PPD is "identified by its cluster of symptoms, their severity and the time of onset. . . . Any one case of postpartum depression can include symptoms from any combination of four subgroups: depression, anxiety, panic disorder and obsessive-compulsive disorder, each of which has its own different assortment of symptoms. Depression is not always a component." Recovery with treatment can take six to 12 months. Without treatment, one-quarter of women sufferers will not recover.[5]

PPP, the most severe of the postpartum disorders, is an actual psychotic state associated with pregnancy and/or birth. It occurs in one or two of each 1,000 births. "It [postpartum psychosis] comes on very quickly usually, and often has been associated with bipolar disorder." Those mothers suffer a chemical imbalance that often causes them to have delusions. "A woman in a psychotic state should be in a hospital. . . . Their thinking is impaired. Their judgment is impaired."[6]

Postpartum illnesses are unique.[7] Their distinctive features include that principally only women are affected. (Recently it has been said men can get postpartum depression too.) Postpartum illnesses appear in women within a year of giving birth, and often within days. These are arguably the most treatable of mental illnesses: with treatment they usually can be effectively cured within months. Postpartum depression and psychosis can appear in women with no prior notable mental health issues, although among the risk factors are prior bipolar disorder, prior depression or prior psychosis. Symptoms in some women can begin during pregnancy, which has led to the broader classification of peripartum onset or perinatal mood disorders. Yet anecdotal evidence indicates the great majority of crimes committed by sufferers are related to postpartum onset, often neonaticide or infanticide.

Being unique among mental illnesses, PPD really calls for unique laws applicable thereto. It makes no sense for a brief mental illness to cause a lifetime of incarceration. Yet until now, no statute in the United States made any accommodation for this illness either in criminal laws or child custody laws.

THE MEDICAL PROBLEM IN THE JUSTICE SYSTEM

A severe form of postpartum depression can leave a mother unable to care for her child, resulting in child protection encounters or even neglect leading to death. It can result in a loss of will to live, in which the mother decides it is best to "take her child with her," even absent a psychotic break.

Such an event was described to this author at the 2017 Biennial Perinatal Mental Health Conference. "Heather" was typical of women at risk for PPP or PPD, as she had long suffered from bipolar disorder. Bipolar disorder is the single most frequent preexisting medical issue associated with PPP. In her depression, Heather chose to take her life.[8] Her depression left her thinking deeply disturbed, but still with rational aspects: She concluded certain of her children but not all could make it without her. The children who could not make it without her would have to "come with her" when she took her own life. She matter of factly discussed with a friend her plan to die with her oldest children by crushing her supply of pills, mixing the pills with a flavored drink, and sharing it with them. Her mental condition was such that she felt her friend would support the plan, perhaps helping her to make her plan more likely to succeed. The friend instead confiscated the pills and, feigning cooperation, drove her to the hospital. As a result of the medical intake reports and hospitalization, the child care authorities "indicated" Heather for potential child abuse. It took longer and involved greater difficulty for her to end the involvement of the child care authorities than it did to recover from her illness. Her illness responded sufficiently for her release from the hospital with medication within a week. Had she completed her plan, her release from needed residential treatment would still only take a week, but her release from the penitentiary might never occur. In Illinois, as in many states, murder of more than one requires a life in prison, without the possibility of parole.[9] Fortunately for her, she did not violate the criminal laws because she did not take a "substantial step" toward the murder-suicide she contemplated.

Criminal laws make no consideration for this disease. Among the many sad examples, Cynthia Wachenheim well illustrates the problem.

On March 13, 2013, lawyer Cynthia Wachenheim jumped to her death from the eighth floor of a New York residence. This case, while only one of countless horrors of the disease, is notable for a number of reasons and should conclusively establish the bona fides of this disease to any rational legislator, juror, or jurist. Wachenheim, a former high school valedictorian and Columbia Law School graduate, left behind a husband, a healthy infant strapped to her chest, shielded by her body from the impact of the fall, and a rambling, mostly incoherent 13-page suicide note. Wachenheim held a $120,000 per year position writing for judges. She had written countless documents in a clear and convincing fashion; the documents were in complete contrast to the incoherent suicide note. She was obsessed with a health issue involving her infant, which was nonexistent according to her doctors. Wachenheim had a delusional belief that she was at fault and blamed herself for his (actually nonexistent) medical problems. She was obsessed with her thoughts of being a failure as a mother. The only way to end her child's and her suffering was for both to die. So she strapped her child to her chest and jumped to their mutual intended death.[10] If the baby died and Wachenheim survived, she would be facing murder charges for the act of infanticide. Is that just and proper? How many mothers are in that position? Only a person whose rationality is more suspect than Wachenheim would argue she was not overwhelmed by a mental illness before jumping to her death with the intent of ending her child's and her own suffering. Yet the internet record shows such people exist and could end up on a jury.

There are believed to be 20 Illinois inmates (out of a total Illinois inmate population in excess of 43,000) who suffered from postpartum issues not reflected in their sentence. If one assumes on average 20 inmates in each state whose sentences did not reflect the actuality of postpartum depression, there are 1,000 women whose sentences are inappropriate and should be modified. This can likely only be done with supporting legislation because of the limitations of coram nobis and its statutory likenesses.

THE FINALITY OF SENTENCES ISSUED BY THE TRIAL COURT

Understanding how ground-breaking this law is requires consideration of the minimal nature of post-sentencing review of the trial courts' original sentences. In Illinois the review of a sentence virtually everyone disagrees with is limited to whether the court considered improper, unpermitted factors, and whether the sentence is within statutory limits.[11] While numerous exceptions exist, in virtually all common law jurisdictions except the United States, appellate review of sentences has been the principal method used to develop consistency in sentencing. The traditional position in this country, however, as stated by the Supreme Court in *Dorszynski v. United States*,[12] has been that "once it is determined that a sentence is within the limits set forth in the statute under which it is imposed, appellate review is at an end."[13] Post-Conviction Act hearings in states where they are limited to the mandate of the U.S. Supreme Court are for constitutional violations only.[14] Thus, in Illinois a post-conviction petition is not available to redress a poor sentencing hearing resulting in a penitentiary sentence.[15] Truth in sentencing laws have taken much, sometimes all, of the authorities' power to release a prisoner predicated upon his post-sentencing maturity and rehabilitation.[16]

THE BEGINNING OF A SOLUTION

PA 100-0574 is a developmental model for legislatures throughout the United States. Its concept provides for a second chance—a resentencing for women whose crimes were committed under the influence of these disorders.

The new Illinois statute is just a beginning. Nearly 30 countries, among those socially and culturally advanced, have even more beneficial laws modeled on the English Infanticide Act of 1938, which made infanticide by the mother a category of offense less severe than murder, substantially reducing the punishment for women who committed crimes while suffering PPP or PPD.[17] There were 49 women convicted under this statute in England and Wales between 1989 and 2000. Only two received prison sentences.[18]

Countries with laws similar to the Infanticide Act include Australia, Austria, Brazil, Canada, Columbia, Finland, Germany, Greece, Hong Kong, India, Italy, Japan, Korea, New Zealand, Norway, Philippines, Sweden, Switzerland, Turkey and the United Kingdom.[19] A survey of countries showed 28 of the 34 countries examined had a specific law regarding acts of infanticide.[20] The laws usually reduced the punishment for the homicide, with an average maximum possible sentence of six years.

THE SPECIFICS OF THE NEW LAW

As initially written, PA 100-0574 was a form of coram nobis under ss 1401 of the Civil Practice Act,[21] and at first glance was just a small change to it. This may have disguised its ground-breaking nature. An amendment switched the basis of the application for relief from the statutory coram nobis, 735 ILCS 5/1401, to the Illinois' Post-Conviction Act (725 ILCS 5/122-1). With that change, and the testimony of Dr. Susan Benjamin Feingold, the bill sailed through the House of Representatives. Dr. Feingold has a vast and comprehensive knowledge on the subject; she literally wrote the book on it.[22] Given only a few minutes to speak, she educated the committee on the prevalence of PPP and PPD, pointing out that these illnesses are beyond the control of their victims and that the disease was overlooked until recent years. In addition, Dr. Feingold told the legislators how treatable the condition can be when identified early. The committee and the House were convinced they should act favorably on the bill.

The Post-Conviction Act, unlike actions brought as a 1401 petition, limits its operation to persons in custody. This means it can be used by only those 20 women who are in Logan Correctional Center plus an unknown but small number who, while not behind bars, are on Mandatory Supervised Release (formerly called parole). They are in custody for the purposes of the Illinois Post-Conviction Act.[23] Later, after some procedural difficulties in the Senate, the legislation finally passed and the governor signed it.

Paragraph 16 of 730 ILCS 5/5-5-3.1—Factors in mitigation, already included:

"(16) At the time of the offense, the defendant was suffering from a serious mental illness which, though insufficient to establish the defense of insanity, substantially affected his or her ability to understand the nature of his or her acts or to conform his or her conduct to the requirements of the law."

The new law adds paragraph (17):

"(17) At the time of the offense, the defendant was suffering from post-partum[24] depression or post-partum psychosis which was either undiagnosed or untreated, or both, and this temporary mental illness tended to excuse or justify the defendant's criminal conduct and the defendant has been diagnosed as suffering from post-partum depression or post-partum psychosis, or both, by a qualified medical person and the diagnoses or testimony, or both, was not used at trial."

PPP and PPD are defined the same as in the modification to the Post-Conviction Act.

The reference to "not used at trial" is used to show a change in the law, which thus would make a petition timely despite the various deadlines under the Post-Conviction Act that doubtless have long passed in the applicable cases. It would have been preferable for the law to have been of more general application, perhaps using the language "was not used at trial or sentencing or the defendant has not yet been sentenced," but any change in the law would have sent it back to the House of Representatives, imposing additional delay at best or causing its defeat at worst.

The new law amends the Post-Conviction Act adding a third paragraph:

"(3) by a preponderance of the evidence that each of the following allegations in the petition establishes:

(A) he or she was convicted of a forcible felony;

(B) his or her participation in the offense was a direct result of the person's mental state either suffering from post-partum depression or post-partum psychosis;

(C) no evidence of post-partum depression or post-partum psychosis was presented by a qualified medical person at trial or sentencing, or both;

(D) he or she was unaware of the mitigating nature of the evidence or if aware was at the time unable to present this defense due to suffering from post-partum depression or post-partum psychosis or at the time of trial or sentencing neither was a recognized mental illness and as such unable to receive proper treatment; and

(E) evidence of post-partum depression or post-partum psychosis as suffered by the person is material and noncumulative to other evidence offered at the time of trial or sentencing and it is of such a conclusive character that it would likely change the sentence imposed by the original court.

Nothing in this paragraph (3): prevents a person from applying for any other relief under this Article or any other law otherwise available to him or her.

As used in this paragraph (3):

'Post-partum depression' means a mood disorder which strikes many women during and after pregnancy which usually occurs during pregnancy and up to 12 months after delivery. This depression can include anxiety disorders.

'Post-partum psychosis' means an extreme form of post-partum depression which can occur during pregnancy and up to 12 months after delivery. This can include losing touch with reality, distorted thinking, delusions, auditory and visual hallucinations, paranoia, hyperactivity and rapid speech or mania."

PA 100-0574 takes note of the fact that the Act contemplates the filing of only one petition. The amendment allows a fresh petition alleging the material facts of PPD or PPP.

(F) Except for petitions brought under paragraph (3) of subsection (a) of this section, only one petition may be filed by a petitioner under this Article without leave of the court.

A FIRST STEP

The Illinois legislation is only a first step. Laws in European countries are far ahead of the United States in recognizing the effects of postpartum issues on mothers in crisis. Many countries have a provision in law for a finding of the equivalent of involuntary or voluntary manslaughter in such instances.

The English Infanticide Act of 1922 effectively abolished the death penalty for women who committed infanticide. The Infanticide Act of 1938 greatly reduced sentences for such women, and is a better model than PA 100-0574. However, in the United States, legislation similar to the English Infanticide Act was proposed only once before, in 2009, in Texas. It failed to pass.[25]

An insanity defense may fail. If it succeeds, it can leave a woman institutionalized for her lifetime. A defense of voluntary or involuntary manslaughter tends not to fit. Relief by legislation or constitutional objections is necessary. PA 100-0574 has a narrow, limited application. However, nine years have gone by since the Texas attempt without any law similar to the UK's Infanticide Act passing in any US legislative body. PA 100-0574 is no panacea, but it is a start. Its limited application may make it more palatable to other legislatures. Perhaps someday the step in England 80 years ago may be made here.

Margaret Mead stated: "Never doubt that a small group of thoughtful, committed citizens can change the world; indeed, it is the only thing that ever has." Hopefully, each state will find such a group within its borders.

The author gratefully acknowledges the efforts of Bill Ryan, Lita Simanis, and especially Dr. Susan Feingold who, in addition to her work on PA 100-0574, reviewed this article.

NOTES

1. Any constitutional argument would involve an extension of *Miller v. Alabama*, 567 U.S. 460 (2012), which referenced the brain of juveniles not being fully developed; a comparison with a temporary psychosis can be made.

2. American Psychiatric Association, *Diagnostic and Statistical Manual of Mental Disorders*, 5th ed. (*DSM-5*) (Arlington, VA: American Psychiatric Publishing, 2013), 112.

3. "Infanticide is most often associated with postpartum psychotic episodes that are characterized by command hallucinations to kill the infant or delusions that the infant is possessed, but psychotic symptoms can also occur in severe postpartum mood episodes without such specific delusions or hallucinations." Ibid.

4. J. Novak, "Moms Killing Kids Not Nearly as Rare as We Think," *NBC News*, April 17, 2011, http://www.nbcnews.com. Cheryl Meyer estimates about 120 infanticides by mothers each year and considers that a low estimate. Meyer and Michelle Oberman interviewed female prisoners in Ohio and concluded that 80 of the 1,800 women incarcerated in the penitentiary were there for killing their children. A news agency analyzed FBI data in 1995 and concluded that five children under age one were killed each week; the data did not identify the causes or persons responsible: "Nearly 5 Babies Killed Weekly, FBI Data Shows," CNN, June 27, 1997, http://www.cnn.com.

5. Susan Benjamin Feingold, *Happy Endings, New Beginnings: Navigating Postpartum Disorders* (Far Hills, NJ: New Horizons Press, 2015).

6. Susan Benjamin Feingold, as quoted in Lisa Black, "Postpartum Depression Fight Frustrating for Victim's Mom," *Chicago Tribune*, January 9, 2013.

7. "The postpartum period is unique with respect to the degree of neuroendocrine alterations and psychosocial adjustments, the potential impact of breast-feeding on treatment planning." *Desk Reference to the Diagnostic Criteria from DSM-5* (Washington, DC: American Psychiatric Association, 2013), 112.

8. It is unclear whether her abnormal thought processes were psychotic or deeply depressed.

9. Forty-nine of the 50 states have life imprisonment sentences in varying circumstances, and 31 have the death penalty. "Life without Parole," Death Penalty Information Center, accessed October 20, 2019, https://deathpenaltyinfo.org. None of these make an exception for PPD or PPP, although it can be a mitigating factor under the general mental health clauses within the sentencing code or by judicial rulings. However, the existence of any mitigating factor is immaterial in the numerous states like Illinois, where life without parole is mandatory in certain situations regardless of the volume or nature of the mitigation.

10. Pam Belluck, "Mothers Mind, Second of Two Articles: After Baby, an Unraveling," *New York Times*, June 16, 2014, https://www.nytimes.com.

11. See, for example, *People v. Alexander*, 239 Ill. 2d 205, 346 Ill.Dec. 458, 940 N.E.2d 1062 (2010). The appellate court twice reversed the case, holding the 24-year sentence for a 16-year-old for the offense of unlawful use of weapons was an abuse of discretion. The defendant fired a gun multiple times, striking no one. He claimed an invalid form of self-defense, a fear of attack not grounded in the acts of his apparent target. The appellate court in the first appeal ordered a resentencing. The trial court again imposed the same 24-year sentence, despite much evidence of rehabilitation of the defendant, who was now 20 years old. The appellate court again reversed, and imposed a six-year sentence. On the state's appeal to the Illinois Supreme Court, the Supreme Court reinstated the trial court's sentence. In affirming the trial court's 24-year sentence, the Supreme Court noted the power of an appellate court to reduce a sentence "should be exercised 'cautiously and sparingly.'"

12. National Research Council, Research on Sentencing (Vol. 1), at 141 (1983). *Dorszynski v. U.S.*, 418 U.S. 424, 94 S.Ct. 3042, 41 L.Ed.2d 855 (1974). See also *Gall v. United States*, 552 U.S. 38, 128 S.Ct. 586, 169 L.Ed.2d 445 (2007), which does allow theoretically for a review of the substantive reasonableness of the sentence.

13. Wayne R. LaFave et al., *Criminal Procedure*, 4th ed. (Eagan, MN: West Publishing, 2016), 945.

14. *Mooney v. Holohan*, 294 U.S. 103 (1934).

15. *People v. Allen*, 40 Ill.App.3d 972, 353 N.E.2d 342 (1st dist. 1976). The court could not reduce a sentence in a post-conviction petition because it was not a constitutional issue.

16. "Truth in Sentencing." Wikipedia, accessed February 2018, https://en.wikipedia.org.

17. England, Wales and Scotland are all similar demographically. All have similar rates of infanticide. Yet England and Wales have an infanticide act, and Scotland does not. M. M. Marks and R. Kumar, "Infanticide in Scotland," *Medicine, Science, and*

the Law 36, no. 4 (October 1996): 299–305, PubMed.gov, US National Library of Medicine National Institutes of Health, doi:10.1177/002580249603600405.

18. M. Frith, “Scrap Outdated Infanticide Law Say Judges,” *Independent*, May 4, 2005, http://www.independent.co.uk. The law was criticized in the article for its requirement that women admit guilt to receive its benefits.

19. S. R. Friedman and P. R. Resnick, “Child Murder by Mothers: Patterns and Prevention,” *World Psychiatry* 6, no. 3 (2007): 137.

20. “All of them indicated that it was always a crime in their country. Mostly it is a mitigated form of homicide, punishable by an imprisonment of up to 10 years. However, in five countries the offender can be sentenced to life in prison. For the remaining countries, the average maximum punishment is 6 years imprisonment.” P. Smit, R. de Jong, and C. Bijleveld, “Homicide Data in Europe: Definitions, Sources, and Statistics,” in *Handbook of European Homicide Research: Patterns, Explanations, and Country Studies*, ed. M. C. A. Liem and W. A. Pridemore (New York: Springer Science+Business Media, 2012), doi:10.1007/978-1-4614-0466-8_2.

21. “Bill Status of HB1764 100th General Assembly,” Illinois General Assembly, accessed October 20, 2019, http://www.ilga.gov.

22. Feingold, *Happy Endings*.

23. *People v. Correa*, 108 Ill. 2d 541, 485 N.E.2d 307 (1985).

24. The word is spelled “post-partum” in the original text. The medical community uses the term “postpartum.”

25. Jessica Farrar, “A Bill to Be Entitled an Act Relating to Creating an Offense for Infanticide,” State of Texas, accessed October 20, 2019, https://capitol.texas.gov.

Appendix I

Sample Letter to Interview Those Incarcerated

The following letter is an example for a person seeking access as a group member, rather than for someone assigned on a single specific case by specific counsel.

LAW OFFICES
BARRY M. LEWIS
ATTORNEY AT LAW
500 NORTH MICHIGAN AVE.
SUITE 600
CHICAGO, ILLINOIS 60611

TEL: (312) 372-2221
FAX: (312) 396-4185
E-MAIL: BLEWISLAW@AOL.COM

Warden
Logan Correctional Center
1096 1350th St.
Lincoln, IL 62656

May 19, 2019

Re: [Name and ID number]

Dear Warden:

Because of the shortage of time, I am attaching this letter, on my letterhead, to the e-mail rather than responding via mail.

Dr. Susan Benjamin Feingold is a clinical psychologist. I am a criminal defense attorney. We are part of the legal committee of Postpartum Support International, Illinois Chapter. Our purpose is to support counsel appointed on behalf of each of the four women we wish to visit. We plan to review records with the above-named women and help appointed counsel with the legal and medical issues these cases present. In no case am I the primary attorney. We are involved in these cases because the legal and medical communities are still developing their understanding of this illness and its ramifications under the law.

Dr. Susan Feingold is a nationally recognized expert on issues of postpartum illnesses. She has been an adjunct professor on this issue and the past president of Depression After Delivery, which effectively merged with Postpartum Support International. Among other presentations, she and I have spoken at Amita Health, the Biennial Perinatal Mental Health Conference in 2017, the American Psychological Association annual meeting in San Francisco in 2018, and the annual meetings of Postpartum Support International in Houston in 2018 and Portland in 2019.

Dr. Feingold wishes to bring to the meetings a single audio recorder. She does not regard this as a mere convenience. It can be important to have an accurate record of the conversation, more accurate than notes permit. Recognizing the safety issue, no video or transmit (cell phone or otherwise) capability will be brought into the institution.

Please consider our application for this meeting, which we hope to have on _____ _____, 20____.

Proof of our credentials is attached.

Very truly yours,

Barry Lewis, JD

BML/v
Enc.

Appendix J

Interview Questions for Logan Inmates

Our intent is to share useful parts of the interview with your defense team and attorney as well as to provide information that can help others.

Prior to the postpartum depression (PPD)/ postpartum psychosis (PPP) incident what, if anything, did you know of maternal mental illness? Can you relate the story of how you came to decide to work on HB 1764 and how you knew how to write the bill that has now become IL PA 100-0574?

1. How did you feel the bill, now law, may (or may not) benefit you directly and other incarcerated women?
2. Can you relate the story of what happened (and when) that led to your being here in Logan?
3. What do you remember about the event (the incident)? Specifically, what were your symptoms before you committed the offense? At the time of the offense? Delusions/hallucinations?
4. When did symptoms start—during pregnancy, at delivery, or at what point after delivery? Was delivery difficult or traumatic?
5. Did you have any differences between the pregnancies and how you felt or how your symptoms appeared?
6. Did you and your family have a history of mental illness? Did this have an impact on you, and how was it related to your own pregnancy or postpartum depression/psychosis?
7. Did you understand that you were committing a crime/homicide?
8. How did you get well? Medication? Which ones?
9. Are you still on medication? What medication?
10. Do you recognize that you had depression or psychosis? How long until you were well?

11. Have you received professional treatment? How soon after the onset of the illness? How long after being incarcerated? What treatment did you receive?
12. Has any treatment been effective? If so, how and what has been effective?
13. Do you have any continuing issues with the illness, depression, or psychosis? What issues?
14. How has it affected you personally? Your relationships, your own mental health, your life's purpose?
15. As a PPD/PPP sufferer, what has been your experience in working with the legal system? Did your attorney or others in the legal system understand that your crime was committed while suffering from a postpartum depression or psychosis?
16. Did anyone in the legal system help you understand the nature of your crime and the ramifications in terms of sentencing, and so forth? (for women with PPP)
17. Has any organization or individuals (i.e., therapists, physicians, nurses, attorneys, etc.) been helpful to you? In what way have they helped you?
18. Were there any positive outcomes at all? Anything learned or good out of this tragedy? Any advice for others?
19. Can you describe your arrest and how you were treated? Specifically, what statements did you make or were made by police? What was the attitude of the police, prosecutors, defense attorney(s), judges, and jury?
20. At trial, did the defense present any witnesses? What do you believe were the strengths and weaknesses of the proofs of the prosecution and the defense?
21. What was your sentence? What issues were raised at sentencing? What went right and what went wrong at sentencing, and why? What did your attorney expect, and what did you expect? Were you subject to the death penalty?
22. How have you been treated in jail by inmates and by authorities (guards, the warden, etc.)?
23. What do you plan to do if you get out of prison as a result of your resentencing hearing?
24. Additional questions:
25. What did your family do and say about your situation?
26. Were there any barriers to the onset of treatment? (i.e., racial, economic/financial)
27. What could you have done differently?
28. Anything you want to add?

Thank You!
Your experience and wisdom will help others.

Appendix K

Report to PRGLAC Task Force on Research Specific to Pregnant Women and Lactating Women

NEW FEDERAL TASK FORCE TO CONSIDER MOOD AND ANXIETY DISORDERS AS A GAP IN KNOWLEDGE AFFECTING PREGNANT AND LACTATING WOMEN

Susan Benjamin Feingold, Psy.D.
February 2018

It has been repeatedly substantiated that Perinatal Mood and Anxiety Disorders, commonly known as pregnancy and postpartum depression, is the most common complication surrounding childbirth, yet all too often it goes unrecognized and untreated.

Perinatal mood disorders (PMAD), or pregnancy and postpartum depression, are the names most commonly used for the psychiatric syndrome surrounding childbirth that includes a variety of moderate to severe mood and anxiety symptoms that require professional mental health treatment.

The clinical presentation often includes many of the following distressing and overwhelming symptoms: depressed mood, severe anxiety, panic attacks, insomnia and/or sleep disturbances, appetite loss, feelings of hopelessness and worthlessness, suicidal thoughts, loss of pleasure or joy, lack of energy and motivation, difficulty functioning at usual level, inability to cope with normal life demands, rumination, and/or obsessive and disturbing thoughts.

Far less common are symptoms of mania and psychosis (1 to 2 out of 1,000 childbearing women) that research has linked to bipolar disorder and is considered the single strongest predictor of a postpartum psychosis.

According to the World Health Organization, depression affects 13% of women worldwide within a year of delivery (*Bulletin of the World Health*

Organization 2012;90:139–149). In the United States and worldwide, the prevalence and incidence rates of PMAD has been estimated at 10 to 15% of women experiencing significant symptoms of depression and/or anxiety during their pregnancy or the postpartum period (Gavin et al., *Obstet Gynecol.*2005;106(5 Pt 1):1071–1083; O'Hara M.W., Swain A.M. Rates and risk of postpartum depression-A meta-analysis. *Int Rev Psychiatry* 1996; 8:37–54).

While the PRGLAC NIH-led Federal Task Force has been assigned the mammoth task of identifying gaps in knowledge and research on safe and effective therapies for pregnant women and lactating women, it is essential to consider perinatal depression and anxiety disorders along with other health and medical concerns. PMAD has enormous implications for the mental health, physical health and the overall well-being of women and their children.

S. Meltzer-Brody (2011) reports that perinatal depression can have devastating consequences for the affected woman, her children, and family (Feldman et al. *J Am Acad Child Adolesc Psychiatry* 2009;48:919–927), and has been associated with serious adverse consequences for the developing neonate (premature birth, low birth weight, and future behavioral disturbances). In addition, maternal depression has been linked to detrimental effects on maternal sensitivity and attachment in the postpartum period; mothers are more likely to have infants with colic and exhibit impaired parenting. Those children exposed to maternal depression have been found to have higher levels of cortisol than infants of mothers who were not depressed. Even nursing can be affected, as Meltzer-Brody reports that curtailed breastfeeding is associated with maternal depression (Meltzer-Brody S., *Dialogues Clin Neurosci* 2011 Mar; 13(1):89–100).

There are numerous research studies corroborating the negative outcomes on children and families of depressed mothers, yet the incredible toll that PMAD takes on the private life of mothers, children and families is not easily measured. Many are unaware of the chaos and havoc caused by PMAD, which results in excessive personal suffering, and the loss of joy in becoming a mother that often accompanies this debilitating mental health syndrome, when it is not recognized early and treated promptly.

In the past few years we have made progress toward understanding various aspects surrounding perinatal mood and anxiety disorders, such as incidence and prevalence rates; development of new assessment and screening tools; predictors and risk factors; clinical symptom presentation; effect on infant attachment and the couple/family relationship; and the efficacy of some evidence-based psychotherapeutic treatment methods.

Yet, there still remains many gaps and much to be learned about the pathogenesis of PMAD, the effect and exposure of various psychotropic medications on the fetus, on infant and in breast milk, the efficacy of evidence-based psychotherapeutic approaches alone or in combination with medication, as well as the usefulness of incorporating complementary and alternative methods in treatment.

From a perinatal psychiatry perspective, Meltzer-Brody (2011, *Dialogues Clin Neurosci* 13(1):89–100) states that more research is needed to address gaps in the literature in the following: prospective studies that further our understanding of the safety of antidepressant exposure in pregnancy and lactation; longitudinal neurodevelopmental studies of children exposed to maternal mental illness, with or without psychotropics during pregnancy; translational research that clarifies the pathophysiology of PMAD with the long-term goal of ensuring the best possible clinical outcomes for mother and child.

In conclusion there is a need for increased awareness of PMAD in both the public sector and with health care professionals. Despite encouraging steps in that direction, we have only just begun to address many significant gaps in knowledge and treatment. We need further efforts to investigate issues of prevention, to identify and promptly refer women at heightened risk, and to research safe and effective treatments for those with PMAD. There needs to be a willingness to explore an interdisciplinary treatment approach, incorporating a combination of alternative and traditional therapies; treatment approaches that consider the risk-benefits of using psychotropic medications when necessary, along with safe, effective evidence-based psychotherapies (http://apa.org/health/briefs/perinatal-depression, 2014) such as cognitive-behavioral, interpersonal, mindfulness-based therapy, couple/family, EMD-R, and integrative approaches, and various alternative methods (acupuncture, nutritional and supplemental approaches, yoga, movement therapy, hypnosis, Transcranial Magnetic Stimulation, etc.) for women's optimal mental health.

Index

Page references for figures are italicized.

About the Authors

Susan Benjamin Feingold, PsyD, is a licensed psychologist, perinatal legal advocate, and author. She is a co-recipient of the 2018 Maternal Mental Health Innovation Award in Policy and Advocacy and a member of the Postpartum Support International Advisory Council (PSI-AC). She has been a specialist for more than twenty-six years in women's mental health issues related to reproductive function: perinatal depression and anxiety disorders, infertility, pregnancy loss, and relationship issues. She is a nationally recognized expert in the field of pregnancy and postpartum mental health and author of *Happy Endings, New Beginnings: Navigating Postpartum Disorders* (2013). Feingold has offices located in Skokie and Chicago, Illinois. You can read more about Feingold at www.drsusanbfeingold.com.

Barry Michael Lewis, JD, is an attorney at law, a perinatal legal advocate, and an author. He is a co-recipient of the 2018 Maternal Mental Health Innovation Award in Policy and Advocacy. His published work includes an article titled "A New Model Law Offers Hope: Postpartum Disorders and the Law" in the *Champion*, the magazine of the National Association of Criminal Defense Lawyers. He has worked for more than forty years in the field of criminal law as a litigation attorney in private practice. He is also past chair of the Chicago Bar Association Lawyer Referral Committee, award winner from Chicago Volunteer Legal Services, and a continuing legal education lecturer. He has offices located in Chicago, Illinois. You can find out more about Lewis and his work at www.BarryLewisLaw.com.

www.ingramcontent.com/pod-product-compliance
Ingram Content Group UK Ltd.
Pitfield, Milton Keynes, MK11 3LW, UK
UKHW040909190926
475560UK00008B/54

9 781538 129852